LOVE FOR LEANING IN

"I'm excited just thinking about all the family members, friends, clients, and professional colleagues I'm going to give this beautifully written book to and how grateful they'll be." —**STEVE CHANDLER**, bestselling author, Creator; master coach; popular motivational speaker

"The most remarkable part of this story is how intuition guided Linda in transcending her grief and finding a new, more mature love and a profoundly effective approach to her counseling practice." —**MARYANN DRESKE**, MBA; former Fortune 50 executive

"In the human design there is a transcendent world, beyond time, space, and matter, which we access through the heart and intuition. Linda touches this world with exquisite beauty and a wicked sense of humor. It's a thrilling ride!" —**SHADRICK MAZAZA**, physician; philosopher; business school academic; founder: African Consciousness Institute

"Linda's internal dialogues speak louder than words for those questioning our connection to God. Her candid storytelling weaves life events into a captivating tapestry... a beautiful blend of love, heart-wrenching circumstances, and the resilience of the human spirit. I feel profoundly changed." —**TERESA WALDING**, BSN, RN, NC-BC, advancing nurse coaching

"Leaning into Curves is a page-turner, with gripping relevance to what we go through in life and love, which kept me hooked till the end. Prepare yourself; this book will touch your heart and soul and trigger insights that transform your life. The ultimate game-changer." —**DENISE HOLLAND**, former national coach, and athlete; leader, spiritual awareness in sports

"Both heartwarming and at times, heart-rending. If you've ever wondered if there's a way back from the loss of a loved one, Linda's story is a reassuring reminder that love itself can never die." —**MICHAEL NEILL**, bestselling author of *The Inside-Out Revolution*

"The transparency and self-revelations in this book make for an insightful read. There are many quotes and nuggets... that readers will remember long after they've finished the book." —**SHERRY CORMIER**, PhD, psychologist; author, *Sweet Sorrow*

"If you've questioned whether there's more to mental health treatment than medication and therapy, more to our current understanding of how our mind works, or simply more to life, then Linda answers this with warmth, love, and raw honesty. Savor each chapter as a gift to your soul." —**DR. JUSTINE CROFT** MB ChB MRCPsych, NHS perinatal psychiatrist

"There are innumerable ways to connect with the infinite peace that lies within us. Linda has experienced and masterfully shared a lifetime of them. You will feel a deep kinship with her, in a way that will settle within you as you read." —**ANDREW McKEE**, author, coach

"More than the story of a single life; it is the story of human life itself. Touching, compassionate, honest, deeply wise, and full of hope, it is about resilience in hard times, joy in good times and an underlying, deep feeling of love through both." —**CHANA ROSENBLATT**, well-being director, Rabbinical Training Academy; director, CR Practice; 3 Principles practitioner

"Linda has poured, with generosity, herself and so many nooks and crannies of her life into this book, and hence, it is a page-turner. This is a wise, rich, and beautiful story of awakening." —**JULES SWALES**, writing teacher and poet

"For anyone whose life has been turned upside down and is desperately trying to find remedies, Linda's calming book points to the driving force of recovery and healing that we can find within ourselves. That driving force is our intuition." —**JOEL SLACK,** leader in the national and international mental health advocacy movement

"Linda points us toward our shared humanity, toward the magic and the mystery that is the source of our experience, the thread that connects us all." —**SARAH HOOK NILSSON,** author, *Holy Days: Reflections of a Travel Pilgrim*

"A jewel of a memoir, a compelling story...told with humility, honesty, and humor. Linda has generously included book circle questions to guide readers as they delve deeper into self-discovery and life's mysteries." —**DEBBIE HARBINSON,** MHI, registered nurse

"An artistically written memoir, where Linda invites us to make friends with the mystery, and to hold with love, our intuitive wisdom." —**DR. PEGGY MOTSCH,** counseling psychologist, professor emeritus of psychology

"If we're lucky in life, we read a book that deeply resonates with our core. A book that seems like it's written just for us. A book we can't put down because every evocative page draws us in and expresses what we've wanted, worried about, wished for. Linda's light-hearted voice reminds us to 'slow down to the speed of love' and pay attention to synchronicities so we 'live the beauty way' ... now, not someday. Read it and reap." —**SAM HORN,** CEO of The Intrigue Agency

LEANING INTO CURVES

LEANING INTO CURVES

TRUSTING THE WILD INTUITIVE WAY OF LOVE

LINDA SANDEL PETTIT ED.D.

Leaning Into Curves
Trusting the Wild, Intuitive Way of Love
Linda Sandel Pettit, Ed.D.

IW
Press

I W Press

First Published in Great Britain by IW Press Ltd
62-64 Market Street
Ashby-de-la-Zouch
England
LE65 1AN

https://www.iliffe-wood.co.uk/

Permissions:
"Love" from Power Through Constructive Thinking by Emmet Fox.
Copyright 1940 by Emmet Fox. Copyright renewed 1968 by Kathleen Whelan.
Used by permission of HarperCollins Publishers.

Extract from the Tao of Pooh used with kind permission from Benjamin Hoff.
Quotes from the teachings of Sydney Banks used with kind permission from Lone Pine Publishing, Judy Banks, and Shane Kennedy.

Significant efforts have been made to obtain permission to quote all material governed by complex copyright circumstances. Any requested adjustments, will be made in future editions.

Cover art by Coizie Bettinger, https://coiziebettinger.com
Author photo by Laura Waugh, www.laurawaughphotography.com
Illustration licensed from iStock by Getty Images - blueberry99d
Cover design by 18 Design Ltd
Interior design by Phillip Gessert

A catalogue record of this book is available from the British Library.

ISBN-13: 978-1-916701-03-8 (Paperback)
ISBN-13: 978-1-916701-04-5 (Hardcover)
ISBN-13: 978-1-916701-05-2 (e-book)

For Luke and Alex
Children of Love and Joy

TABLE OF
CONTENTS

FOREWORD

By William F. Pettit, Jr., M.D., Psychiatrist

HOP ON FOR a rich, sweet, exhilarating ride through love, loss, and healing into the mystery, joy and understanding of the spiritual theater of life.

In my twenty plus years of sharing my life with Dr. Linda Sandel Pettit, I have been blessed in many ways. She has opened all my senses to wonders of creation that I had been oblivious to prior to meeting her.

In this personal and powerful memoir, she initiates the reader into the richness of life, to the sweetness that remains always present and the exhilaration that comes naturally in those moments each of us has the courage to step fully into the now. Like a deft motorcyclist, she navigates us through the universal experiences of profound love, devastating loss, and welcomed incremental healing.

Like passengers who rejoice when the pelting rain has ceased, clouds are lifting, and the sun is peeking through again, we readers find ourselves holding on tight with hopeful expectation.

With an open heart, Linda conclusively invites us to share in the profound mystery, heart filling joy and illuminating understanding she has come to appreciate in a full and trusting acceptance of the spiritual theater of life.

You *will* be *grateful* for having hopped on for the ride!

A WORD ABOUT MEMORIES...

L*eaning into Curves* is a work of creative nonfiction. Memory is subjective; no two people will remember a given experience in the exact same way. Sometimes the differences are striking. Because we think and focus through unique filters, we construct reality in separate ways.

I have taken small liberties to create dialogue and scene details around the clear snippets of memory that I have. In a few instances, scenes are composites of experiences. Some names have been changed for privacy. Through creative detail, I have tried to convey the truth, the feeling of the tale as it lives in my heart and mind.

"...lean into curves.
Don't fight the flow of life. Go with it.
It's a little scary sometimes, but it makes for a sweet ride."

Eulogy for Jim Pfeffer,
Linda Sandel Pettit, Ed.D. [1999]

PROLOGUE

I HELD MY dead husband's Christmas gifts to my chest and sobbed. Unmoored at the age of forty-six in a sea of bereavement, waves of sorrow swamped me.

My last glimpse of Jim in his gifts—a brown plaid flannel shirt and gold suspenders—is paired with the click of the lid of a bronze casket as it closed our human life together. It was a twist of fate that I found the right clothes to bury him in just days before his sudden death.

The violent winds of change that Jim's death ushered in cracked the shutters over my heart wider. There was a treasure carried on those winds—the mystical keys to seeing a little bit more about the mystery of life, to seeing more about love, and to seeing with certainty that love is who I am, who *we* are, at our shared core.

This is a therapist's tale of finding love—at home and in my work—by listening to the intuitive wisdom of my heart. It is a tale of losing the beat in the noise of mistrust, exhaustion, resentment, and grief. It is a tale of how love, a brilliant force, uses life as medicine. It is a tale of forgiveness. It is a tale of how intuitive wisdom pointed the way around blindsiding curves and dark mountains.

We are given *everything* we need on our wild rides through life. Our safety is guaranteed when we lean into curves and flow with love through life's mysteries. Trust is the path. Beauty is the destination.

This is everyone's story—we are guided through life by love.

CHAPTER 1

MISSIONARY PRIEST

"**I**'M THE ICE man," Father James Noel Pfeffer said, and chuckled, as he came through the front door of his sister's house in 1977. His black leather jacket was sheathed in snow. He wore chaps of ice over his faded jeans.

A biker to the core, he had ridden his motorcycle to dinner through an unexpected Michigan snowfall in early winter. *Who does that?* I wondered.

A tall man, he was muscled and lean, with dark hair trimmed close. Tiny icicles dripped from his nose and chin.

Jim had the eyes of an old soul, chocolate brown pools of a child, magician, and sage. I was mesmerized by his hands. He pulled black leather gloves off long, graceful fingers that were expressive and sensitive. He wore a silver five-strand puzzle ring on his left hand. His smile, a little crooked, sparkled with innocence.

"I've come to share my last date with Jim Beam," he said, and swung a whiskey bottle wrapped in a brown paper bag into the soft light in the cozy house, as though raising a toast to life.

His sister, Denise, had invited me to share dinner with her and her boyfriend, Larry. She was a schoolteacher and a former Dominican nun who left her religious order during the great exodus in the 1970s when Vatican II modernized the Catholic Church. Larry, a Jesuit priest on leave of absence from his order, was youth minister at St. Patrick's Catholic Church in Brighton, Michigan – the parish I belonged to. Larry had asked Denise and me to help him form a young singles' group for the community – our work together on the project cemented what would become a lifelong friendship.

Denise mentioned that her oldest brother, Jim, would join us. He was a Catholic priest in the Maryknoll order of missionaries. She explained that while working in the jungles on the Philippine Island of Mindanao, he had developed a problem with alcohol. The following day, he would begin treatment at Guest House, a recovery program for clergy, in Lake Orion, Michigan. At age forty-four, he was twenty years older than me.

"Jaime, welcome," Denise said. She referred to her older brother in the Filipino version of his name. Her deep affection for him rang in her gentle laughter, which twinkled like diamond dewdrops in morning sunlight. Arms outstretched, she went to the door and hugged him, ice, and all. He rocked her in a big bear hug.

Larry watched them sway in the doorway from where he stood at a kitchen island, slicing tomatoes, and green peppers into a salad. His Black Russian, Kahlua and Vodka on ice, rested next to the wood chopping block. A crumpled cellophane wrapper was discarded on the counter. On the dinner table, melted Brie and almond slices waited on a cheese board.

"Had to get one last ride on the motorcycle, eh?" Larry said, his soft laugh conveyed understanding. Larry and Denise shared Jim's love of biking.

"Got that right," said Jim. He shrugged off his leather jacket and revealed a blue plaid flannel shirt that snugged broad shoulders. He was tanned bronze, in sharp contrast to the rest of us, who wore winter white skin. My guard was up as I watched Larry and Denise greet Jim. I felt awkward and inferior when meeting

2

men. Jim's presence intruded into the comfortable sense of belonging and acceptance I enjoyed with Denise and Larry.

"Jaime, meet Linda," said Denise. Jim's eyes had taken me in but now they met mine. I felt anxious and inadequate, self-conscious, as a *woman*. I reacted to Jim as though he were a romantic interest. I felt uneasy about this; the sensations were a total surprise and didn't fit my moral code. He was a priest, off-limits. He was several generations older. He was an alcoholic.

I was aware of the olive green and white striped sweater and jeans I wore. *Did I look ok? Was my make-up good? My waist-length red hair could be frizzy; was it laid flat?* A blush burned my cheeks. I was embarrassed by my tendency to turn red at the drop of a hat; it betrayed my shyness.

"She's a member of our young singles' group," Denise said. Jim crossed to where I sat at the round dining room table in a circle of light from a stained-glass chandelier. He carried the smell of wet jeans and fresh snow with him. He reached for my hand.

I stopped fingering the small gold cross at my neck and reached for his.

When our hands met, I felt a strong electric current, a magnetic charge that pulled us together. It was as if I had known him forever—that we had a timeless connection and I had recognized him. My heart skipped a few beats and desire rose in my body. I was shocked by the strength of the sensations—Jim didn't fit any definition I had of a soul mate.

"Hi, Linda," he said, his voice a husky tenor with a hint of hesitance. I later learned he loved acapella music and that he did a mean Louis Armstrong imitation. *What a Wonderful World* was his favorite song and his signature.

That night, Jim shared his exploits as a young man in the seminary who loved hockey and girls, about the friends he made as a priest in training, and about his preparation to be a missionary at the Maryknoll headquarters in Ossining, New York. His training had taught him farming and carpentry; he'd even done stints sewing people up in New York City emergency rooms! Jim's humor was funny, self-effacing, spiced with irreverence. Social justice for the poor and oppressed was embedded in his heart. His tenderness for the Filipino people he ministered to oozed as he described them.

I watched him with deep curiosity. He was gentle, sensitive, and wise – traits that seemed uncommon in men my own age. His depth of feeling, the heart he wore on his sleeve, was rainwater to a parched soul.

I didn't say much that night. The milieu Jim lived in was quite different from the youngish, free-wheeling early tech corporate culture that formed a backdrop to my work as a corporate communications specialist for a company in Ann Arbor, Michigan. I was immersed in innovation, travel, perks, bonuses, and generous salaries. My life was organized around journalistic writing, photography, and promoting timesharing—an early version of Cloud computing.

Years later, I asked Jim what he remembered of our first meeting. "You were beautiful," he said. "I was preoccupied with the treatment I would begin the next day, but I was attracted to you. I was ashamed of that. You were so young."

We wrapped up an hours-long evening with Jim Beam whisky. Jim poured shots for each of us. The burn, a little bit vanilla, a little bit sour, was my first drink of bourbon. It was Jim's last, ever.

Later that night, at home, I lit candles, drew a bubble bath, and relaxed in the warm water. I held my journal above the suds and wrote, *"I've just met the man I'm going to marry."*

I stared at the words in disbelief. I was a young and pious Catholic woman. I never missed an opportunity to visit a Cathedral, for God's sake—I *lived for* stained glass windows, fragrant incense, religious rituals, and Gregorian chant. I had flirted with thoughts about joining a convent, a cloister no less, from the time I was a small girl.

Catholics knew that priests could not marry. Priests were off limits. Priests were sacred to their congregations, their leadership carried great trust. As if to ward off my irreverence, I shook my head.

But I did *not* discount that a guiding power connected to love had just shown up and pointed me toward a possibility. At the time, I called it intuition. My connection to this power felt inconsistent, mysterious and nonrational, but I had reason to trust it—I had seen that when I followed it, life unfolded in magical ways.

Even then, I associated intuition with a *beautiful feeling* of "rightness" or wisdom.

A *beautiful feeling* had looked *through me* at Jim with soul-fired love. That beautiful feeling had blown open the shutters over my heart—the shutters of my inadequacies, my religious beliefs, my judgments, my certainties about "right" and "wrong." From the depth of that feeling, I glimpsed *beauty and Truth*.

My knowing was that I'd stumbled upon a fork in the road. The dictates of my religious upbringing and the wisdom of my heart had collided.

CHAPTER 2

FIRST MEMORY

"IT'S LAURA'S TURN for a bath," my Ma said, as she squeezed a soft pink infant's washcloth in her right hand and watched warm water fall in rivulets down my baby sister's back.

It was the summer of 1956. I was three. Laura, six months old, sat in the kitchen sink; soapy water lapped against the folds of her belly. Perched on the laminate countertop, my feet dangled into the same water. I was fresh-bathed and naked, snuggled into a downy cotton towel.

The compact bungalow I lived in was set in a fresh-built tract housing suburb of Detroit, Michigan. The small kitchen was awash in the soft yellow glow of summer sunlight. Bright curtains fluttered in the bank of open windows that wrapped around the corner behind the kitchen table. White roller shades were pulled down about a third of the way; they fluttered in intermittent breezes and tapped a sociable rhythm against the sills.

The kitchen was pristine. My Ma, true to her Polish roots, took great pride in a tidy home. My little mind's eye noticed the order, simplicity, and colorful beauty of it all.

Ma, age twenty-four, stood close to the counter; she squeezed me in to prevent a fall. A flowered shift with short sleeves draped her body, belted at the waist. She was barefoot. Lively brown eyes danced behind dark glasses; she was never without them.

I knew that my mother loved us without reserve. My love for her, and for my sister swelled in my chest. There were times when I wanted to pinch my infant sister because she required so much attention and I was certain Ma loved her more, but not in that moment.

"Would you like to help, sweetheart?" Ma said, and she offered me the washcloth. I dunked it into the water and dribbled suds over my sister's shoulders. Laura laughed, angel's music from a baby's lips, and I giggled.

This first memory recorded by my conscious observer left three delicate lifelong impressions. *A safe mother is the center of the world. Life is beautiful. Love is a gift.*

CHAPTER 3

THE BIG ASK

S OME OF US are born Protestant, Jewish, Hindu or Muslim. I call this religion "by accident." I was born Catholic by accident. I am a "cradle" Catholic—my religion was adopted for me by my family. Until I was in my late forties, I also chose it and I still identify with it. Catholicism had shaped me in immeasurable ways.

Early on, I became afraid of a God who was intent on punishing me for my imperfections. I was haunted by a belief this easy-to-anger and vindictive male power was going to take my life early. I don't know why this was so.

"You're a quiet and deep one, sweetheart," Sister LaSalette said. The young nun knelt to look into my eyes, after I confessed to her that at seven years old, I was scared I would die with sin on my soul. Her ankle-length black habit fell into a layered drape on the speckled linoleum floor. A sturdy black shoe poked beyond the hem.

The classroom was in a public school in Garden City, Michigan, a suburb of Detroit, where "Catechism," religious instruction for Catholic children, was held on Wednesday nights. The parish my family belonged to in 1960, St. Mel's in Dearborn Heights, did not yet have a school, so the Catholic Church borrowed the public classrooms after school hours. I loved Catechism and I loved Sister.

Sister's slender face, open like a sunflower, was pinched between the sides of her starched wimple, her white headdress, covered by a black veil. Her pretty cornflower blue eyes sparkled, and her lips curved into a smile's hint. She smelled like spearmint.

"And still waters run deep," she said. Braided strawberry blond pigtails lay against the pink plaid seersucker blouse that fell over my skirt. Clutched to my chest was a copy of the "Baltimore Catechism," the official book of Catholic doctrine for children in the United States.

I was required to memorize that Catechism. It was written in the form of hundreds of questions and answers. "*Question:* What is God? *Answer:* God is infinitely perfect spirit. *Question:* Why did God make me? *Answer:* God made me to know him, to love him, to serve him in this world and to be happy with him forever in heaven. *Question:* What other effects followed from the sin of our first parents (Adam and Eve)? *Answer:* Our nature was corrupted by the sin of our first parents, which darkened our understanding, weakened our will, and left us in a strong inclination to evil."[1]. I fell in love with a perfect God. I was also terrified of my corrupt nature.

Sister's job was to prepare me, a second grader, to receive the Catholic sacraments of Penance (Confession) and Holy Communion. After receiving the sacraments, I would be allowed to accompany my parents to the communion rail to receive the body of Christ. That made me happy. The teaching, called transubstantiation, that the one-inch, paper thin round communion wafer was the actual body of Jesus puzzled me. Crunching on the body of Jesus smushed into a quarter-sized wafer seemed bizarre to my young mind. I was taught this was a miracle.

"Your communion day will be special, Linda," Sister said. She cupped my cheek in her hand. Her voice was melodic and kind.

"God will be nearby. Ask him to help you be good and make a special wish," she said. I surveyed the possibilities: a bike, maybe;

a Barbie, a good option; another sibling—nope; two sisters and a brother were enough.

Sister tapped my nose and sent me out the door to walk the four blocks home. For weeks, I weighed what I would ask for from God.

The Big Day arrived. To prepare, my mother, Ma, and I had made a trip in a city bus to downtown Detroit; we visited the flagship J. L. Hudson department store. A Black man, an elevator attendant in a crisp blue uniform with gold epaulettes and buttons welcomed us into a car and punched the switch for the eleventh floor. The door opened to a sea of circular racks filled with fancy white dresses and veils.

On my First Communion Day, Ma slid the lace dress I had chosen over my head. "This is a special day for our family," she said. It was May and the bedroom curtains fluttered in a lilac-scented breeze. We were alone. Ma had helped me fasten on my new white patent leather shoes. She knelt in front of me in her best dress in mauve, her favorite color. An intricate gold dragon necklace with a large amethyst stone was fastened around her neck. Dad had brought it back for her from Japan, where he served during the Korean War as an Air Force radioman, legendary for his trouble-shooting abilities. She wore that necklace only on special occasions. Ma fluffed my curly shoulder-length hair. She bobby-pinned a crystal and pearl studded tiara into it. The veil, layers of waist-length crystal-studded gauze floated around me. "You are beautiful, honey," she said. Her brown eyes sparkled. "I'm so proud of you."

All four of my grandparents had emigrated from Poland and we observed many Polish traditions. Our house smelled of the savory kielbasa, fresh and smoked, that simmered in the canning pot on the basement stove. After I received my first communion in church, my relatives on both sides of our extended family would come over to share a Polish meal and to bring gifts.

Ma had worn herself ragged over the past few days cooking every morsel our large family would eat. We had cleaned the cement block basement and decorated it with white crepe paper. The high rectangular windows sparkled. A store-bought cake decorated in pink and white icing sat on a thin cotton towel placed over the washing machine. The money spent on that cake was a sacrifice.

"You stay calm," Ma said. Even at the tender age of seven, I got migraine headaches when I felt anxious or excited. I could see in the mirror of the dresser that my cheeks were flushed. I worried that an awful headache was brewing and was alert for the first sign—flashing lights in my vision, followed by searing pain, nausea, and vomiting. "I'd better go turn on the roasters so the food will be warm when we get back from church," she said.

When Ma left, I saw my chance to make my big ask of God—the God who was too busy most of the time to care, but today, would listen in on my prayers because I was about to eat him. I still had no idea what to ask for.

I screwed my eyes shut, knelt on the floor beside my bed and folded my small hands, fingers bitten to the quick, in prayer. I went to a place inside myself that I was familiar with—a place of quiet reverence, of awe, of timeless peace.

"Dear Jesus," I said. Sunlight fell on a white plastic rosary and a scapular, a long string necklace that connected two small pictures encased in plastic, one of The Blessed Mother, and one of Saint Simon of Stock, her devotee. These, along with a prayer book, were part of my "First Communion kit." Later in the day, a priest would place the scapular around my neck and consecrate me to Mary, the mother of Jesus.

Breathy and reverent, I heard my girlish voice pray. I was surprised at what came out. With a little heart wide open, reaching beyond the fear that I would die young, I prayed:

"Please God. I want to know what the fullness of life means."

CHAPTER 4

ORIGIN STORY

T HE BIG SANDEL clan, my dad, his nine siblings, their spouses and my many cousins were gathered in Grandma's and Grandpa's basement in 1964 waiting on our traditional Polish Christmas Eve dinner.

The spicy aroma of pierogi pan-fried in butter, the savory fragrance of Golumpki, cabbage rolls in tomato broth stuffed with ground meat and green peppers, mixed with the nutty scent of coffee brewing in a three-gallon aluminum pot, wafted up the stairwell. I loved belonging to a boisterous Polish family. I thought we were fascinating people—colorful, giving, religious and proud of our roots in the Old Country.

I was in the living room of the modest bungalow in a Polish neighborhood in Detroit. The home was familiar; we visited every other weekend. I had slipped upstairs to look out the front picture window to see if I could glimpse Santa and his reindeer.

I peeked around a wide, real Christmas tree lit with bubble lights, small candle-like fixtures that fizzed up from the bottom. A tiny musical train ran through a miniature village on the snow blanket beneath the tree. To my eight-year-old eyes, it was magical. Lights twinkled around the window.

My family, Ma, Dad, me, and now two younger sisters and

two younger brothers, one a newborn, had made the snowy drive from the suburbs to Grandma's house. We would have dinner here and attend midnight Mass at nearby St. Hedwig's, a cathedral-like church, a hushed, dark place with a vast, vaulted interior that echoed the smallest sounds, gold-rimmed alters, twinkling votive candles and stained-glass windows. My grandpa had helped to build the church. After mass, we would return to home in the suburbs to open our presents. By contrast, Christmas day was quieter. We would rest and visit some of Ma's family, also Polish.

My army of aunts proclaimed that dinner was ready; it was time to break Oplatek, a Polish word meaning sacred bread. I knew Grandma would soon circulate among the family downstairs with a silver plate holding stacks of pink and white square wafers embossed with the Christian Nativity scene. Adults and children alike would pair off, break pieces off each other's wafers and share good wishes, sealed with a hug and kiss.

"May you live long. May you get the best grades in school. May you be happy. May you be a good girl." These were the wishes I would hear. I loved and disliked the breaking of Oplatek. Loved that it was unique and Polish, loved the connection with family. Disliked that I never quite knew what to wish adults and disliked the smell of alcohol on their breath – by that time of the night, my adult relatives could be quite tipsy, and their wishes could become lectures.

I turned to go downstairs but stopped for a moment in front of an unusual picture I loved of the Blessed Mother and Jesus. They were *Black*. I was curious about this—in most pictures, the Lady was White. I reached up to touch the picture, to trace the gold filagree on the trim of the Madonna's royal blue gown. She was magnificent and beautiful.

Jesus, dressed in crimson, sat on her lap. Both of their heads were rimmed with bright gold halos. Jesus had a book in his right hand and his left hand was held up to his mother. His index and middle finger pointed at her, like he was her teacher.

I didn't realize Grandma had come up behind me until she

placed both her hands on my shoulders. I sank into her comfortable folds. She spoke Polish. When she immigrated to America, she refused to learn English; she hadn't wanted to leave the Old Country. I don't know why I loved that about her, maybe because it mirrored my rebellious nature. I didn't understand her words, but the feeling behind them was reverent, awed.

A bounteous woman with a generous bosom, Grandma wore a flowered print dress covered with a white apron. There were smudges of flour on her arms. I looked up at her; behind her wire-rimmed glasses, her eyes were wet, and a tear slid down her rounded, wrinkled apple cheek.

Aunt Jenny, one of Grandma's youngest daughters, a warm, fun-loving, and pretty woman with red-gold hair like mine, came up alongside us. I was very fond of her.

"Grandma says this is Our Lady of Czestochowa [chess-ta-hoe-va], the Black Madonna," Aunt Jenny said, her voice low and like a melody. "Her home is in Poland. Grandma prays to her always. She says you should, too. The Lady will protect you, as she does all Polish people. Some day you must visit her. She helps us to love and heals all sorrow." She translated for Grandma, who continued to weep.

"Why are the Lady and Jesus Black?" I asked Aunt Jenny. The coo-coo clock on the wall chimed and a little bird flew out of a brown birdhouse. "This picture is a copy of one in Czestochowa which was burned in a fire," she said. "It survived, and that was a miracle. The black is soot." I thought it was odd that only the faces were black, but before I could ask for an explanation, Aunt Jenny said, "It's time for Oplatek."

She and Grandma hurried downstairs, but I stood in front of the painting a while longer. Something in Grandma's voice and presence, a love, a certainty, faith, had connected me to the beautiful, quiet feeling in my heart a place silent, and holy.

I'll be like Grandma and be the Black Lady's daughter, I thought. This exemplar of love and healer of sorrow felt far more approachable than a punishing male God. I vowed in front of that picture to visit the Black Madonna someday, to let her know how much she meant to me and my grandma. I kept my promise.

My quest to know the Divine Mother had begun.

CHAPTER 5

THE DARK OF MY EYE

I *will be in an accident. I will lose an eye. I will die.*
As these thoughts bloomed, I was consumed by terror in my ten-year-old body. Terror was a monster that chewed my gut and spit nervous energy from the tip-top of my head to my toes. I would not tell the school counselor who sat across from me about this monster. I would keep my hell private. I had picked up a belief founded on mistrust and being the butt of jokes, that Polish people best took care of their own business.

The terror monster had started to chase me months before, after I watched an episode of *Dr. Kildare*, a popular weekly medical drama that aired between 1961 and 1966 about a young, handsome intern in a metropolitan hospital. In the episode, *A time for every purpose* ² a teen-aged girl lost her eye due to an injury in an automobile accident.

After watching the show, I bolted to the small bathroom in our bungalow. I stood in front of the mirror of the medicine chest and stared at my reflection. My freckles stood out against a bleached face. I moved closer to gaze into the center, the iris, the dark of the eye that I was certain God was going to take from me. A foreboding took root in my body, a tailspin into an abyss of panic.

I couldn't fall asleep that night. I tossed in my bed and re-imagined the show. For the first of dozens of nights to come, I crept down the carpeted stairs from my bedroom and sought safety in the hub of the house, the kitchen.

"Somebody help me," I prayed and sobbed. In my flannel nightgown, I sat down next to a heating register in a small cubby between the stove and the hallway. I curled into the heat on the linoleum floor, leaned against the kitchen counter, and crossed my arms on my chest to stop shaking. I hadn't bothered to turn on the overhead light; I sat in the dim shadows cast by a fluorescent night light on the stove. I wanted to wake up my mother or father. I wanted their comfort. I wanted them to make the terror stop.

No matter how hard I tried, I couldn't be a good and perfect kid. I felt certain God intended to punish me in an accident.

"What's the matter, Lin?" Ma said as she rounded the corner from her bedroom. Her dark hair was tousled, and her sleep-puffy features were worried. She sank to the floor next to me and slipped her arm around my shoulders. She did her best to listen and to comfort me that night and on many such nights, but she couldn't expunge the monster.

I acted out at school. In my anxious state, it was hard to grasp analytical concepts; fourth grade mathematics were beyond me. My teacher was impatient, and her irritation fed my panic. I masturbated in my classroom. I knew I wasn't supposed to do that in public, but the sensation of orgasm gave me relief from tension. I had discovered this guilty pleasure early. My Ma had caught me doing it at home and had told me it was an activity for the bedroom alone. It was the masturbation that got me referred to a school counselor.

"You can tell me anything you want," Mrs. Gast said. She was kind, middle-aged, with a comfortable, padded body. I sat on a wooden chair at a wooden desk between us. The compact office was framed in cement blocks painted a nondescript color. I didn't want to tell Mrs. Gast about the Dr. Kildare thing. Doing so would make me relive the nightmare and I felt stupid that a TV show had bothered me so much.

Our session was a respite from my fourth-grade classroom and my sad and irritated teacher. The counseling office was sterile, absent of homey touches. Rectangular florescent lights glared from the ceiling. A wide window framed the empty playground behind the school. I bent my head and picked up a crayon to draw a picture.

I would hold out in my rebellion against counseling for many months, until summer vacation interrupted the cycle of nighttime terrors and daytime anxiety. Once I got absorbed in the freedom of bike riding, baseball games, tree climbing and friends, I felt better and could sleep again—a miracle.

Now, though, I had something else to be afraid of—anxiety itself. Anxiety became an endless rabbit hole. From that point on until I was in my fifties, the fear of it was never far from the edges of my awareness. It could consume me at any time—and it often did.

Ordinary human things became hard. In public rest rooms I was afraid that others might hear me pee. Sometimes I would be near desperate to pee, but I could not relax. If I thought I was taking too long in the bathroom, causing someone else to wait, it became even more impossible.

I learned that counting the tiles on floors or ceilings helped. Counting, counting, counting, anything and everything, became one of my "go to" solutions for managing.

For years, I hid the severity of my anxiety. Its origin baffled me. Some people had very real traumas, mine had been a television show.

I was sure God abandoned me in that time, and in every time when anxiety swallowed me. Anxiety became a reoccurring dark night of the soul. I prayed and God did not answer.

A vicarious catastrophe about an accident and a lost eye coalesced a central question of my life: why and where does God hide when we hurt?

CHAPTER 6

CONFESSION

I WAS A juicy sapling, a ten-year-old in love with life.

I wanted to shimmy up the maple tree in the backyard and feel the rough bark scrape against my thighs as I climbed toward my favorite crook in the canopy of summer green. I wanted to play Old Maid up there with my best friend, Susie, and eat fuzzy peaches.

Instead, I rode my bike to church in 1963 on a brilliant warm Saturday, to make a confession. I had sinned too much, and my soul was stained, or so I'd been taught. It was time to seek God's mercy in the sacrament of Penance, where Catholics whispered their shameful secrets to a priest and begged forgiveness.

My sins were venial, minor traffic violations. Unlike mortal transgressions, which could rack up points against my license to heaven and even cremate my soul in hell, venial sins, unforgiven, could consign me to purgatory.

Purgatory was limbo, a torture of ambiguity. God decided how much expiatory suffering he needed before the soul was pure enough to enter heaven. His sentence was classified information. Aware that death could come anytime, I went to confession often to keep my soul squeaky clean.

I had a conspicuous "attitude" that adults did not like. I had sassed my parents. I had lied—created minor fabrications to jazz up stories. I had masturbated—a guilty pleasure I couldn't resist. I felt humiliated about my sins. The benefits of the confessional were lost on me. I went because I was terrified of dying in an unforgiven state, unshriven.

I parked my bike in the rack and strained open the wide glass door of the church vestibule. My rubber-soled sneakers sucked and released against the floor as I crept toward the front of the church and the confessionals.

St. Mel's Church was empty, hushed in the late morning on a Saturday. The quiet mirrored the way I felt inside when I was alone in the sanctuary. The feeling was so delicious; I shivered. A whiff of cedar incense leftover from services hung in the air. Sunlight filtered through the stained-glass windows high on the vaulted walls and dappled the pews with prisms. Wooden beams in honeyed oak gave the church an informal warmth.

I knew every inch of that church because I had cleaned much of it. All-wise church fathers had decided centuries before that I was not worthy of being an altar-boy, so I served in the way girls of the time did—as a pint-sized housekeeper.

Earlier that week, I had cleaned the sacristy, the sanctum of power, where priests dressed for mass. It was a task reserved for trustworthy children (or maybe the most compulsive cleaners). I could never be a priest, I knew, but I folded the embroidered stoles they wore around their necks, with reverence. I fingered their chasubles made of jewel-toned brocades and silks, violet, rose, sapphire, and gold. I imagined myself wearing them. I draped a stole or two around my neck and budding breasts. Another sin, I'm sure.

At the front of the church, I genuflected and made the sign of the cross. I slid into the wooden pew and chewed my nails. Finally, it was my turn to confess.

Heavy maroon curtains made a door to the confessional; I pulled them aside and plunked down on the wooden kneeler. My weight, insubstantial as it was, triggered the switch that turned on a small red light on the outside of the cubicle. Catholics knew the glowing scarlet bulb meant do not approach, do not go in, do not disturb.

The priest, my confessor, was in an adjacent box. Another penitent was in a box that matched mine on the other side of his. She had begun her confession and I heard her say it had been three months since her last one.

This priest, the parish pastor, was grey-haired and stooped. He scowled a lot and seemed irritated most of the time. He stalked around in a severe black cassock and white collar. I thought he didn't like children. He was a razor wire fence I had to get past to reach God's forgiveness. I was terrified of him and his power and did my absolute best to stay out of his way. My heart had sunk that day when I realized that he was on duty for confession rather than his associate, who was jovial and kind.

The other penitent, a grown-up, poured out anguish about something called an "affair." To eavesdrop was a sin, another sin to confess. To listen might even be a mortal sin; it was *that* bad. I had to find a way to block her out. With what teachers called my "outside voice," I belted out, *"I'm a Yankee Doodle Dandy. A real doer, do or die! A real, live nephew of my Uncle Sam, born on the fourth of July. Oh, I'm a Yankee Doodle sweetheart..."*[3]

My hands rested on the ledge of a small rectangle window covered by a thick screen. This screen was the portal to the box where the priest sat on his throne. It was only a folding chair, I knew because I had dusted it, but I thought of it as a throne.

When the wooden door on the window that separated me from the priest banged open, the sound reverberated in the empty church, and I jumped.

"Shut up, for God's sake," the priest said. "What's wrong with you, singing in a confessional?"

Father's voice was raspy. The rancid smell of alcohol on his breath pushed me back. I had smelled it on the breath of relatives, and I knew it meant their behavior became unpredictable, even aggressive. My extended family drank heavily when they got together. One of my aunts had blemished my First Communion Day with an angry, drunken outburst. I felt uneasy. *"Do priests drink, too?"* I wondered. *"I thought they were too holy for that."*

The priest, a personification of Jesus, had yelled at me; I had committed another sin, a big one; mortal. I knew I should just begin, "Bless me father, for I have sinned." But I could not find my voice.

An exigent thought said, "run."

I stood up and the pew creaked beneath me as the light above the door extinguished. I brushed aside the velvet curtain. I ran past sympathetic St. Joseph with children at his feet. I ran past the big Jesus slumped on the massive wooden cross above the altar. I did not pause to genuflect in front of him like I was supposed to. Another sin. I ran past my beloved and beautiful Blessed Mother on her side altar and caught a whiff of the fresh roses at her feet. The votive candles around her flickered as I whooshed past.

My heart was torn. Although young, I had a deep, felt sense of a magnificent God who showered me with love. I felt a warm, personal relationship with the perfect spirit that the Baltimore Catechism had pointed me to. I yearned to understand that God. But I was terrified of the exacting, punishing God my religion had also handed me. Which God was the Truth?

The day of my confession mishap, I ran to a God who didn't judge children so harshly. I ran to a God of forgiveness and understanding. I ran to a God of forever and always love.

I wouldn't have a sure fix on that God until I was forty-seven years old. Redemption would have to wait.

CHAPTER 7

FIRST KISS

S EVEN MONTHS AFTER we met, Jim bent to kiss me. The light, gentle touch of his lips was flavored with the bitterness of guilt, the spice of desire, and the sweetness of love. I opened my lips and melted into all of it.

"I'm sorry, Linda," he said as we pulled apart. Our hips touched on the splintered top of a weather-beaten picnic table at a roadside rest stop in early summer of 1978.

The sun was high and hot. A blur of breezes whispered against my skin; the protective coverlet of a just-sprouted tree canopy provided shade. Jim's shiny black Honda motorcycle was parked on the gravel drive in front of us. "I shouldn't have done that," he said, his voice rubbed with regret. We had crossed our first Rubicon.

I had wanted to show off my body, so I'd worn cream-colored short shorts and a coral-colored halter top. He wore jeans; he'd taken his shirt off and stuffed it in the bike's tank bag; he loved to ride without it. My arm was wrapped around his naked back. I felt the warmth of his skin and smelled the Hawaiian suntan lotion I'd rubbed on him earlier. A child's ponytail ring lay in the just-mowed grass. Birds chattered in the background. "Be gentle with yourself, Jim," I said as I looked up at him. "You're human. Let *me* take care of *me*."

The look on Jim's face was part happiness, part chagrin. He was afraid he had betrayed my trust in him as a priest and friend. I assured him he had not. Later, I worried that we'd broken a taboo, but in that moment, there was only a peaceful feeling of rightness, a sense of deep connection to the quiet place inside me.

After meeting Jim at dinner at his sister Denise's home that winter, I had tried not to think about him. He was away for three months at the alcoholism recovery center for priests. I learned from Denise that when he was discharged, he asked Maryknoll for a sabbatical from mission work and got a job as a chaplain to students at Siena Heights, a Catholic College in southeastern Michigan. He wanted time to strengthen his sobriety. He moved into a small cottage on a side street near the college supplied as part of his contract. His housemate, Jon Taylor, a priest, was a professor of theological studies. Jim was busy adjusting to his new life.

I worked long hours at my job; it was absorbing and stretched my talents and skills. I conceptualized, wrote, and designed a slick internal employee magazine that came out monthly. I travelled often to do interviews and photography for my stories. My work ethic had been noticed and I'd been put on a fast track for performance evaluations, salary adjustments and bonuses. My salary today would have the purchasing power of a six-figure income.

My non-working life was organized around religion. I made time every week to teach Catechism, religious instruction for children, at my local Catholic parish and to attend weekly meetings of the Young Singles group I'd co-founded with Denise and Larry, Jim's sister, and her boyfriend. I attended training to become a master catechist and a lay minister to young, single adults.

But I had also begun to question my Catholicism. In my final semester at Michigan State University, where three years before, in 1975, I earned a bachelor's degree in journalism, I had enrolled in a class on the philosophies of world religions.

As I explored the beautiful cosmologies and theologies of other religions, I questioned my belief, which I'd accepted as a child, that Catholicism was "the one true religion." It now seemed right that there are many paths up the mountain to home, to God.

In the world religions course, I was also introduced to the thinking of Carl Jung, who had observed that there were "archetypes"—patterns of understanding, recurrent mental images or motifs held in a "collective unconscious" that showed up across religions. I wondered if there was something universal behind life that was the same but was thought and written about differently depending on culture. I liked that my heart felt more open, wider, with my musings. It was exhilarating!

Jim became a regular at the Young Single's Wednesday night dinner meetings. After a pot-luck meal, we pulled encounter exercises from personal development books like *Values Clarification* [4] and *What Color is Your Parachute* [5]. Our sharing was intimate; we got to know each other's hearts well. We talked about religion and spirituality; it dawned on me that the two were connected but not the same.

"I know I'm religious," Jim said, at one such discussion, "but I don't know if I'm spiritual." About twelve men and women lounged in a comfortable patchwork circle in the living room of Denise's cottage. Some were on the couches, some in bean bags or just cross-legged on the floor. The room was paneled in pine, miniature lamps spilled muted light into the early evening darkness. We were dressed in jeans and flannel, or sweatshirts to ward off the fall chill.

After our group discussion, Jim celebrated Mass. It was time for the homily, and rather than preach, he often led a conversation. The room was quiet. We listened with attention. Candles flickered on the tables. "I have a hard time with a God who stands silent when people suffer," Jim said.

I was surprised that a priest didn't have a handle on God. I was drawn to his candor like a moth to flame.

I mused that everybody searched to understand the nature of the spiritual. I was less of an oddity than I thought. I adored Jim's humility, and self-effacing humor. He was real and I wanted to be like him. If I were, I would be unafraid, unafraid of death, unafraid of life, unafraid to be myself, embracing questions and imperfections. There was reason to hope.

When summer arrived, Jim invited me on a motorcycle ride, but I was crushed to learn he'd also taken a spin with another woman in the Young Single's group. He invited me again, however, and by July we were riding at any opportunity we could carve out of our schedules.

I teetered every day between an intuitive trust of the gentle feeling unfolding between us and doubt fueled by rational questions. Questions about the strength of his sobriety. Questions about his conflicted vow to be celibate. Questions about just how far God's understanding of our humanness could be stretched.

Could He forgive me and a priest for falling in love?

CHAPTER 8

TURTLES

C OUNTRY ROADS, FREE of traffic, unfolded in front us as Jim and I moved on his motorcycle through Michigan and Indiana on our way to Shipshewana in Amish country. Stalks of sweet corn fringed in silk waved in the endless ocean of ripening summer fields. Crickets chirped into the late June day in 1978.

Weeks before, Jim had been "deadheading"—his word for motorcycle rides taken with no planned route or destination in mind. He had discovered the Das Dutchman Essenhaus, an Amish style restaurant he wanted to share with me. So, we arranged our first weekend road trip several weeks after our first kiss. I was ecstatic and nervous.

I felt uneasy that I'd lied to my parents about where I'd be that weekend. Even at age twenty-four, I went home almost every Sunday for dinner and had fabricated an excuse to explain my absence.

On our way to the restaurant, a 300-mile trip, we'd paused for rest breaks and our conversations turned to Jim's struggles with his priesthood and the Catholic church.

There were deep, strong currents of unresolved questions, mid-life conflicts, moving in Jim. I remember wondering if I had jumped into a river that might dash my heart against boulders.

I never considered pulling away in self-protection. When I listened *within,* I felt a quiet peace and a curiosity in the face of the unknown.

"The Vatican is intent on building churches in the jungle," Jim said, as we sat on a picnic table at a roadside rest stop, the bike parked in front of us. My royal blue half-helmet, which we called "the turtle," and oversized sunglasses were on the seat of the motorcycle. Jim had fastened white, fuzzy sheepskin to the saddle to pad my seat. Long rides were tough on our bottoms. His faded jeans and navy-blue T-shirt were topped by a red bandana. His face had the vague look of faraway and yesterday. He was with his heart, back in the Philippines. A cigarette smoldered in his right hand.

"Poor folks don't need buildings for worship," he said. "They need food, homes, access to fresh water, someone to care about them." He rubbed and twisted the pewter Celtic puzzle ring on his left-hand ring finger. I now wore a similar ring that he'd given me on my right hand.

"They also need help resisting a repressive government," Jim said. Jim loved the Filipino people, loved serving them and loved their culture. He was disgusted by the corruption of their government and the United States' support of their rich dictator leaders, Ferdinand Marcos, and his wife Imelda (famous for her big closet filled with over three thousand pairs of shoes). He intensely disliked the CIA's involvement in the country. He grieved over his parishioners who had disappeared, presumed victims of clashes between the Marcos regime and anti-government communist death squads.

Since returning from the Philippines, he had participated in strikes for higher wages for migrant workers, and against lettuce and grape growers in California, led by Cesar Chavez' National Farm Workers Association. He searched newspapers to follow their struggle. He looked for opportunities to protest the Vietnam War.

Jim admired Daniel Berrigan, a Jesuit priest, antiwar activist, and Christian pacifist, and took me to one of his anti-war lectures in Ann Arbor, Michigan. I was unsettled by an experience I had as we arrived and entered the conference hotel.

"How odd," I'd said to Jim as we passed under a portico into the lobby. A man had jumped out of the crowd and taken our picture with a flashbulb camera. He wore a dark suit, shined shoes, and a fedora. Super fit, he had broad shoulders and was tall. His face was solemn, and the energy about him was not friendly. He didn't fit the crowd, a mix of young people dressed in the hippie look, tie-died t-shirts and bell-bottom jeans; University of Michigan college professors; priests, and nuns. Jim wore jeans, his biking boots, and a navy t-shirt, his cigarettes were rolled into one of the sleeves. I was in shorts, a blouse, and sneakers. The day was humid and sunny. A spent flash bulb lay crushed on the sidewalk.

"Your picture has just become part of an FBI file," Jim said, with a dry laugh. "Berrigan is being watched." I was horrified. I did not share Jim's activist heart. I *was* interested in learning about liberation theology—about a view of Jesus as a champion of the poor, a crusader against injustice and about a God who had an intimate concern for the suffering of "the least among us." But I was not keen on brushing with power and government.

Jim interrupted my reverie about the FBI encounter. "Hey Lin," Jim said. "Let's get rolling so we can get to the Das Dutchman before the dinner rush." He slid off the table, stamped his cigarette under his scuffed biker's boot, raised his leg over the bike and stood square and firm as I climbed aboard. He watched from the rear-view mirror. He looked happy; being on the bike seemed to help clear his mind of brooding thoughts.

I loved our rides, both dead-headers and destined. I reveled in the adventure and fun. I was thrilled to be out of my comfort zone and taking more risks.

Jim taught me how to be a good biking partner, to lean into curves and surrender to the dip and weave of riding.

On our first rides, I'd resisted the dynamics of the bike by leaning in the opposite direction of a curve to maintain a sense of balance. This destabilized the bike. After a ride or two, Jim had said, "Lin, hang onto me tight as I lean into curves. Go with my body. It might feel scary, but it'll be easier for me to navigate the curve and the ride will be sweeter, more fun for both of us."

It was late afternoon; soon the smell of green would come out. By this time, we'd taken enough motorcycle trips that I knew about a time—just at the point when day yields to dusk, when the fragrance of nature rushes to meet the cooler air. I looked forward to this mystery; I'd pull the scent into my nose and try to hang on to it. This was the aroma of heaven. I smiled back to the rear-view mirror; I was ready to greet what I came to call "the time of green."

We rounded a curve, and I leaned deep into it. Jim braked the bike and stuck out his legs as we coasted to a stop. "I have to get off for just a minute," he said. I dismounted, as did he. He strode ahead in his loping way as I watched.

Golden rays backlit the trees and threw deep shadows over the road. I saw Jim bend over and pick something dark up in the middle of the road. He carried it with both hands to the opposite berm and laid it down. He returned a moment later.

"It was a turtle," he said. "I stop and move them, so they won't get run over," he said, sheepishly. His sunglasses hid his eyes. I fell in love with him even more. His smile was shy, tentative. "I notice which direction they're going and move them to safety. I imagine they are trying to get to their families. Sounds silly, I guess," he said. He turned, mounted the bike, and stood tall so I could climb behind him. I rubbed his back. "Not to me," I said. He paused for a moment, his gloved hands at rest on the rubber hand grips.

"I'm like a turtle—shell on the outside I carry with me wherever I go. Inside, soft, and vulnerable," he said. He reached to switch on the ignition and then stopped. "I like you because you help me get where I'm going," he said. He glanced at me in the rearview mirror and smiled. I melted. And with that, we were off.

At the restaurant, we sat at a round wooden table savoring the mouth-watering aromas divulged by platters of golden broasted chicken, savory mashed potatoes with gravy, applesauce, pickled beets, and chilled coleslaw. Over dinner, Jim turned the conversation to our relationship. He measured his words.

"I have strong feelings for you," he said, "and I don't want to hurt you." An invisible barrier snapped up, a place in him where I could not go. I shivered, though the air wasn't chilly.

"I fell in love with a woman in the Philippines," he said. His voice was quiet; he broke my gaze and looked down. I wasn't surprised. Jim was charismatic with women. In a time where we were held in place far more than now by male dominance, his gentleness and egalitarian *being* were breaths of fresh air. In the security of that lived equality, I, like so many other women, could relax and self-express. Yet, shutters snapped over my heart. *How much had she meant to him? Was he still in love with her?*

I put down my fork and stroked his hand. "I told her when I left that I intended to stay a priest and that I didn't know if I would return to the Islands. I hurt her," he said. "I don't want to repeat that."

CHAPTER 9

ZIPPERS

W EEKS LATER, THE murmur of distant campers on the Leelanau Peninsula drifted toward our pup tent on a stiff breeze tinged with the musty scent of Lake Michigan. The chirp of insects sounded in pulses. A shadow of flickers from the dying campfire played on the pitched walls. Jim and I had escaped into anonymity on another weekend trip.

Our green nylon tent was small. We snuggled close for warmth. Jim drew me to him and kissed me. His hands moved to my breasts. We were about to cross another Rubicon. He pulled on the zipper of my sleeping bag. It stuck fast; the zipper would not budge. We took that as a sign to go slow.

"Guess the bag has a better idea!" Jim said. We laughed with exasperation and relief. "Keep the zippers up," became our metaphor for abstaining from intercourse.

We settled into a peculiar relationship waltz: one step forward toward intimacy, one step sideways to grapple with guilt and doubt, one step back in restraint and retreat, and another step to get our bearings and move forward again.

A month after the zipper got stuck, we took a longer motor-cycle ride together, a week of vacation. Jim was eager for me to experience Skyline Drive and the Blue Ridge Parkway through the

Appalachian Mountains of Virginia and North Carolina; it was his favorite bike run.

He packed one saddlebag with his clothes, the other was for me. We loaded a miniature stove and lantern, and kitchenware, into the trunk box and strapped sleeping bags and pads, and a tent stuffed into a duffle bag, on top. The tank bag held our toiletry items and my cosmetics. We "nook and cranny" packed small stuff wherever we could find a place. I loved to watch the amusement and amazement of other campers as a fully equipped campsite sprang from the bike. I was proud of our ingenuity!

Our first night out, we found a rustic campsite, no showers, or toilets, in the Monongahela Forest on Cheat Mountain in West Virginia. We munched hot dogs, no buns, and Campbell's pork and beans, and finished off with cookies we'd purchased at an Amish bakery along Route 250 through Ohio. We wiggled into our sleeping bags and reached for each other.

"Can you do this, Jim, without beating yourself up?" I asked, as our caresses grew more urgent. Light from the ebbing campfire diffused a sheen on the skin of his arm. The crackle of the fire was the top note in the symphony of our quickened breathing, the roar of crickets and the sound of the nearby Monongahela River. I traced a scar on his left shoulder from a past motorcycle accident. "Can you?" he asked.

The zipper on my sleeping bag was still in place. But it wouldn't be for long. I knew I loved Jim. It felt to me like we had known each other across many lifetimes, though, at the time, I had given little thought to the notion of past lives.

"I can no longer believe in a God who could punish any human being for loving someone," I said. My heart hammered underneath my t-shirt. I'd already slipped off my jeans and panties. I was prepared; I'd gone on birth control weeks before, sure that we were headed toward sexual intimacy. Everything around me had receded. The moment was just all that was me and all that was Jim, suspended in this desire to merge.

"I can't promise I can stay with you," he said, his voice filled with regret and conflict. Clouds of desire and uncertainty shrouded his eyes. I reached for the zipper on my sleeping bag.

"I'm not asking you to stay," I said. The fire of love burned in my chest, a peace beyond understanding settled in my bones. "All I need to know is that, right now, you love me and that what we're about to do is coming from that place."

Tears slid off his face and splashed on his sleeping bag. "You're clearer about love than anyone I've ever met," he said. He kissed me. "I want the certainty you have. I'm finding deeper feelings inside—it's new and exciting. I do love you."

We escaped our zippers and slipped, naked, into the arms of Eros.

In the morning, we bathed in a rippled pond, surrounded by shagbark hickory pines, sycamores, and red oak trees. Sunlight streamed through the wisps of early morning mountain fog. *This is heaven,* I thought. I wrapped my arms around Jim's waist. A laugh burbled up from my core.

"What's so funny?" Jim asked. His hair was slicked to his head. Rivulets of water poured down his neck. "You do realize that we've now made love twice on *Cheat* Mountain! A bit of an irony for a Catholic priest and his lover," I said. He nuzzled my neck and was quiet for a moment. "Well, if this is cheating, I'm guilty. But I've never felt less so."

In my journal entry for that day, I thanked God for our relationship. "You write a new chapter on loving in the book of my life," I wrote. "Love is so simple to speak, yet so difficult to master. It is the true language of the human tongue—it has many different dialects—including the one Jim and I create for ourselves."

Lovemaking that day pulled me deep into my body. I experienced a whole-body surrender—there were no questions, no doubts, no insecurities to distract from pure sensual pleasure. I explored womanhood and God in new ways, as the complement to Jim's masculinity. "He delights in my femininity," I wrote, "It is good, it is whole, and it is holy."

CHAPTER 10

FREE PEOPLE

"TIME TO GO say mass," Jim said as he dressed one Sunday morning after a night of lovemaking. He had donned black slacks, a black short-sleeved shirt, and a white clerical collar. As I watched Jim fasten the collar, I felt pangs of guilt. I was naked, wrapped in white bed sheets in the tiny bedroom of the cottage he shared with Fr. Jon near the university campus where he served as a chaplain.

Was I being selfish? I wondered. Later that day in my journal, I wrote, "I'm not going to run away from the chance to love Jim. It's unorthodox and controversial. It's also an invitation to growth, self-discovery and—perhaps—it can make a significant difference in his life, too."

Jon was in the kitchen making breakfast; the aroma of coffee and fresh bread was delicious. Whenever I visited, Jim's house-mate welcomed me and assured me that it was wonderful to have a woman around the house.

"Would it be ok if I came to mass?" I asked Jim. "Of course," he said. "You'll inspire my sermon." Jim was known for earthy homilies that included stories about his life and his friends; he was willing to be vulnerable and took delight in self-effacing humor. "Just don't mention *me* in your sermon," I said.

I got an ardent kiss before he walked out the door. "Free people, free people," Jim said, as he released me from a hug. "Your freedom to give love is freeing me to find it and give it, too. I feel freer to be me in everything I do."

Jim headed out the door toward the University. I dressed and walked the several blocks over and slipped through the back door of the chapel.

I took a seat in a back pew and thought about the magical and mysterious synchronicity that Jim's journey had led him to a chaplaincy at a college, now a university, named after Catherine of Siena. I'd chosen Catherine to be my patron saint at my Confirmation, one of the Catholic Church's seven sacraments or rituals where divine grace is imparted to the recipient. In the Church's eyes, my full name became Linda Marie Catherine.

When I was deciding, at age eleven, which saint to pick, I was given a book about the lives of the saints. Catherine was described as a mystic, a counselor, and a doctor of the church. She was said to have "*fortitude.*" When I read that, I experienced a strong intuitive hit. A force shot through me; the hairs on my arm stood on end. I remember thinking, *I don't know what fortitude is, but I'm going to need it.*

With Catherine's fortitude on my mind, I watched Jim walk out of the sacristy in full priest gear. He wore a floor-length white garment, an Alb, and, over it a chasuble, a long, brocaded satin poncho in a jeweled color that symbolized the Church's liturgical season (i.e., white for Easter, purple for Lent, green for Ordinary Time). Around his neck, he had draped a royal blue and emerald stole he had brought back with him from the Philippines.

He greeted the congregation with warmth and humor. People around me broke out in big smiles. As they reacted with appreciation for his humanity, his warmth, his collegiality, I felt another strong pang of guilt.

This was my teeter-totter, the up-and-down and back-and-forth between guilt, shame, and peaceful certainty about the rightness of our love for each other.

"Our relationship has drawn me into awareness that, in love, all that I do is of you, God," I wrote in my journal that day. *"I am the I am. We are inseparable. I have faith in...miracles. The beauty and growth evolving from our attraction must be you in action."*

I tried to wrap my head around this Truth.

CHAPTER 11

DISCLOSURES

J IM AND I were honest people, not prone to dissembling—we didn't like being secretive. We were also crazy in love and wanted to share our happiness with others.

Soon after we made love on Cheat Mountain, we decided to tell our families about our relationship and face the music. On a weekend in late July, two months into our courtship, we set up separate times to talk with our parents. I decided it was best to face my parents alone. Jim invited me along to talk to his folks. We told our parents we wanted to allow our relationship to evolve but had no idea where it would take us.

Mine were aghast. For them, it was unthinkable that I was involved with a priest, and they were taken aback by the age difference between us. First, they refused to welcome Jim into their home. We went through a period of détente; we didn't talk about the relationship, but there were no overt fireworks. I was upset but determined to maintain my connection to my folks and stand firm in my love for Jim.

My mother softened first, several months after my disclosure. She stood in the kitchen washing pots, looking out the window at a wide expanse of green lawn dotted with maple and oak trees that rolled into the lapping waters of Strawberry Lake.

"Linda, there's something I want to say," she said. She wore her favorite faded light pink buttonless boucle cardigan, over a light purple knit top and slacks. The sweater sagged around her arms and the elbows were threadbare, but she wouldn't part with it. It was a gift from my sister Carol, who has an eye for clothes that please Ma. Because of her boundless reserves and work ethic, Ma was known in our family as the energizer bunny. Homemade spaghetti sauce bubbled on the stove behind her. The spicy aroma was delicious.

Ma's lips were pursed. That wasn't a good sign. "In church on Sunday, I prayed to know what to do about you and Jim. I'm troubled by your relationship because my religion says it's wrong," she said. Afternoon light filtered over her young-looking face, which at that moment was serious. I stood at the kitchen counter, a MacIntosh apple in hand, and waited for a bomb to fall.

"It occurred to me as I prayed that I welcome into my home your sister's husband, who is drinking too much and not always kind to her," Ma said. I was frozen in my tracks. I waited, still, at the butcher block counter. "He sits at our dinner table. Yet we ostracize Jim, a man who is gentle and kind, who has spent his lifetime so far serving God." She hesitated for a moment.

A football game blared on the television in the den adjacent to the kitchen, where dad was watching. Behind her glasses, Ma's brown eyes were clear in a face puzzled with emotion. "That doesn't make sense. As far as I'm concerned, Jim is welcome here and I will work on your father," she said. Relief flooded into my chest and my heart stopped pounding. I was grateful for my mother's change of heart. I pulled her close and she hugged me hard.

Work on my father she did. A week later, Jim was welcomed for Sunday dinner. Ma was warm to him; my dad was silent.

We also disclosed our relationship to Jim's parents, Jim Sr., and Lil. We sat with them at their large mahogany dining room table that Lil kept covered with a lace tablecloth under a glass top. There were newspaper and magazine clippings under the glass, recipes she wanted to try, or articles she had read and wanted to bring to her children's attention when they visited.

Jim's dad, slender and greyed, in his seventies, still pulled his milk route in Detroit. He wore his uniform, brown shirt, and brown twill trousers. "I suppose I could be a little disappointed because I've been proud of having a son who is a priest," he said. Jim Sr. attended Mass every Sunday and prayed the rosary often. His son had inherited his father's gentle and loving nature. The light from the chandelier reflected off Jim Sr.'s glasses, his eyes beneath them had misted. "But the most important thing, Jim, is that you're happy. That's all that matters. I already know I love Linda." My Jim, beside me, choked up and coughed. These words touched my heart and grew my already deep love for Jim's dad.

Lil spoke up, her voice high and thin. "The church took you far away from me when you went to Maryknoll and the missions, and took my daughters, too, when they entered the convent," she said to Jim. During Denise's and Ann's postulant and novice years, the first two steps on the way to full profession of vows as religious women, Lil had seen little of her daughters. She and her husband had driven many times to Adrian, Michigan and parked on a dirt road that ran alongside the motherhouse of the Dominican sisters. They'd hidden behind some lilac bushes until their daughters came out for a recreation period, just to get a glimpse of them. That picture scraped my heart; I couldn't imagine a mother having to do that.

"That was so hard," Lil said to Jim. "As far as I'm concerned, I'm happy if it works out and I have you around here for good."

And that was that. Lil rose and offered us a slice of her delicious lemon cake with thick chocolate icing poured over the top. Serving food was one of the ways Lil shared love. The matter was settled. Not another word about it would ever be said.

Denise and Larry, who had both navigated the transition from religious life to secular life, created an oasis of love and understanding around us. We told several other friends we were sure would understand. A small circle of people created a safe space for us to be ourselves and to love out in the open. It seemed that the love we were given by our families and friends amplified our own. We floated along, full of joy, for at least a year in this deep, clear river of unconditional love.

CHAPTER 12

PSYCHODRAMA

T HE CURRENT OF that river carried us to one of the last weddings Jim performed. He introduced me to the bride and
groom, Bob Brady, and Linda Brewster, who were psychologists
and adjunct professors in the counselor education program at
Siena Heights College.

They would grease the wheels of Jim's transition to the field of
addiction counseling and coax me out of the public relations field
and into mental health work. They were guardians at a threshold,
mentors to a new way of life. Jim had told Bob that we were a couple. A sincere Catholic, he encouraged Jim to ask me to their private wedding.

At the time, I lived in South Lyon, about an hour's drive from
the university. My job at the tech company had changed. My
beloved first boss had left the firm to start a dressage ranch. Her
replacement and I did not have an easy relationship. I transferred
to a marketing communications department to serve as a writer
and project manager. The work involved technical writing and
was not the best fit. I contemplated quitting.

As part of his compensation package for the chaplaincy at
Siena Heights University, Jim was offered free tuition and started
a master's degree in Counselor Education.

Either Bob or Linda, both consummate psychologists and warm, loving people, taught most of Jim's classes. Bob was passionate about psychodrama: a combination of psychology, sociology, and theater, created by Jacob Moreno, a Romanian American psychiatrist and psycho-sociologist. The technique facilitated insight into psychological dilemmas by enacting inner dramas as theater—as scenes and plays on a stage. Jim and I hurried, late, to a weekend psychodrama workshop that Bob was holding.

"This psychodrama stuff is fascinating," Jim said, as we approached a classroom in a building that would soon become like a second home. The hall was long and darkened. We passed chemistry and biology laboratories, this was the Science Building, and the smell of old books, sweaty students and preserving fluid was strong. Jim loped along next to me in jeans and a blue and rust ski sweater, his long, lean legs took big strides. "I hope you enjoy it," he said. I had zero idea what psychodrama or counseling were about. I just wanted to be with him.

I spent most weekends with Jim and his roommate, Jon, a professor, and theologian, cerebral and kind. He encouraged me to begin classes at the university, and in 1979, I enrolled in a master's degree program in Religious Studies. My first class was called "Methods in Theology." I didn't know what I would do with the degree; I started it because I wanted to know more about spirituality and philosophy, partially so that I could keep up in conversations with Jim and Jon.

After dinner one day, Jon drew out a book by Alfred North Whitehead, a mathematician and philosopher and read a passage: *"The foundation of reverence is this perception, that the present holds within itself the complete sum of existence, backwards and forwards, that whole amplitude of time, which is eternity."* [6]

"What do you think about that, Linda?" Jon's shaggy brown hair fell over the collar of his baggy blue sweater; his face wore not-yet-shaved stubble. He had on jeans and frayed suede slippers. We sat at a small table over plates that held the remnants of savory

Moroccan Chicken with couscous and crusts from the sourdough bread that Jon had baked that afternoon.

Jon was a fantastic gourmet cook, and the three of us often shared his creations, delectable dishes from a wide variety of cuisines—Moroccan, Vietnamese, Thai—exotic to a Polish girl. I was dressed in jeans and a Siena Heights sweatshirt and sat next to Jim, who had his arm around my back. A caramel flan sat on the cracked yellow laminate counter waiting for us. There was a discarded match on the floor by the gas stove, which was covered with pots and pans.

"Gosh, it sounds like Whitehead is saying it makes sense to live in the *now,* that in the *now* we can access all the knowledge of the past and intuit the future," I said, a bit hesitant, though I knew Jon well enough to know that he'd never judge an answer. "Precisely," Jon said, "you're a quick study. You should read more of Whitehead."

I did and was enthralled with Whitehead's deep, searching writings about the nature of God and religion.

Jim, Jon, and I had long conversations about heady topics like liberation theology, values clarification, and feminism. At the age of twenty-six, I was Alice in Wonderland, dropped through a hole into an intellectual, diverse world of shared scholarship.

When I expressed thoughts, which was infrequent, Jim and Jon, both in their forties, listened with care. They challenged and encouraged me to have a viewpoint. Their thoughtful consideration of my self-expression was refreshing and liberating.

A male executive at the tech company where I was employed had told me the only way I'd be taken seriously was, "to cut your hair, put a pair of glasses on your startling blue eyes, stop wearing dresses, and hide your body under a business suit." I'd had plenty of experiences of misogyny in the corporate world.

By contrast, Jim and Jon reveled in my femininity and scholarship. Their unconditional regard, along with exposure to graduate-level theology and philosophy, fermented vague dissatisfaction with the corporate milieu of my work-life.

Jim was enthralled with helping others and had begun to see a future as a chemical dependency counselor. He shared his excitement about all that he was learning with Jon and me. Jim talked often about Bob, who ran a successful private practice near Toledo, Ohio. Jim admired Bob's proficiency and power as a helper, as well as his depth as a human being.

Jim and I entered a large classroom; the psychodrama workshop was about to begin. Bob stood in the center of the room, silhouetted by the morning sun that gleamed into the big empty space. All the desks had been pushed out of the way, against the wall.

"You're late," he said. Silvery-blonde hair, permed into an afro style, framed a handsome, craggy face. He was an impressive man, tall and broad-shouldered. A soft beige sweater, cashmere, I thought, draped over his khaki cargo slacks. The sleeves were pushed up to reveal sturdy arms, wrists, and a gold watch. Students lounged around him, most sat on the floor.

Bob radiated charisma. He had a presence that I felt drawn to and afraid of. *He is intense,* I thought, *confident, even arrogant.*

"Welcome, anyway," Bob said. His hands were in his pockets. He slouched a bit. He appraised us with hooded eyes that penetrated — I swear he saw right through me — and then smiled at Jim. "Let's get going." The classroom quieted. An empty Styrofoam coffee cup was perched on the edge of the blackboard ledge.

"Who wants to work?" Bob asked. Dead silence. He waited.

Bob was the director; the class was the audience. Actors would either volunteer or be chosen to help the "protagonist" explore his or her challenges. The students in the classroom fidgeted, the atmosphere was pensive, as each considered whether to take the "stage."

"I do," said Jim and everybody in the room breathed a sigh of relief, now off the hook. I don't remember much of the psychodrama that Jim created, except for one dramatic scene when he sat on a pretend toilet and challenged the authority of the Catholic pope: "We both crap on the toilet the same way," he said, with sarcasm to a fellow student who he'd chosen to play the role of the pontiff. "Who the hell do you think you are?" he asked

Bob asked me to "double," to stand next to Jim and be one of his "alter egos," one of his feeling states. "Be his anger," Bob said. I was frozen, tongue-tied. The eyes of the audience were on me and watched with intent. "I can't," I said, and felt a bit of nausea. "Unless you tell yourself you can't, you can," Bob said. His words sounded strange; but in an odd way, they rang true. "Get still and listen inward. Say what comes to mind without censoring."

I had known Jim for two years, but I'd never seen him express anger in a direct way. He could be critical of injustice, but in quiet, muted tones. The day of that psychodrama, I channeled his anger, speaking it into his ear and for the audience to see and hear. His anger at his vow of celibacy. His anger at his sexuality. His anger at his alcoholism. His anger at injustice. His anger at God. It was like I was connected to him via an invisible matrix of empathy. His anger made visible was potent. His body shook, and he cried. The psychodrama climaxed.

"You are not a victim, Jim," Bob said at the apex of Jim's distress, his voice an ocean of understanding. "Nor does God expect you to take on, to fix, to be responsible for even the smallest sliver of the world. You're not that important. All God asks is that you live true to the love you are." The silence in the room was deafening.

The theater shapeshifted into an over-heated classroom. We, the audience, and Bob, the director, gathered in a circle around Jim, introduced ourselves as our "selves," and stepped out of our roles as characters. We offered Jim love and respect for his authentic sharing, his courage, and listened as he explained his insights. He saw that, for him, anger signaled that he was repressing deeper truth.

Jim was never the same. He had found more peace. He loosened the ties to his past, his priesthood, and explored a revised life that might include me, with lessened guilt and without shame. That night, our lovemaking felt more free, less restricted by the sense of breaking a taboo. For both of us, the psychodrama was pivotal.

I lay in the dark in the afterglow and thought, *so that is psychodrama. People can grow. People can transform. People can be freer. I can be freer. I want that for myself, and I want to help others be free, too. I felt a longing to serve. I felt called...*

CHAPTER 13

IN SERVICE

WEEKS AFTER THE psychodrama workshop, I applied to the counselor education program at Siena Heights and was invited to an admissions interview with Sr. Dr. Miriam Stimson, OP, the Dean of the Graduate College, and an Adrian Dominican nun.

"Doctor Sister Stimson," as I thought of her, elevated my vision of what was possible for women.

Stimson was a force, wizened and bent. She didn't tolerate whining. She was the first woman to graduate from the University of Michigan with a doctorate in chemistry and only the second woman to lecture at the Sorbonne. She played a role in our understanding of DNA.

"Miss Sandel, why do you want to be a helper?" she said, her voice rusted steel. She pinned me with her direct look over gold wire-framed glasses. She wore casual street clothes, not the habit of a nun and her wiry graying hair was pulled back in a messy bun. I withered under her intensity. "I don't know that I do," I said, and blurted the truth. "I have been asleep to something and during the psychodrama workshop I woke up to it. I felt alive. At the very least, a degree in counseling will help me listen and communicate better."

Before the psychodrama workshop, I thought of psychology as a field of research and theory. I had no idea that there was a profession of psychology, a profession of helpers, a profession of listening.

A new director of public relations had come on board the company where I worked. I was rehired into that department and promoted to a manager's position.

The company offered employees a generous tuition reimbursement program and when I petitioned for financial support to seek a counseling degree, my request was approved.

I suggested I could use my studies to help develop an employee assistance program for the firm's growing workforce. I took pleasure in listening to the personal and professional challenges of the people I worked with, including executives on the company's leadership team. Perhaps I could work in human resources, a division just established at the firm.

Dr. Stimson asked me about critical incidents in my personal development and I stumbled through answers. I felt acute discomfort, a fear of being "not enough" when sharing my innermost thoughts and reflections with an authority figure.

After listening, Dr. Stimson twisted in her old, wooden swivel chair to scan the volumes on her bookshelves. She selected the book she had been looking for and turned to face me.

"You are a scholar in hiding," she said. Under a professional business suit, my heart hammered, wild. "Read this and come back to me in a month with an opinion about it," she said. The book was *The Aquarian Conspiracy: Personal and Social Transformation in Our Time* by Marilyn Ferguson.[7] It opened my eyes to the metaphors of quantum physics, the limitations of religion, the possibilities in spiritual understanding, and to the sea of change occurring in human consciousness.

"Welcome to the Counselor Education master's degree program," Dr. Stimson said, her voice a stew of a teacher's authority, a counselor's warmth, and a spiritual director's sincerity. Although she accepted me into the degree program that day and facilitated my transfer out of the Theology program, she was an advisor through and through. True to her word, she scheduled monthly appointments with me to challenge my intellectual growth and to make sure I made a smooth entry into Counseling.

I rose from the dull green leather pad on the old steel chair. My legs, encased in panty hose, were jelly and I was grateful to hear that I was accepted. Still seated, she appraised me. "You have a fine mind," she said. "It's time to put it in service to others."

CHAPTER 14

COUNTRY ROADS

"WE'RE ABOUT TO cross into West Virginia," Jim said. I cuddled against his back to absorb his warmth as the night-chilled wind whistled past our motorcycle.

It was 1980; we had been a couple for two years. Seasoned co-riders, we leaned into the curves that carried us beside creeks and between hills on a dark country road in southeastern Ohio.

"Do you need a stretch break, Lin?" asked Jim. His tenor voice was tender. He smiled at me in the round rearview mirror that peeked out from behind the bike's windshield. The night sky glittered with stars, and the moon was a creamy pearl. "No, I'm ok," I said. I was eager to make it to our destination.

We were on our way to visit his sister Denise and her husband Larry. They had followed their dreams, left their religious orders, married, and moved from suburban Detroit months before to deep rural West Virginia.

This was my first visit to their new digs. They were renting a 125-year-old farmhouse and had warned me to be ready for a rustic, wild experience.

The evening was thick with the blink of lightning bugs and the stink of muddy river. It had been a long ride down Route 33; we pulled into the tiny village of Pomeroy around midnight. Like a night light, a dim streetlamp illuminated our path; the shuttered town was fast asleep, not another soul was in sight. Appalachia seemed ancient, stricken, and poor, a different world from the suburbs I grew up in. I felt its raw, primal beauty.

Jim's leather jacket was smooth against my cheek. My scalp itched under my blue half-helmet. "We've got another hour and a half to go," Jim said.

Jim throttled down the Honda motorcycle and stuck out long, jeaned legs and heavy black boots to slow the bike for a red traffic light. The 500cc motor thrummed between my legs. The wide, mighty Ohio River rolled in front of us, a silent indigo current that reflected lights from the town huddled around it on the opposite bank.

As we waited for the red light to change to green, something mysterious yet tangible happened. It was as if I looked at life through a slow-motion camera. I felt pulled toward something new by a current of magnetic, palpable energy.

When the traffic light changed, we continued through the small town headed for Ravenswood, West Virginia. The name conjured images of poets and magic. About a half hour later, our headlights silhouetted a stout historic bridge that spanned the Ohio River. As we drove across, the grated structure rumbled under us. Mid-way over, a sign came into view: *"Welcome to West Virginia, Wild and Wonderful."*

A sharp thrill snaked down my spine and bolted into my sneakered feet. Every cell in my body tingled. This was intuitive wisdom, another experience of the eyes of love opening in wide certainty to see beauty and possibility.

That bridge tumbled me into a new life. For the rest of my days, West Virginia, a land of forests, mountains and rugged, wild, close-to-the-earth living, would be the home of my heart. My taxi along the runway of early adulthood had ended; my landing gear had retracted, and I was in the air on a flight path of my own choosing.

CHAPTER 15

OF A PLACE

A S WE CROSSED into West Virginia, life shapeshifted. The headlight of the motorcycle spotlighted raw natural beauty. Strong stone cliffs guarded the edges of the road; luminous mosses clung to them, and spidery ferns draped their sharpness. Small waterfalls cascaded around the rocks, feeding a creek that ambled alongside the road.

The road had changed, too. Sensual curves that had snaked around lesser hills now coiled into tight serpentine loops around rocky outcrops and more dramatic mountains and hollows.

The night air flew around us and pushed the earthy, loamy fragrance of the dirt, clay, and wildflowers up our noses. Lightning bugs, flies and mosquitos spattered to their deaths on our goggles.

From time to time, I caught a sharp whiff of natural gas, a pungent odor I associate with the state. I would later learn it came from miniscule leaks around the old wells and crusty, rusted natural gas pipelines that crisscross the hills and forests.

We moved past a smorgasbord of buildings. Modern and well-built homes were kissing cousins to rustic cabins, manufactured housing, and trailers. Some homes were neat and made pretty with country touches; some homes wore the hand-me-down dress of poverty. Some homes and lawns looked like junkyards littered with old cars, tractors, toilets, washing machines, pipes, and plain detritus. It struck me that the churches looked well-kept and flush. I couldn't keep up with the impressions that rolled by as fast as the tires on the bike. Deep rural. Old. Musky. Rugged. Poor. Fierce. Untamed. Littered. Ugly. Exquisite. Powerful. Raw. Wild.

With each passing mile, I grew more excited to see Denise and Larry. Their relocation had left a gaping hole in my life. I was eager to experience their new lifestyle. Shocks were ahead.

The first seismic wave crested as we bore right off the two-lane main highway onto Sycamore Road. The "road" to the farmhouse was little more than a path, two dusty dirt strips separated by a threadbare patch of trampled weeds, in Appalachia, called "two-tracks." I leaned and whispered into Jim's ear, "Is this the right way? This road is little more than a cow path." I'd never seen a cow path, so calling it that was funny.

After we negotiated multiple steep curves and hills, the two-track flattened. We rounded a bend, and, on the left, a two-story blue-green farmhouse clad in asbestos shingles designed to look like bricks came into view. Behind a weathered split-rail fence, the porch light was on. Cheerful lamplight spilled from the windows.

"This is it," Jim said over his shoulder as he killed the engine of the bike at the end of the drive, behind the house. He knew because he had helped Denise and Larry move. The silence roared. No sirens. No cars. No city sounds. The insects were quiet. The birds were asleep. The faint wash of a creek burbled in the background. I smelled grass and wet leaves; it was early spring. My breath hung, vapor on the cool night air.

"You guys are here!" Denise said as she ran out the side door to greet us. Larry was right behind her. They enveloped us in big hugs and welcomed us into the warmth of their country home.

The house smelled pungent and musty, a bouquet of old wood, dry rot, and moss. It was toasty; heat shimmered from the blue-yellow glow of a three-burner ceramic gas heater on the wall that looked like a mini fireplace. The house was warmed with "free gas" from a local well.

The kitchen of the farmhouse, owned by the McDonald family, was large and cozy and emptied into a dining room which Denise and Larry used as a living room.

"We don't use the actual living room. It's not insulated and too cold," Denise said, as she opened a folded curtain and revealed a dark, drafty room beyond. "But we'll take you through it on your way to the upstairs bedroom."

The house was "Jenny Lind" constructed, a simple build on piers of stone that made judicious use of nails. As we walked across the living room floor, I saw the dirt below the house through cracks between weathered boards, where chinking, mortar made of clay, common in West Virginia, and mud or sand, had crumbled away. A bulky metal gas heater jutted from a generous fireplace constructed of large square cut sandstone, outlined by a sturdy wood frame. The back of the fireplace was formed of large rocks that had been mortared together.

Old amber glass lamps attached to copper gas pipes jutted from the walls on both sides of the fireplace. Their mantles gave off a soft hiss and poked a dim orange light into the dark of the room. On both sides of the fireplace, floor-to-ceiling mahogany-stained cupboards of rough-hewn wood, built in perfect square and beautifully finished, formed the uninsulated wall. The boards were uneven in size but tight.

Nothing in my suburban upbringing in a tract home had prepared me for this glimpse of old Appalachia. I was transfixed—my body responded to it like a tuning fork resonating with perfect pitch.

Exhausted by our 400-mile trip, Jim and I grasped the thick railings of the staircase and climbed into a large bedroom, also finished in dark mahogany. We collapsed into bed. Wasps buzzed in lazy circles in the old rafters, but I was too tired to care. I pulled a soft handmaid patchwork quilt around my ears and was soon asleep.

Ka-thump, ka-thump, ka-thump, ka-thump. The distant drone of a repetitive pounding awakened me to the smells of morning and coffee. Jim had already left our bed. I heard the murmur of voices downstairs.

I padded to a screenless window to look around and caught my breath. A huge, old maple raised its arms to the heavens. Green hills and forest undulated in every direction. Dew blanketed the grass; to my left a faint cloud hung in the treetops, a remnant of the morning mists that had veiled the mountains; the sun peeked through it, rays like beams of a giant flashlight visible against the vaporlike backdrop.

In that moment, West Virginia imprinted herself on my heart. My intuitive wisdom told me I had found an earthly home. I became what mountaineers call "of a place."

CHAPTER 16

FORESHADOWED

I PULLED A blanket around me as I stood at the window of the old farmhouse and flashed back to a memory of when, at the age of eleven or twelve, I first laid eyes on the Appalachian Mountains.

"It's too much to take in," Dad said, awe in his voice as we surveyed layers of mountains, hazed in dusty blue and dusky purple against an infinite sky. A barrier of boulders prevented onlookers from tumbling into a canyon dotted with purple and yellow wildflowers, profuse scrub bushes, and an army of trees.

We were on vacation motoring along the Blue Ridge Parkway, a scenic byway that snakes through Virginia into North Carolina. Dad had driven the family's blue Ford station wagon into a pull-off overlooking the dramatic beauty of Shenandoah National Park. He, Ma, and my four siblings piled out.

"God's creation, nature, sure is beautiful," Dad said; his voice hitched in his throat.

The air was hushed, fragrant with green. Dad's arm was warm, wrapped around my chest. I heard the crackle of the cigarette pack in the pocket of his white T-shirt against the back of my head.

Next to the immense mountain backdrop, I felt small in my

shorts, blouse, and sneakers. An acorn was perched at the edge of the sidewalk. I twisted to look up at my dad. I knew that, like me, he was both there, and not there, transported to some place where boundaries disappear. His gaze was soft and open.

"Someday I'm going to live in these mountains, Daddy" I said. I was as certain of that as I was that my name was Linda. Tears of longing gathered in my eyes.

"Ka-thump, ka-thump, ka-thump." The sound interrupted my reverie, my wonder at this childhood memory and my prescient knowing. Here I was, in West Virginia, surrounded by the beautiful Appalachian foothills. I grabbed my robe and headed downstairs, lured by the smell of coffee and the voices of people I loved.

"What's that ka-thumping sound?" I asked. Coffee bubbled into the glass knob of a stainless-steel percolator. Denise, in her robe, scrambled eggs at the stove. Larry, in jeans and a denim shirt, was frying up savory sausages. Jim, in a Siena Heights sweatshirt over jeans, chopped green peppers at the kitchen island. Denise was good at getting her guests involved in cooking.

I stood in the wide doorway, took in the scene, and thought my heart would burst with affection. "That sound comes from the oil and gas wells all over these hills," Larry said. "If you look outside the kitchen window toward the creek you can see a blue derrick and rusted yellow tanks. When the derricks pump, they pop like that." They were metronomes, extracting fossil fuels from a resource-rich land.

"Can you put the toast in, Linda?" Larry said. "Or are you too special?" he asked, a tease in his voice. Before they'd left Michigan, Denise, and Larry, Jim and I had studied the Enneagram, an understanding of personality with ancient roots in the far East. We had enjoyed learning about it by listening to tapes and books by Richard Rohr, [8] a Franciscan priest. We spent hours discussing them. I had self-identified as a "4", the creative individualist, most often introverted, who loves beauty and wants to feel special.

"I'll make the toast as long as you keep your one-ness away from my work," I said, and teased Larry back. The Enneagram "1", the idealist or perfectionist, has a strong desire for justice and likes to be right. Denise sputtered with laughter in the background. "If you have trouble, Linda, I'll come over and help both of you feel good about yourselves." She had self-identified as an Enneagram "2", a giver, who liked to please. "And if you all can't work it out," Jim said, and piped up from his chopping position at the butcher block, "I'll make the peace!" He had self-identified as a "9", the peacekeeper, an accepting, trusting type who values inner peace and hates conflict. We all laughed aloud!

I felt so blessed to know Jim, Larry, and Denise. Our friendship was like favorite slippers or the best, most aromatic cup of coffee on a perfect morning. I was happy to be with them in this wild, raw, and rustic natural beauty.

From that day forward, when Jim and I visited Denise and Larry every couple of months in West Virginia and then left to return to Michigan, I cried as we rode away. I felt ripped out of the place where I belonged. I wanted to stay. But I couldn't fathom how.

CHAPTER 17

SINKING SPRINGS

"**M**ARY, IT'S TIME we get these sleepyheads into bed," Mike said to his wife as he corralled three youngsters. We were visiting Denise and Larry again over the New Year's holiday and their friends, Mike and Mary Franek had invited us to dinner.

As I helped to clear dinner plates, I looked around, astonished at the dilapidated, but cozy log cabin. I couldn't fathom how people could embrace living so simply the way our hosts did. Bitter cold wind and infinitesimal snowflakes whistled through gaps in the chinking between the logs. Colorful newsprint from the comics section of a newspaper had been stuffed into the cracks.

The chilly, humble structure was a stark contrast to the warm love that permeated every corner of the little house in Sinking Springs, West Virginia.

Once the kids were quiet and dishes were tucked away, Jim and I huddled with Denise and Larry and their friends on mismatched chairs and rockers pulled up to a wood stove; the cast iron doors had been opened to release heat; a cheerful fire crackled behind a screen.

The flicker of the flames and the glow of candles illuminated the darkened living room. Wood smoke hung in the chilly air, mixing with the fragrance of the dinner we'd just eaten—homemade chicken soup, fresh-baked crusty bread, and delectable brownies. Except for Jim, we held jelly jar glasses filled with wine.

On our many visits, Denise and Larry pulled us into their circle of friends, fascinating people like Mike, a musician, and Mary, a teacher. Before moving to West Virginia, both Mike and Mary, like Jim, had been associated with the Maryknoll mission organization. Mike was a seminarian, Mary a nun. All three had been deeply influenced by Maryknoll's values, including bringing social justice, hope, and love to those most in need.

Mike and Mary, like Denise and Larry, were part of a wave of kindred spirits who, in the 1970s, moved to the solace of the rugged mountains to choose a simpler back-to-nature lifestyle. Artists. Dancers. Musicians. Doctors. Nurses. Teachers.

As we sat around the fire, Denise, Larry, Mike, and Mary traded stories about their life in West Virginia. A picture emerged of a tightknit community, a mix of long-standing hill dwellers and these free-spirited transplants who loved rural life.

"Mike, tell Linda and Jim about the time you tried to shoot a raccoon that was making a racket on the porch," Larry said. He leaned forward in a rocking chair, his mustache and beard framed a wide smile as he waited in delight to hear the story, again.

Mike's blonde hair grazed his shoulders as he threw his head back and laughed aloud. He wore faded jeans, a baggy sweater, and slippers. He was a good-looking, trim man with a wide smile and a gentle manner. His wife, Mary, a striking woman with kind, perceptive eyes, had pulled a faded pieced quilt around her legs.

"Well, now, that's a tale," Mike said. His guitar rested against his chair. He'd promised to play for us later. Snow gathered on the wavy windowpanes. Mike reached for a piece of wood and tossed it into the fire. Sparks spit onto the stone hearth.

"This enormous old raccoon was making a mess of our trash," Mike said, relishing the story. The feeling in the room sparkled with lightheartedness. "He would clamber around on our porch, make a racket, and keep Mary and I and the kids awake. I tried dozens of ways to dissuade him and decided the only remedy was my shotgun."

Denise giggled, anticipating the next bit of the story. "Denise, I haven't gotten to the funny part yet," Mike said. That got us all laughing. Mike continued, "Every time I got out of bed and grabbed my gun, that raccoon would scamper away before I could get out the door," Mike said and took a sip of wine. "One night, I outsmarted him. I took aim from inside the cabin and shot at him right through the glass window. Blew the window out and I still missed!" Mary shook her head and rolled her eyes. "Did you say you outsmarted him?" she asked and raised her eyebrows. Denise laughed so hard she snorted, which got us all hysterical.

"Can you see Mike in his long johns shooting right through a window?" Larry asked. "And still missing the raccoon?" We all howled again. "Yeah, and now there was a window to fix," Mike said. "I think that coon laughed all the way back to his family."

When the hilarity subsided, we were quiet until Mary spoke.

"Tell us about you, Linda," Mary said. "What's your life like?" Tongue-tied as usual with people I didn't know well, I pushed past shyness to explain that I traveled to interview clients of the company I worked for, wrote about computer software applications for business magazines, and produced marketing videos.

"That wouldn't satisfy me," Mary said. "Is it meaningful for you?"

Chagrin tightened my chest. "It's a great job and it pays well," I said, on the defense, though my answer seemed lame.

The conversation went in other directions, but I was stuck on Mary's comments. I enjoyed my work colleagues more than a little. But we weren't connected the way these people were. These beautiful souls valued intimate relationships. They valued family, nature, solitude, simple living, service, and community. They valued spirituality, creativity, self-expression and, above all, love. They were my people.

CHAPTER 18

THE FISHBOWL

"WHAT WOULD YOU like to talk about?" asked my professor, Peggy. I sat across from the petite youthful woman, a counseling psychologist, with short, curly blonde hair. She wore an embroidered teal tunic with a mandarin collar, over black slacks.

We were in a "fishbowl"—a training exercise where two people volunteer to do the "work" of counseling while a class watches. Peggy conveyed interest and curiosity. Her posture matched mine, legs crossed at the ankles, hands in her lap. I had learned that this unconscious postural matching suggested we were in rapport. I liked her a lot. She was a brilliant counselor educator who went the distance for her students.

"I've lost interest in my job," I said, "and I struggle to meet deadlines." This was my first counseling skills class; we learned to listen, to reflect content and feelings, to summarize, and to ask open-ended questions that moved disclosure forward.

I was dressed in a business suit and pumps. I'd driven forty-five miles from my job in Ann Arbor to Siena Heights, after a full workday. I would participate in two back-to-back three-hour classes that finished at 10pm, and then return to Ann Arbor. I was nervous, conscious of the classroom full of students who sat in a circle around us. We'd only met for a few sessions, but I'd realized I had a lot to learn about listening. Like all my fellow students, when listening to others, I tended to pay attention to what *I* was going to say next rather than to what *they* were sharing.

"It's hard to stay motivated," I said, as Peggy leaned in. The world outside the windows of the classroom was dark, it was early winter. In the fishbowl, in our hard, wooden student desks, Peggy and I were bathed in fluorescent light. Peggy followed my every word. I was sure she was going to tell me that I was depressed or lazy. I held an orange book, "The Skilled Helper" by Gerald Egan[9] on my lap.

"You sound unhappy and discouraged," Peggy said. My spine stiffened; I sat up straight. *She's right,* I thought, surprised. *"I am far from lazy. But I'm no longer passionate about what I'm doing."* In a flash, I realized that I while I felt fortunate to have a worthy job working for a great company with interesting colleagues, writing about computer software was not satisfying. *I was no longer in the best job for me!* Peggy's deep listening and reflection of my feelings created the conditions for an insight that hit a target in my heart. The ground under my feet fell out and I was in free-fall.

After the fishbowl, my classmates and I were paired into threes, triads—one person took the role of a counselor, one of a client and a third person observed the interaction so that he or she could later provide constructive feedback to the "counselor." Peggy served as the observer in my triad.

Afterwards, the class took a rest break. I met Peggy in a bathroom made stuffy and hot by old steam radiators. "Linda, you're a natural at counseling," she said. Under the dim bulb of a single light that bounced illumination off the cement blocks, she washed her hands at an institutional sink. "I encourage you to explore it as your career path. You have what it takes," she said. It still strikes me as funny that one of the most transformational moments of my life happened in a women's restroom. I stood in front of a metal towel dispenser on the wall and dried my hands on scratchy sheets of brown paper.

"Do you really think so?" I asked. Peggy faced me square and put her hand on my arm. "My dear, I know so," she said, certain. In that moment, she became a mentor, and we began a friendship that endures.

In the next semester, my career switch was sealed in a group leadership laboratory class taught by Bob, the psychodrama professor. Each of my classmates and I had taken turns co-facilitating our group with him. We'd weathered laughter, anger, and lots of tears as we explored the terrain of our inner lives.

We'd also participated in weekend marathon psychodrama groups facilitated by Bob and Linda at their comfortable home on a lake in Michigan. During marathons, we stayed up all night creating psychodramas, helping each other to get free of stories, perceptions, and beliefs, obstacles that limited our personal freedom to live self-expressed. All this was professional self-development. We practiced what we would do with clients on ourselves. The Siena counseling program rested on the assumption that the health of the helper was sacred. We were taught we had to "keep our instrument"—the self—tuned to health. We were taught that our presence trumped technique.

In our last class, Bob taped blank sheets of paper to our backs, and we milled around writing supportive feedback to each other. The feedback was meant to be anonymous, but I knew Bob's handwriting. By that time, he'd read and commented on many of my papers.

"Linda, your potential as a helper is unlimited," he wrote. "I love you a lot." Bob was not prone to effusiveness, nor was he disingenuous. I knew he wrote from his heart. His words meant the world to me.

From that moment, I was on a mission to become the best counselor I could be. Listening would be my life's work. I never looked back.

CHAPTER 19

DECISION

"WOMEN CAPABLE OF a new and deeper love ethic will need to be *somebody in their own right*," I wrote in 1981 in a paper entitled "Womanhood Transformed", a topic I'd chosen for a final paper in my lifespan psychology class.

Somebody in their own right—it seemed to me that those words came from a source deep inside, an ineffable place of knowing. What did they mean to me?

I had begun to own the prophetic nature of Dr. Stimson's observation that I was a scholar in hiding. I loved knowledge. I loved learning. I loved finding patterns and connections in information and drafting first-rate papers. I would earn the "Outstanding Counseling Student" award when I graduated with my master's degree. I mastered the techniques of counseling, but I also devoured books that explored the personhood of the counselor. I came to see counseling as a sacred *way of being* that required high levels of presence and self-awareness. To serve my growth, I participated in dozens of experiential groups and training opportunities.

I truly did become a person in my own right due to my counseling training—and with that came the wisdom that it was time for me to ask Jim to choose between his priesthood or our relationship. We had been a committed couple for three years.

My biological clock was also ticking; I was twenty-eight. I wanted to have children.

When I mentioned the future, I could feel Jim's anxiety. One night I took a risk; I told him I didn't want to hurry his decision, but I needed to take care of myself and move on. As I said that, I felt like my heart was breaking, but I stood firm.

The next day, Jim called me from a pay phone at a nearby gas station and asked me to meet him in the parking lot of my apartment complex. He didn't want to come inside.

"I'm taking off on a long ride; a deadhead. I don't know when I'll be back," he said. "I will use the time to make a decision."

We stood under the aluminum canopy that protected my parking spot from snow and sun. It was early fall. I pulled my sweater close to ward off the chill I felt, inside and out. I was terrified about what he might say next. Bright red-gold leaves on a nearby maple tree fluttered in an autumn breeze. A few leaves skittered across the cracked asphalt pavement. Jim leaned against his black Honda motorcycle; his hip covered by faded blue jeans. His black leather jacket was zipped. He had tears in his eyes, and I could not stop myself from crying. I didn't like feeling that vulnerable.

He pulled a small ceramic jar, periwinkle blue, the size of a coffee mug, out of the bike's weather-beaten black tank bag. I recognized the jar as a knick-knack he'd made during his recreation time in the alcoholism treatment program. It had a tan rubber-clad stopper.

"I've put two slips of paper inside," he said. Tears slid down his cheeks. I couldn't breathe. I slouched against my baby blue Camaro; my legs were like rubber. On one slip, he'd written, *my promise to be a priest*, on the other, *my freedom to choose another path*. "Pray for me to make the right choice," he said. He did not want his decision to be about our love, in his mind's eye, that shifted responsibility to me in an unfair way. He wanted to choose his path and then choose a companion. I was too filled with emotion to say anything, except, "travel safe." I didn't want him to worry about me or feel burdened by my pain.

Jim lifted his leg over the motorcycle. He stood sturdy in his black biking boots. He turned the key and revved the engine. I watched him ride out of the parking lot. I leaned over, held myself and cried. I was twenty-seven years old, and I'd insisted that we step up to this threshold. But I was terrified he'd just said good-bye. I put the blue ceramic jar in the middle of my coffee table.

Jim was gone weeks and I had one note from him, from Florida. He said if he left the priesthood, his future would be uncertain. He wondered if I would be better off with a younger man who could offer me more security. He said he was certain he loved me. He was on the move, so there was no way for me to reply. He didn't call.

That stretch of life, a passage through the dark unknown, was a spiral through moments of desperate fear that I would lose Jim to his priesthood and a rock-solid knowledge that I could face whatever music came. Later I would learn the time was a very dark night of the soul for Jim, a final wrestling match between the call of two loves, his vocation as a priest and his desire to be a man free to love, free to enjoy sexual intimacy, free to choose.

Relief flooded through me when the phone rang, and he was on the end of the line. "I'm back and ready to talk," he said. I looked around the hand-me-down furniture in my apartment in South Lyon, Michigan. Bright orange pillows and an orange candle broke the white of the walls and nubby-textured couch. Pale sunlight that carried a hint of winter shone through the sliding glass doors. I was frozen inside, braced for what Jim would say next. But he was noncommittal. "Can I stop by your place later tonight?" he asked.

I picked up around the apartment in an absent-minded way as the minutes marched toward Jim's arrival. When I opened the door after his knock, he hesitated and then scooped me into his bear hug. "I've written Maryknoll to ask for a leave of absence," he said into my ear. "This is the final step before I ask to be released from my vows." Relief flooded through me, and I hugged him back hard. He had chosen me; he had chosen our love; he had chosen our unlimited future. We clung to each other for a long time and moved to the bedroom.

Jim graduated from the counseling program, left his job as a campus priest, took a position as an addiction counselor at Flower Hospital in Sylvania, Ohio, and moved into his own place, a small basement apartment near the hospital. He seemed lighter, easier.

I was living in Ann Arbor with my sister, Carol, and her two-year-old son, Mike, at the time. By day I worked at the computer technology company and at night and on weekends, I continued my counseling studies and progressed through supervised training experiences called practicum and internship.

Although I had my own place, Jim and I lived together much of the time. His humble apartment was our love nest and an experiment in living together, a first for both of us.

CHAPTER 20

TWO WEDDINGS

W E HAD TWO "weddings"—one was a civil ceremony in front of a judge in Ann Arbor, Michigan, on April 16th, 1982. The other was a lovely self-designed liturgical service celebrated with our friends and families in a VFW [Veterans of Foreign Wars] hall in South Lyon, Michigan on April 17th.

Because of Jim's priesthood, we could not be married in a Catholic Church. Jim had to seek release from his mission order, Maryknoll, and request formal dispensation from his vows as a priest—in the Catholic Church, a process known as laicization.

Maryknoll was quick to support him. Other priests, including his superiors, reached out to acknowledge his love and to share his happiness. The order also sent along the laicization paperwork—a thick packet.

"To be laicized, I have to declare that I was mentally ill or incapacitated or that I lied when I professed my vows," Jim said, as we pored over the papers.

His hand cupped his forehead, his elbow was on the table as he read the pertinent section of the paperwork. There was no window in the kitchen, and we sat under a bright overhead light.

I stared through the holes of the latticed metal grate that separated the kitchen from the living room. A drawing of three colorful clowns hung on the wall to my left. A plaque of the serenity prayer "*God grant me the serenity to accept what I cannot change and the courage to change the things I can,*" hung on the wall near the refrigerator. A squeezed tea bag lay on a napkin on the table.

"I can't do that," Jim said. "I would be notarizing a lie. I made my vows in good faith and had every intention to keep them." His voice was firm and agonized.

"How important is my laicization to you, Linda?" Jim asked me. I answered without hesitation or reflection. "It is not at all important," I said. "It's hard to believe in a God that would be rule bound. These are the rules of men, subject to change."

"How important is laicization to *you,* honey?" I asked. Jim sat back in his chair and stuck his long legs out under the table. He was quiet and thoughtful for a while. He rubbed his hands up and down jeaned thighs. "I'd rather stand by the truth of my vows," he said. "I propose that we move forward without it."

We had learned that laicization, while freeing Jim from his duties as a priest, did not undo his vow to be celibate [water under the bridge] or give him permission to marry and have children. That would take a special dispensation! In the church's eyes, a man, once a priest, was always a priest. The processes of laicization and dispensation, the paperwork said, could take up to ten years to proceed through the local hierarchy and the Vatican!

We were consigned, in the eyes of the Catholic Church, to live in permanent "concubinage" until Jim's vows were formally released, and he was dispensed from celibacy. We looked at each other and shrugged, a mutual "so be it!" We chose to be respectful, but to forge ahead based on our own inner knowing of the Truth of Love.

Resigned that we could not have a church wedding, we planned a beautiful sacred ceremony. It was important to both of us that we have a wedding that celebrated our love in a holy way. We didn't talk a lot about religion or spirituality; the honoring of God was simply implicit in how we lived.

Our wedding aisle was a scuffed linoleum floor between rows

of wooded folding chairs set up in a humble V.F.W. [Veterans of Foreign Wars] hall in South Lyon, Michigan.

No church organ played. The crescendo of Pachelbel's Canon in D pealed from an audiotape through speakers that my audiophile brother, Jim, had built. The music transformed our humble space into a cathedral as grand as any I've ever been in.

I walked up the aisle, between Ma and Dad, toward the "altar," a raised band platform. Candles flickered in the darkened, hushed hall. Just behind me, Jim walked between his parents. They put our hands together in front of our celebrant, a nun, Sr. Sue, a dear friend.

"Are you ready to do this?" Jim asked; his eyes brimmed with tears. He looked sharp in a taupe suit with a vest, the only suit he would ever own in his adult life. I wore an Alfred Angelo dress, ivory, with a pleated skirt, crystal-studded bodice and sheer sleeves that puffed into long cuffs with satin buttons. I felt like a medieval princess under my fingertip veil.

Our journey to this moment was unconventional. *What intrigue awaited us? What would life bring? What would we create?* I could not wait to peek deeper into my lover's soul, this solid, romantic man who looked at me as though I were the only woman in the world. "I'm so ready," I said, in a whisper. "Are you?"

"With my whole heart," he said, "I've never felt happier." We turned to face 125 of our dearest friends and family. My father had made his peace with our marriage; my mother had overseen making a huge Polish meal for our guests.

"As Linda and Jim share the vows they've written, they'd like their immediate family to come up and gather around them," Sr. Sue said. The diminutive woman in a blue pantsuit opened her arms wide to the crowd. Her voice was loving and strong. I felt the soft touches of our families on my arms, back and shoulders.

We began our married life connected to the people we loved.

CHAPTER 21

RED HAIR AND BLACK LEATHER

DAYS LATER, JIM and I sat at the small hand-me-down kitchen table in our love nest, counted our wedding gift money and considered what to do with our unexpected windfall. Our guests had been generous!

He turned his lopsided grin my way and said, "Could we use this cash to buy a bigger motorcycle?" At first, I thought he was joking. The sensible thing to do was put the money in savings. But I wanted Jim to be happy, and I'd also fallen in love with the motorcycling. We picked out the bike together—a deep, maroon-colored Honda Gold Wing Interstate, 1100 ccs of horsepower and plenty of chrome. It purred like a kitten.

Some men gift their new wives with negligees; mine gave me a tight black stretch t-shirt with the words, "I'm a motorcycle mama—a real mean ole' lady" emblazoned on the front. It was sleeveless; the armholes and hem were lined with sexy black lace! I never wore it, but kept it wrapped in tissue paper in my underwear drawer, and wished I had the guts.

A month after our wedding we set off on our Gold Wing on our honeymoon—we pooled all the vacation time we could muster into a four-week trip from Michigan, through the Midwest and down to the Arizona desert, over to California and up Highway One to the northwest, and back across the plains to home.

The weather turned mean hot and steamy, in the low 100's Fahrenheit, on our way across Kansas and Nebraska. We rode from rest stop to rest stop, jumping off the interstate system at every opportunity to drink water. Jim took off his white helmet and filled it with water in the bathroom. He'd bring it out and we took turns dumping it over our heads to douse ourselves. We called it "highway air-conditioning" and we smiled, happy rebels, when onlookers stared and chuckled.

As forests, deserts, canyons, and oceans rolled by, I got bit hard by the long-distance bike travel bug. From that point forward, whenever we could, Jim and I hit the road—we put 200,000 miles on the bike, most of it in the first few years of our marriage. We traveled every weekend, long holiday, and vacation break. We often rode in the evenings after work.

On some of our rides, we soloed. On some, Denise and Larry were our vagabond companions—we traveled easily together. Jim made up a phrase, "pother mot" that became our rallying cry as we started each leg of a ride with them. It was nonsensical, two words paired together that showed up often in the crossword puzzles we worked on together.

During our relationship, Jim and I crisscrossed the United States multiple times, and explored the far reaches of Canada, including Nova Scotia and Quebec's Gaspe' Peninsula.

My pinnacle experience on the bike came on the dramatic cliff road that bites into the edges of the North American continent on the Gaspe.' We rode through elevations immersed in fogs so thick we couldn't see more than a few feet in front of us.

"Are you ok?" I said to Jim as we moved through the heavy mists. I leaned forward into him, my bright rubber yellow rain suit squeaking against his blue Gore-Tex duds. Fog droplets pelted my face. I was cold and a bit nervous. He was cold and calm. Water dripped from his chin. "Yeah, I have to concentrate, but we're good," he said and smiled.

In the next second, we swooped down a heart-stopping stretch of road and fell just beneath the fog into brilliant sunshine. A small fishing village shimmered in a distant harbor. From our elevation, it looked like diamonds sparkled on the ocean around bobbing fishing boats. The embrace of a small French village circled the harbor. I could not breathe; the beauty was so intense. Jim pulled off the road and we stopped to drink it in.

"I would not have seen this if it weren't for you," I said and kissed him hard. "I am so grateful."

Biking wasn't always a bed of roses. We spent uncomfortable moments huddled under overpasses, waiting for pelting rainstorms to pass, and fried under devilish sun. We shivered through bone-chilling cold snaps and endured numb butts when extralong deadheads took us to places where finding camps or lodging wasn't easy.

But on our honeymoon, those experiences waited down the road. Being newlyweds was an outer discovery of the art of longdistance cycling and an inner introduction to the nuances of partnership. Both were eye-opening.

One dark, starless night we rode into a campground just outside Ouray, Colorado, in the middle of a fierce thunderstorm deluge. The host of the campground, a big guy dressed in faded jeans and a holey t-shirt, eyed us, and took in our bedraggled appearances. "Can't believe you were out on your bike in the middle of that lightning," he said, as he surveyed our drenched wet suits.

I was exhausted, cold, and not looking forward to setting up camp in the heavy rain. "Only camp I have left is near the river," he said. Jim reached for a pen on the desk to fill out the registration form, "We'll take it," he said. The camp host filled out the green ticket we would clip onto the camp's numbered post. He handed it to me.

"If you hear a loud noise tonight that sounds like heavy thunder on the river, get the hell out of that camp fast," the host said.

Both Jim and I shot each other quizzical looks. The camp owner pulled in a drag on his cigarette. "That river comes down outta the Rockies. In heavy rains it'll carry dead logs with it and when them logs roll by it sounds like thunder and shakes the earth. Good luck."

We set up our tent in record time and crawled into our sleeping bags. Jim was exhausted and out like a light in no time. I was awake most of the night listening for logs that never rolled in. Life with my new husband would be an adventure.

CHAPTER 22

MIRACLE MAKERS

O UR RELATIONSHIP WAS smooth until it wasn't!
We were both introverts, both liked order and gave each other lots of space. We didn't fight but we had moments of difference and disagreement. Jim was a night owl; I was a morning person. He was immersed in politics; I avoided them like the plague. He liked salty and I liked sweet. Jim deferred to me to avoid conflict; I liked consensus and the process of getting to it.

We *were* united in our devotion to the counseling profession, to helping others. After graduating with my master's in counseling, I secured a job as an addiction therapist at Flower Hospital, where Jim worked. He worked in the inpatient unit; I helped to build an outpatient program. We attended many continuing education programs together, part of our search to find healing modalities that were efficient and effective. One such program was a Reality Therapy Workshop in Cincinnati, Ohio with a well-known trainer and psychologist, Dr. Robert Wubbolding.

At the workshop, we stared at an 11X14 white paper that had six squares on it, each drawn to look like a television screen. We had been instructed to create a storyboard—a visual picture of a goal and the steps needed to achieve it. Reality therapy emphasized staying in the present, clarifying wants, being responsible and doing the next right thing to realize dreams. It eschewed the concept of mental illness and proposed that everyone could make good choices. Jim and I were drawn to Reality Therapy's notion that everyone has the same ability to live from wisdom.

"Let's draw our dream to have a baby," I said. Jim's brown eyes twinkled. His mouth turned down at the edges as he feigned the look of "that's a scary thought!" He looked relaxed and handsome in his sweater, the color of pumpkins, and faded Lee jeans. We'd been married a little over a year and were trying to get pregnant. I stared at the magic marker in my hand with a thoughtful expression.

"You're a better artist than me," Jim said. "You draw the pictures." Our first picture was of us in bed doing what must be done to conceive a baby. We snickered as we drew stick people having intercourse. The second picture was us searching for a bigger apartment; the next of us moving. It was fun to draw the setup of a nursery. The final picture we drew was of a baby girl in a red and white striped dress next to the bottom of a lit Christmas tree. We were both tearful as my markers drew that picture. We'd been instructed to feel the realization of our dream. We closed our eyes and felt the gratitude and joy it would bring. We squeezed each other's hands.

I was twenty-nine and he was forty-nine. Could miracles happen? By the next Christmas, it was clear to us that they could and did.

CHAPTER 23

CONCEPTION

J IM'S BODY, LONG, lean, and sensitive, delighted me. Our lovemaking had been gentle and sweet; he drifted into sleep, and I
relaxed into a blissful, lazy haze of satisfaction, my body radiant
with the after-effects of sexual pleasure.

Half-asleep, I sat upright as an iridescent, transparent pink
orb, about two feet around, materialized out of thin air in the
dark corner of the room and floated toward me. It merged with
me, and I was jolted, hard.

It was February of 1984. Somehow, I knew the apparition
carried our daughter's soul. I was in awe—I'd never heard other
women talk about such an experience, but I accepted it without
question. I had a sense that there was much that occurred beyond
the visible world, hidden under an invisibility cloak or a veil. Others thought of these kinds of things as "woo-woo" but I did not.
They were spiritual and as tangible for me as the world of nature.
Many years later, I learned that I had experienced a "conscious
conception." It isn't rare.

Oh my God, I've just become pregnant. I thought. I lay back,
astonished. I felt joyful and alive; awed at the mystery of the
moment. I was suffused with whole-hearted thankfulness. I had

just become a mother. No matter what happened with this pregnancy, nothing could take motherhood away from me.

An upper respiratory infection flattened me two weeks later. I
coughed so hard I developed a painful pleurisy, an inflammation
of the chest wall, which propelled me to the emergency room. The
young ER doctor explained why I was in pain and pulled out a
prescription pad.

"Wait!" I said. "You need to know that I'm pregnant." Early
pregnancy, pee-on-a-stick tests were not yet available, so the doctor asked, "How do you know?"

"I just do—it's early. I'm only about two weeks along." His
hurried movements paused, allowing his white lab coat to catch
up to the moment. His dark eyebrows were raised; he was dubi-
ous.

"Well, let's be sure," he said, as he sensed my certainty. "I'll
order a blood test." When the young physician called forty-eight
hours later to confirm that I was expecting, the surprise in his
voice was unmistakable. "And you're right, the hormone levels
confirm that you're only about two weeks along," he said and then
added lamely, "I guess sometimes women just know." His tone was
guarded, as though he had encountered witchcraft.

Jim and I welcomed Laura into our arms nine months later at
Toledo Hospital, after a difficult twenty-two-hour labor.

"OK, I've got this!" said Dr. Purohit, the petite Indian obste-
trician, her gown speckled with blood. Scrunched next to her
in the small theater between my legs was another physician, Dr.
Arvin, who'd been with me since I'd arrived at the hospital. In
the mirror above the table, I could see their heads bent over large
metal forceps and a yellowed suction cup with a long silver handle
that cupped around the crown of a dark-haired scalp and pro-
truded out of my body. "Can you believe it's taking two of us
strong women to pull this little one into the world?" Dr. Purohit
asked, and the two women physicians giggled. Their light-heartedness eased my distress.

I watched our baby's head pop out of my body. I saw my

daughter's perfect rosebud mouth and dark, almond-shaped eyes look straight at me. A thunderclap of love rolled through me, so strong it took my breath away. The pain of birth was forgotten.

"She's here and she's beautiful, Mama!" Dr. Purohit said and lifted Laura for me to see her before delivering her into the hands of the pediatric team. A moment later, Laura took her first breath and said "yes" to life. Her wail quivered but it was lusty.

As I felt Laura's feather-light weight against me, the instant love was fierce, protective. I glanced up at Jim and I saw that above his blue surgical mask, my husband's eyes had formed a river of tears that melted down his face and pooled on his protective gown. "I've been called 'Father' all my adult life," he said, "but now I know what that word means."

Two months later, we snapped a photo of our daughter, born in November, in an infant carrier under our beautiful Christmas tree. She wore a red and white lace-trimmed dress that I'd bought at Kmart, over white tights and knit booties. She was the best Christmas gift ever, our beautiful pride and joy.

Funny thing was, we had forgotten about the storyboard we'd created at the Reality Therapy workshop. Years later, I found the storyboard and we were shocked that, apart from my rudimentary drawing, it was a near exact replica of the picture of our daughter that we snapped Christmas of 1984.

We didn't pretend to fully understand the mystery of our experience. Had the Divine plan flowed through us as an image to open our eyes to a possibility, or had we co-created a heartfelt dream, one thought, one choice at a time? We couldn't answer that question, but we knew we'd participated in magic.

CHAPTER 24

BECOMING A MOTHER DOCTOR

E ARLY MOTHERHOOD WAS a fast ride on an out-of-control roller coaster into the unknown, sometimes thrilling, sometimes terrifying, non-stop, no way to hop off. One minute I was in love heaven, the next minute in the unrelenting hell of newborn squalls, poopy diapers and spit-up.

Jim had stepped up to fathering. His willingness to football-carry Laura during her fussy times or take her for a drive in the wee hours of the morning to put her to sleep, was without end. He changed diapers as often as I did. I pumped breast milk for bottles so that Jim could feed her, which he loved.

Good enough parenting and caregiving required creativity, ingenuity, and inner resourcefulness. Jim and I matured a lot as a couple, and as individuals during Laura's early years. Even so, I was unprepared for the tumult of her toddlerhood.

"Mama no, not that dress," Laura said, petulant. She would only wear dresses. She pulled at the pink polka-dotted sundress I'd just slipped over her head. She did not have much hair yet, but the dress emphasized her dark, expressive eyes. She was an early talker and was quick to develop a prodigious vocabulary. I sat next to her on the bed in khaki shorts and a flowered olive-green print pullover. Every morning, our dressing tussles raised my blood pressure. I had to take a deep breath to master my impatience. She glared at me. "I want the blue one with flowers, Mama," Laura said. It was a navy pinafore with red and yellow flowers on it, edged in white lace. That was the only dress she wanted to wear. I washed it every day. That day it went on dirty; I was no match for her will.

I did not feel like myself. My emotional world tilted in uncomfortable directions: toward low-grade irritability, a chafing sense of sadness, and impatience in the face of her tantrums. I reached out to my mentor, Bob, for help.

"I love Laura so much, but I dislike these tugs of war," I said. I sat in Bob's office, where Native American artifacts roosted right alongside books on psychological testing and psychodrama, and poured out my concerns about parenting a precocious, expressive toddler. I was sure no "good" mother experienced anything but perfect, gentle, calmness in a relationship with a child she was head-over-heels in love with. A dream catcher twisted in a draft; a Native American talking stick made of polished wood and tied with feathers and beads sat on a bookshelf. "Let's have Laura tested to make sure her tantrums aren't due to sensorimotor difficulties," Bob said.

The tests showed her development was advanced. In written and expressive arenas, she showed precocious gifts.

Reassured that Laura was either right on or well ahead of schedule as a toddler, I thought Bob would focus on my parenting. When I met with him to discuss the test results, I was surprised by the direction of his questions.

"What are you doing to pursue your own dreams and interests?" asked Bob, in his slow-motion drawl, with a hint of Southern. I flinched under his direct stare. I was motionless in a bamboo rocking chair.

"What do my dreams have to do with Laura's tantrums?" I asked and fiddled with my wedding ring. Bob's desk was neat, with papers stacked in organized piles. He had turned to face me. A desk phone with multiple lines blinked behind him. "I need help with those!" He stared at me, as though he was looking straight into my soul. There was no hiding.

Typical for him, Bob's reply was direct, "This isn't about Laura or parenting. She's right on schedule to assert her independence and you're a good mother," he said. He chuckled and pointed a finger in my direction. His voice went a little exasperated. "You're over-focused on her and not paying attention to the parallel rhythms in you! What do you want to do about *your* need to separate and follow your dreams?

Along the short drive home from Bob's office, I fumed over his lack of helpfulness, but I was also curious: *could he be onto something? Did my over-analysis of Laura's behavior and my own response to it mask wisdom that it was time for me, too, to separate, just a bit, from her so that I could turn to new creative endeavors of my own?*

I sat with my questions over the next several days and noticed that doing so returned me to a place of equilibrium and wiser responsiveness to Laura's struggle to be her own little being. I kept a journal, and felt surprised when I wrote, "I want to go to doctoral school in psychology."

Doctoral school? Me? I'm not smart enough for that! How could I do that with a child? Where would I find the money? We're ok but have little savings. That's just not possible!

A week later, I returned to Bob's office, upset again. I rocked in his bamboo chair and let him have it: "Well, I thought about the separating thing and you're right. I want to go to doctoral school in counseling psychology. But I don't have the money and I'm not smart enough." I glared at my mentor; my permed red hair, which had gone more auburn after Laura's birth, was extra frizzy.

Bob sat back; his chuckle was dry. "There is no question in my mind that you have more than enough smarts to complete a doctorate," he said. His look was of the "give me a break" variety. Books by Carl Rogers, the father of counseling, lined his bookshelves along with others considered to be masters in the profession. "If you want a doctorate enough, you will find a way to do it and you'll be supported," his tone was confrontational, but kind. He spoke with conviction. "Start the process, Linda," he said. "Take the first step and let the path unfold. I'll help you any way I can."

As I followed my intuitive niggles to grow, to evolve, the annoying irritability I'd felt about Laura's natural stretching vanished. The psychic energy that was drained as I resisted love's evolution was released into the freedom to move forward.

The first steps were to take the Graduate Record Exam and to apply for admission. One path I saw was to do my doctorate nearby so that we could continue our lives in Toledo; the other led to West Virginia University at Morgantown. The denial letter from Bowling Green came back pronto; my scores on the mathematics, analytical and psychology sections of the Graduate Record Examination (GRE) were not high enough to qualify for admission to their program, the off-the-chart scores on the verbal/expressive sections didn't count. I didn't get an interview.

The Director of the Counseling Psychology program at West Virginia University, Dr. Jeff Messing, was a former classmate of Bob's. Bob called him to put in a good word for me. I got offered an opportunity to participate in a day of intensive interviews with faculty and students. In the end, I was admitted as one of a cohort of four chosen from two hundred applicants. I was going to doctoral school.

Jim and I were elated. The bridge to West Virginia had appeared. Now we had to find the funds to pay the toll and cross it.

CHAPTER 25

JUMPING OFF

Exhausted, Jim and I faced each other on the bed in the Comfort Inn in Morgantown, West Virginia in late spring of 1987. We had spent the day searching for a place to live during the three years it would take for me to complete doctoral coursework in Counseling Psychology.

Laura, now thirty months old, was sound asleep in the bed next to us in blue pajamas with feet. We'd put pillows around her so she wouldn't fall out of bed. She clutched her pink Care Bear. Her fine, shoulder-length brown hair spilled across her face and onto the pillow.

As part of my admission, I'd been promised funding to cover my tuition—an assistantship to do either teaching or research. But the department's two graduate assistantships had been awarded to other students in my cohort of four. We had driven down to Morgantown to find housing with no secure funding to bank on.

"Should we make the commitment to go forward?" Jim asked. Beyond the sheer window curtain, the contours of the mountains were shaded by the fall of dusk. It was late spring; white dogwoods and purple-pink redbuds flowered amidst their green tree cousins. I wore cotton pajamas and Jim wore a navy T-shirt and underwear; he was under the duvet; I was on top.

"It's a risk," I said. "Dr. Messing said he might not know for sure about my tuition waiver and stipend until right before classes start."

We spent the afternoon with a real estate agent, looking around Morgantown for suitable family housing. She'd taken us to student housing flats, built into the hills around town. Students referred to West Virginia University as "Thigh Master U" because navigating the campus meant climbing up and down hills. Several of the flats were multiple floors up, with rickety steps, impractical for a family with a small child. In one, the smell of marijuana was so strong we all got high. The real estate agent had depleted her portfolio.

Before she left us, the agent took out a piece of paper and printed the name and phone number of a friend on it. She said, "Fred is a landlord who's built new townhomes about ten minutes from the university, but they're probably above your budget and may not be ready."

Laura was asleep in our blue Toyota Tercel 4WD wagon, toys scattered around her. The agent, her suit crisp, her hair a just-right flip, took in our drooped shoulders and dejected features. Her resignation said our search for affordable family-friendly housing was futile. We stood in the parking lot of the real estate agency, surrounded by Morgantown, a curious mix of old mountain town and bustling university center on the banks of the ancient Monongahela River. "It's a long shot, but it can't hurt to give him a call."

We found a pay phone and made the call; Fred invited us right over to see a rental he was painting. The spacious two-bedroom townhome, a new build on a quiet street high on a ridge, was perfect. The backyard overlooked a lovely hill with dogwood and redbud trees. The rent was a reach but do-able. Fred saw us suitable tenants, but he wanted the place occupied within a month, by June 1st and, no, he couldn't wait until school started in late

August. Crestfallen, we asked for twenty-four hours to see if we could produce a plan.

"Linda, every time we've faced a cliff and jumped off," Jim said, "we've landed." His eyes were tired, but lively. His hair had begun to thin out, but his energy was strong. "I'm fifty and about to build a life from scratch again," he said. "This is the bridge we've longed for, to West Virginia. I think we should cross it." He would have done anything for me and he, too, longed to find a way to be closer to Denise and Larry.

I reached over and brushed his hair from his forehead. "But we don't have the money," I said. The reality of our slim bank account made both of us exhale. Despite the money I earned doing child-care for a friend, the salary from the part time work I did in the evenings as an intervention counselor to families trying to get a loved one into substance abuse treatment, and Jim's salary, we lived paycheck to paycheck. Mental health is not a lucrative field.

Jim lay back on the bed and stared at the ceiling. "What about if you quit so that you and Laura can move down here and get situated?" Jim said. I held my breath as a plan seemed to dawn in both of our minds at the same time. The air conditioning in the hotel room hummed. "I could keep working in Toledo until August, right before school starts," Jim said, his voice quickening with quiet excitement and confidence. "I'm sure I could bunk with my friend Charlie to save money," he said. Charlie was a co-worker at the Flower Hospital addiction treatment center where we both worked. Laura stirred on the bed and hugged her Care Bear tighter. "By then, you should have funding, and, with luck, I'll have found a job," Jim finished.

My heart sped up. That could work. "But that means Laura and I will spend three months alone down here without you," I said. The thought was daunting. How would I manage being alone in a new place without friends or family? And on my own with a toddler? I began to doubt the plan. "I'll ride down every weekend on the Gold Wing," Jim said. "You know how much I'll hate that!" We both laughed. We decided to sleep on the idea.

That night I mulled over a quote attributed to W. H. Murray[10] a Scottish explorer of the Himalayans, which had become a guiding beacon in my life:

"Until one is committed, there is hesitancy, the chance to draw back, always ineffectiveness. Concerning all acts of initiative (and creation), there is one elementary truth the ignorance of which kills countless ideas and splendid plans: that the moment one definitely commits oneself, then providence moves too. A whole stream of events issues from the decision, raising in one's favor all manner of unforeseen incidents, meetings, and material assistance, which no man could have dreamt would have come his way. I learned a deep respect for one of Goethe's couplets: *Whatever you can do or dream you can, begin it. Boldness has genius, power, and magic in it!* Begin it now!"

When I awoke the next morning, in the freshness of morning and a peaceful mind, I knew our plan was the next right thing to do. Jim called Charlie, who was quick to offer the use of his attic bedroom, free of charge, for several months.

Fred met us at the townhome the next day, and we handed him a check for the security deposit and first month's rent, which depleted our savings account. Just before we climbed into the car to head home, Jim and I high fived each other and crowed to Laura in excitement, "We're moving to West Virginia!"

CHAPTER 26

PROVIDENCE

Tᴴʀᴇᴇ ᴍᴏɴᴛʜs ʟᴀᴛᴇʀ, the week before doctoral school was to begin, Jim called me from Toledo, his voice hesitant and uncertain.

"Lin, there haven't been any positive responses to my job inquiries. Have you heard on your assistantship?" he asked. My heart sank. I admitted that I had talked with Dr. Jeff Messing, the program director, that morning and he said he had not yet been able to secure my funding.

Jim wondered if he should go to his supervisor at work and ask if he could stay on a few more weeks. "I think my boss will be open to it; I know they haven't hired a replacement yet." I couldn't imagine how I could manage an almost three-year-old toddler, doctoral classes, and studies without Jim's help.

Silence hung in the air between us on the phone. My stomach contracted and my throat felt tight. *Had we made a huge mistake? Should we turn back?* On one level, I was afraid, but in a deeper place within, I felt an unshakeable confidence that we were meant to be in West Virginia and that my doctoral studies were the next right step. Previous experiences, including meeting and marrying Jim, had taught me to lean into curves and have faith in my heart's knowing that all would be well.

"My vote is that you get on the bike and come down here for good," I said. I looked around the beautiful kitchen of the new apartment. Warm air filtered through the screen of the back door. I never got tired of looking at the forested mountains that enveloped the little subdivision, nor took them for granted. Laura played happily at the kitchen table, absorbed in artmaking with crayons and paints. Paint brushes sat in a clean glass of water. A small saltshaker rested on the floor next to the microwave stand. Laura flourished here, though she missed her daddy. I'd found a wonderful childcare facility for her. She loved Pleasant Day School!

"We'll work out whatever comes from here in West Virginia," I said. "I trust that we were guided to be here." An owl hooted from its perch in a tall pine tree. "Some way, somehow, we'll find a way to support ourselves."

Jim exhaled, relief in his voice, "I agree. That feels right, and I want to be back with my family." Eight hours later, in the middle of the night, he arrived home, saddle-sore, and weary, but his hug said everything: "*I'm home. We're home. At last.*"

Sunday, we racked our brains to produce backup plans if our "no job" status persisted.

The kitchen phone rang first thing Monday morning; it was the director of the counseling psychology program; his voice was kind and upbeat. "Linda, my colleague, Dr. Anne Nardi, needs a teaching assistant in the Educational Psychology Department, and she wants to meet you," he said. "Can you interview with her this afternoon?"

Anne met me in her office in Allen Hall on the West Virginia University campus; she sat behind a large wooden desk piled high with books and papers. "I'm thrilled to meet you," she said. "I've spoken to your mentors, Bob and Peggy, and they think you have strong potential as a teacher."

The Director of the Ed Psych program, Anne was a lively brunette, a wise academic with a warm, no-nonsense manner. She appraised me from behind dark-rimmed reading glasses at the end of her nose. The interview was less about what I had done and more about who I was. I relaxed in the face of her good will and common sense. We hit it off. By the end of the interview, Anne had decided. "I'd like to offer you a teaching assistantship," she said. "I will help you grow into teaching at the university level."

I left her office flushed with excitement and with a big stack of textbooks in my arms, assigned to teach two introductory courses in educational psychology, about which I knew next to nothing. I had two weeks to prepare for my first class. I was awarded a full graduate tuition waiver and a modest stipend. In the end, the assistantship was a three-year gig that funded my entire doctoral program, taught me a ton about teaching, and gave me access to many supportive mentors.

Divine Providence smiled on Jim, too. Three times that week, the phone rang and the caller on the end was the director of an addiction treatment center who offered Jim a job he'd interviewed for. That support from life overwhelmed us with awe. Jim accepted an addiction counseling position at Fairmont General Hospital, thirty minutes south of Morgantown.

We celebrated our good fortune with Laura's favorite food, pizza, at the Pizza Hut in Sabraton, a subdivision of Morgantown. Jim and I clinked our glasses of Pepsi as Laura dug with enthusiasm into a slice of cheese and pepperoni. Our leap into the unknown had been rewarded. The bridge materialized after we jumped! We were Mountaineers.

CHAPTER 27

DEGREES OF FREEDOM

Counseling Psychology programs are based on the "scientist-practitioner" training model. They are designed to turn out professionals with skills for both conducting and interpreting research, and for the art and practice of counseling. I was terrified that I didn't have what it took to manage the science part but felt confident I could become a respectable practitioner.

The words "degrees of freedom" and "analysis of variance" were Greek to me, a foreign language. My statistics professor, Dr. Parker, medium height, slim build, early fifties, thick brown hair, had written them on the board and turned to face the class of about forty students. He had patches on the elbows of his tweed jacket, the quintessential picture of an academic.

"Is there anyone in the class who did not take a statistics course during their master's program?" he asked. My heart skipped some beats. Sunlight shone through the tall windows of the psychology building, Oglebay Hall, on the downtown campus of the University. The room was warm, my permed hair was frizzed by the humidity. A heavy stack of books sat in a plastic bag stamped with the WVU logo, by the side of my desk. I'd just visited the bookstore to purchase my textbooks. I could not believe how many of them there were, nor how thick! I wore white shorts and a pink and white striped top.

The professor's reading glasses had slid to the end of his nose; he looked over the heads of his students with warmth and curiosity. I raised my hand. My degree program at Siena did not include a statistics course. Only one other student raised his hand. "You two will have to play catch up," the professor said. My mouth went dry.

After class, I approached Dr. Parker's desk. "Could you recommend a tutor for me?" I asked, my voice trembled. "I had a tough time following much of what you talked about today." The room behind me had cleared of students. The professor's fingers drummed his desk.

"Give it some time," he said. "Let's wait until after the first test. If you need a tutor, I'll find one for you or do it myself." His voice was kind. The scratched brown top of his old wooden desk stared at me.

In the first months of my doctoral program, I felt overwhelmed. I didn't comprehend it yet, but I had started an educational marathon that would last almost six years before I would earn my license as a psychologist. The reading load was enormous. The road ahead was full of hurdles: course work, comprehensive exams, supervised practicum, dissertation proposal, research, dissertation defense, internship, supervised practice, written national board exam, oral licensing exam! To keep my funding, I had to manage my assistantship by learning the ropes of teaching college students as well as mastering educational psychology, a terrain unfamiliar to me.

Laura struggled to adjust to full-time daycare. She cried hysterical tears every time I left her at Pleasant Day School. This was heart-wrenching, and I felt horrible guilt over leaving her when she was distressed. I watched through the school window and if she didn't calm down, I'd go back to comfort her, sometimes several times, until the director pulled me aside and with kind firmness told me she was fine as soon as I left and could I please just drop her and go, not prolong the leave-taking!

Jim struggled to adjust to his new job. He and one of his colleagues, like oil and vinegar, were an uneasy mix. My life became one of classes, teaching, parenting during the day, cooking, and cleaning, getting Laura to bed, and then assuming my position at the kitchen table until the wee hours of the morning when it was quiet, and I could study uninterrupted. I lapsed into chronic exhaustion.

My statistics course was a make-or-break threshold. If I couldn't clear it, I would be dropped from the program. An iron-clad belief that I could not be good at math had gotten lodged in my brain after a painful fourth grade experience when a teacher had ridiculed me for not being able to "get" long division. I overcompensated, I memorized formulas and practiced statistical calculations until I saw them in my dreams. The professor would not let us use calculators. "I want you to understand the math and principles behind the calculations," he said. I was convinced he enjoyed torture.

Dr. Parker walked between four rows of our students to hand back our first tests. He slapped the exam upside down on each student's wooden desk. When he got to mine, he paused. I felt light-headed. He slapped my test papers down. I turned them over. He had written and circled "100%—A" in large letters with a bright red China marker at the top of the page. "You earned the highest grade in the class," he said. I fought not to cry on a wave of relief and incredulity. "Still think you need a tutor, Ms. Sandel?"

Proficiency might take me longer and I might have to work harder at it, but if I pushed myself, I could compete with the best and brightest! I completed my three years of coursework with straight "A"s and earned my cohort's award for the "Outstanding Counseling Student" when I graduated. The price tag was a perpetual knot in my stomach, fatigue, irritability at home and a feeling that I jumped through senseless and unending hoops.

CHAPTER 28

CHRONIC DISTRESS

T HE DAYS OF deadheading on the motorcycle were over. Jim and I snuck away from jobs and doctoral studies whenever we could, but the pickings were slim.

Our trips now looked different: Jim was on the motorcycle, and I was in the car with the camping gear and our precious daughter. I tried to be "ok" with this. Jim was stressed about his job—I knew he needed the outlet biking brought him. But I wasn't consistently good at it.

We packed for a weekend trip to Rocky Gap State Park in northern Maryland, a quiet oasis [at least until a casino was built at the Lodge] of glacial rocks, a lake and endless hiking trails. My shoulders dropped their load and my heart lightened as we made the ride over Route 68; the mountain and forest scenery were breathtaking. Laura played happily in the back seat with books and Barbies. She loved to read and was an easy traveler.

We arrived at the park, set up the tent, and enjoyed an evening around the campfire. Contentment filled my heart as I looked at my sleeping toddler and husband snug as bugs in a rug in their sleeping bags.

"Would you mind if I took off for a ride?" Jim said, as we cleaned up dishes from the breakfast I'd cooked. A surge of resentment tightened my solar plexus. I had hoped we'd spend the day at the lake's beach. *Jim needs this relief*, I thought. *But what about me?* The sun climbed steadily into a bright blue, cloudless sky; the day promised to be a scorcher. My jean shorts felt a stitch too tight—I'd put on weight since starting doctoral school. A pop top from a soda can shone in the dirt next to the blackened metal campfire ring.

"No, go, enjoy," I said, and lied. Jim sighed with relief and, in short order, took off on the bike. Laura was distressed to see her daddy drive off, but I distracted her with the promise to spend the day swimming, got her dressed and we headed for the water.

I assumed Jim would be gone for a couple of hours, but the morning sizzled into the afternoon and cooled into evening. No Jim. *Had he had an accident? Had he forgotten he was a father with responsibilities?* There were no cell phones to text and stay in touch, and we were in the middle of nowhere.

As the day wore on, I brewed a cauldron of righteous anger and frantic worry.

I thought about my perception that I did more than a fair share of the housework, cooking, and parenting tasks like taking Laura to day care and dental or medical appointments. Jim was emotionally available to Laura and loved to spend time with her. He wasn't a disciplinarian, though, and avoided conflict with her, and with me, like the plague. When I expressed anger, he withdrew. I often felt isolated and stressed.

We were also in constant financial distress. It was tough to stretch his salary and my teaching stipend, both modest, to cover our budget.

Laura had developed persistent ear infections that required her to be on an expensive dose of prophylactic antibiotics. "We don't have the money to cover Laura's next round of prescriptions," I said to him after I'd paid the bills on a Saturday, also my job. I sat in my robe at the kitchen table next to a stack of envelopes and checks. Jim lounged against the kitchen counter in jeans and a sweater. He had just poured a mug of coffee; he drank it black. "How much do we need?" he said after a pause. When I told him, he swallowed the rest of his coffee, grabbed a black plastic trash bag, and left the house.

He came home hours later with a stack of bills to cover Laura's prescription. "Where did you get that?" I asked, as he stood there in his navy down jacket and brown winter cap with a bill that snapped to the lid. "I walked along roads, picked up plastic bottles and cashed them in at the grocery store," he said. He cried, and I sobbed into my hands at the table.

The following week, he asked for a raise, and I took on additional teaching to earn more money, which also eroded my reserves and time. Throughout the day, I ruminated about our hardships. From that stressed place, Jim looked more and more inadequate, and I felt more alone.

As I sat at the Rocky Gap campsite waiting for Jim, my resentment grew. When he rolled in around dinnertime, he wore a big smile on his face; he'd enjoyed hours of a good deadhead ride. I met him with stony silence. After we got Laura bedded into her Disney-themed sleeping bag, we faced off over the campfire.

"How could you have thought it was ok to be gone all day?" I asked. I could not see straight. Fatigue narrowed my vision; what I saw in front of me was a man who did not care. He buried his head in his hands. "You said it was ok for me to go," he said, in disbelief. He looked up; firelight shadowed his eyes.

"Not for a whole day," I said in an angry whisper; I didn't want to wake Laura, who slept in the tent behind us. "Did it even occur to you that I might need a break for a walk, or some time alone?" I asked, as a dull fog of resignation rolled over my heart. My needs did not seem to matter.

"I'm sorry, Lin," Jim said. "I am so preoccupied with all that's going on at work. I thought you would enjoy an entire day with Laura." I gave up, went to the tent, and slithered into my sleeping bag. There didn't seem any way to bridge the gulf between us. There was something wrong with me that I couldn't seem to manage parenting, a marriage, managing finances and doctoral studies without seething inside. I felt terribly stuck. I was knee-deep and just crossing the mid-line of the process of becoming a psychologist—I didn't want to quit. I couldn't change the external circumstances; I couldn't change Jim and couldn't see any way to change my resentment. The best I could do was soldier on.

In my second year of coursework, I enrolled in a required course: "Behavior Pathology" a study of the many faces of mental illness described in the *Diagnostic and Statistics Manual* (DSM)[11] used by helping professionals to categorize and code such disorders. In my stressed, anxious, and tired state, I perceived many of the disorders in myself. This frightened me.

I was on a collision course with a psyche that seemed broken and a struggling marriage.

CHAPTER 29

THERAPY

O N THE WAY to my first therapy session to spill the beans about my growing distress, I pulled off the road a quarter mile ahead of my destination to vomit.

The migraine headache I developed as I crossed the steep mountains to Barb, the therapist, reached its zenith. My purge was symbolic of the poison I would spill and a warning that I was making myself sick.

I entered the old Victorian home that housed Barb's office. A sign at the bottom of the narrow steps explained she was "in session" and invited me to be seated in the living room. The purple, mauve and creamy colors were calming.

The steps creaked as the previous client exited, and Barb descended. An angel had arrived to listen. She was past mid-life, neither tall nor short with generous curves, had silver-blonde short-cropped hair and a serene face.

"You must be Linda. Please go upstairs and enter the first door on the left," she said. "Take a seat in the leather chair. Would you like some tea?" I was too nervous to say *yes,* and that I needed liquid to excise the bile from my mouth. I lied and said, "no, I'm fine." I asked to use the bathroom first so I could rinse my mouth.

She headed toward the kitchen and called over her shoulder that she would be up in a minute.

Barb's office was comfortable; books lined a wall, a long window splashed sunshine into the room. The leather chair, of Scandinavian design, had a scooped seat. I plopped into it and lost my balance when I underestimated its depth. The headache throbbed behind my eyes.

Barb, a social worker, practiced from a grounding in the work of Carl Jung, and in family systems theory. As part of my doctoral studies, I explored Jungian thought and found it reflective, and spiritual. It relied on the use of imagination, fantasy, and dream analysis to access information from the unconscious.

I was curious to see how our sessions would unfold, how Barb would integrate Jung's understanding into psychotherapy. Some schools of thought suggested that psychology and spirituality shared common boundaries. Jungian psychology offered a way to explore those commonalities and integrate them.

Barb shuffled in with tea in a flowered cup and saucer and settled into a chair across from me, at an angle. She pointed to a footstool in front of my chair. "Would you like to put your feet up?" she asked. "No," I said. That seemed too relaxed, too familiar, too vulnerable a position to be in with someone I didn't know. "I'm fine," I said, and lied again.

"Did you have any dreams last night?" she inquired. She sat still and bent forward a bit. Her hands rested in her lap; her face was tilted a bit as she studied me. Inside, I felt a buzz of enthusiasm and wonder; her question heralded a journey into the unknown. I had a feeling that there was no turning back from another level of intuitive knowing.

"I dreamt I was at a summer camp, at the swimming pool, standing at the edge of a diving board," I said. I could feel the skin of my legs below my shorts sticking to the leather chair. The air-conditioned room was cool, sweat tricked between my breasts under my summer shirt. I stared down at my sandals and unpolished toes. My stomach was jumbled with unsorted feelings.

"At first, I felt a deep happiness in the dream. The water was crystal blue and clear. I jumped in, came up, and paddled over to the side. A man stepped to the edge of the pool where I was climbing out. He carried a knife. He intended to kill me, and I was terrified."

"What do you make of your dream?" Barb asked. "I am not sure," I said. "I'm new to Jungian dream analysis. I guess the killer is the anger I feel that I'm turning against myself."

We explored my anger. I felt crushed by the pace of nonstop doctoral courses, and I strained to balance studies with teaching, marriage, and mothering. I drove four hours a day, three days a week, to get to and from my training Practicum. Practicum involved rigorous supervision of clinical work. I had started my third year in the doctoral program, so I was also working on a dissertation. I'd chosen to research the development of empathy in psychotherapists. Most days, I muscled through with four to five hours of sleep. My insides felt pressure-cooked.

Barb listened for a while and then said, "Water is an ages-old and universal symbol of the unconscious, of intuition and emotion. It is a symbol of the Divine Feminine. It interests me that when you are in the water, you have a deep feeling of happiness." She studied me, "But your dream suggests that a part of you, the inner masculine, which is meant to support and receive the wisdom of the feminine, instead threatens it, tries to kill it off. What do you make of that?"

I could not see my situation from the level of impersonal interpretation of symbols at that moment. My life was not a play that I could detach from and observe. I wanted to blame someone or something for my pain and I was sure the source of it was outside of me. I focused on Jim.

The way I saw it, he just wasn't doing enough to help me. I gave little thought to how he also struggled with demanding work situations and that I was no longer very present to him.

Barb listened; her nonjudgmental presence and kindness comforted me. I don't remember that she offered much else in that first session—I didn't give her a chance to get a word in edgewise. Having a place to spill stress felt good. With the valve open, the pressure inside eased. She suggested that we meet every other week and asked that I keep a dream journal.

I cried all the way back to Morgantown. For fifty minutes, the so-called "therapeutic hour," the flow of caregiving reversed. I was the one cared for.

I cried because I was exhausted. I cried because I no longer felt punch drunk in love with my husband. I confessed to Barb that we hadn't made love in months. He seemed more like a roommate than a husband. This loss of connection was devastating. I cried because I felt alone.

CHAPTER 30

ULCERS

I T WAS TIME for a break. My therapist, Barb, had encouraged me to take better care of myself. Being in graduate school with life organized around a university calendar brought me opportunities to get away that Jim's job did not afford. With his support, I packed our blue Toyota Tercel station wagon and headed for my parents' home near Ann Arbor, Michigan for a week-long summer holiday.

Several days in, on our daily call, Jim's voice seemed weak. "Are you ok?" I asked. "I'm fine. I just woke up and haven't coffee-ed up yet," he said. We chatted about his frustrating struggles with his co-worker. He spoke with Laura, who was about four years old, and we hung up.

Hours later, my play time with Laura was interrupted by an emphatic thought: *Go home. Now!* I argued with the thought. *Go home? It's only Wednesday. Why leave now?* I ignored it and went about my business. But the thought was insistent: *Return to West Virginia now!* I felt a surge of apprehension.

Mom was bewildered when I said I had to cut short our visit, that Laura and I needed to head back to Morgantown. I told her that something school-related had come up, but that all was well.

She was disappointed but helped me load the car and kissed us goodbye.

Jim did not get out of bed to greet us when we arrived home eight hours later. That was unusual, but he mumbled *welcome home,* so I wasn't worried. I hustled Laura into bed and crawled in next to him.

Less than an hour later, a loud crash from the bathroom startled me awake. I sprinted out of bed and knocked on the bathroom door. When there was no answer, my heart hammered, and I flung the door open.

"Honey, what happened?" I asked. Jim lay in a crumbled heap on the white linoleum floor. Blood ran from a deep gash on his forehead. There was blood on the silver rail of the sliding glass door to the bathtub; he had hit it as he fell. He was conscious, but his eyes were dazed, far away. "I don't know," he said.

I knelt on the floor next to him. His skin was clammy; he was pale. His hair was slick with sweat. "I got dizzy, and I blacked out." I tried to help him up off the floor, but he was too weak to stand. I double-hopped down the stairs to get to the kitchen to call 911.

The arrival of the emergency paramedics, and the ride that followed to Fairmont General Hospital are a blur, but the words of the ER physician are not. "Your husband has a bleeding ulcer," he said. "He was down four quarts of blood, so we've transfused him. Another hour and he would not have survived."

Laura stirred in my lap; her head was buried in my shoulder. Strands of her fine brunette hair spilled over my chest. I'd had no one to leave her with, so I'd thrown on clothes, bundled her into the car in her Little Mermaid pajamas, and we'd hurtled through the dead of the night following the blinking red-and-blue lights of an ambulance. I felt alone and scared in the waiting room, which was quiet and institutional, bare of comforts. I couldn't comprehend that if I hadn't driven home to Morgantown, I might have lost my husband.

After he was stabilized, Jim confessed he hadn't felt well for days. He'd had tarry stools but ignored them. He said, "I didn't think it was serious. I figured if the dizziness happened one more time, I would call my doctor. I didn't want to interrupt your trip or bother anyone."

I had mixed feelings. I was grateful that Jim was alive. I was grateful that I'd followed my intuition. I was also angry that Jim had ignored the warning signs that his body was in trouble.

In my therapy with Barb, we focused on my anger and Jim's denial. I wonder, now, because of what I've since learned, how the course of my relationship with Jim might have changed had we focused instead on the beautiful, mystical connection between us that had called me to him.

I wonder if a focus on what was right and good might have helped more than the search for the relationship's ulcers. I wonder how life might have been different if we'd seen that, in our stressed states, we'd begun to send sewage rather than nourishment back and forth over the pipeline called communication.

I can only wonder. At that time, my focus on the negative made the negative seem true, the only reality worth discussing, to both me and my therapist, Barb.

Jim healed and our relationship sputtered along. I finished my doctoral course work and my proposal to do my dissertation on the development of empathy in seasoned psychotherapists was accepted. It was time to leave Morgantown so that I could do my research and complete a year-long internship in Columbus, Indiana.

My year of therapy with Barb ended. I was grateful for her unconditional love and compassion. She had helped me own my inner beauty. She had helped me own and trust my intuitive, creative nature. She had deepened my understanding of Carl Jung's mystical psychology and helped me see ways to weave spirituality into my practice as a therapist. She had listened to me when I was drowning in pain. I was, and remain, grateful for her loving kindness, her presence, and her professional expertise.

However, I did not find the understanding needed to fix my marriage.

CHAPTER 31

COPPERHEAD COUNTRY

O UR YEAR IN Indiana passed with the speed of light. I was immersed in a busy doctoral internship, a big step toward completing my doctorate, at a community mental health center and psychiatric hospital.

We settled into a comfortable three-bedroom townhome in south Indianapolis so that Jim and I could split our commuting distances. I rotated through placements in a behavioral health and addictions center, in two rural outpatient clinics, and on the psychiatric unit. Meanwhile, I conducted the interviews that were needed for my dissertation research on self-understanding and empathy development in therapists. Jim was immersed in a demanding job at an addiction treatment center in northern Indianapolis. Laura settled into a home daycare and thrived.

Jim and I were lulled by the rhythms of life and tensions in our relationship receded. As we wrapped up our year, we knew we wanted to return to West Virginia.

My entire family of siblings, their partners and my parents drove down to our suburban, brick townhome in Indianapolis to help us pack our moving van for the journey back to the mountains. We had decided to move to Millstone, where Denise and Larry had built their home on a mountain ridge, known as a hog-back.

Mike and Mary, their friends who we had met in the Sinking Springs cabin, had been first to build a home a quarter mile down the same ridge. However, they now had six children and had decided to move on a temporary basis to an area in New York where jobs were more plentiful. It was fortuitous that they were willing to let us rent their home.

Our caravan wended up the rocky, dirt hill road to a rustic, vaulted two-story structure covered with weathered cedar and topped with a silver tin roof. It was surrounded by forest; no neighbors were visible. We tumbled out of our cars and headed through a thick, heavy, hand-made wooden door.

A gossamer Copperhead skin, wafer thin, shivered in the whoosh created by the door I'd just opened to our new home. The skin twisted in the draft where it hung around two slats of a walnut stained banister on the second-floor balcony.

"Oh my God," said Ma, who walked in behind me. She spotted the snakeskin right away. Dad, next to her, was silent, his hands tight balls in the pockets of his khaki shorts. He shook his head in disbelief. "What have you gotten yourselves into?" Ma asked.

I felt defensive. "Snakes are symbols of wisdom and healing," I said, with a nervous laugh. I was taken aback by the sight. Copperheads, a poisonous viper, are frequently found in the mountain state.

"Wisdom or not," my sister, Laura, said as she eyed the hanging snakeskin. "Let's get rid of that thing. It's giving me the willies."

The ceiling of the great room soared two stories and light from tall, wide windows poured into a room paneled in wood. The walls were constructed of wide planks laid at angles and weathered to their natural patina, as were the pine slats that formed the ceiling. The floor was red-stained concrete. Everything about the house trumpeted one-of-a-kind and organic. It was rustic and wild. Large cobwebs hung in the eaves; it had been unoccupied for months.

The silvery snakeskin portended a life chapter of shedding old understandings and sliding through life on a fresh, pink underbelly, sensitive to raw experience. It was, indeed, an auspicious omen.

"That stonework is cool," said my sister, Carol. She pointed to a massive and unique fireplace that rose two stories. The stones had been harvested from the surrounding acreage and placed by a local masonry artisan. He had fashioned a planter at the top; long, thick philodendron vines and glossy leaves draped the stones. The fireplace cupped a squat wood stove with woodland animals sculpted into the cast iron. Well-used fireplace tools rested on a black iron rack on the raised stone hearth. "That's our heat source," I said. "We will need to tend a fire 24/7 in the winter."

"Are you serious?" asked Ma. She stood next to the fireplace in her print blouse, shorts, and sandals. Hair dampened by the humidity of an early September day clung to her forehead, which was wrinkled in astonishment. Her eyes behind her stylish glasses were wide, mirrors of dismay. "There's no furnace?" she asked.

I explained that the stove was the only source of heat in the house, except for a small, box-like chestnut brown gas heater in the downstairs bathroom. The gas was turned on by an old-fashioned copper faucet nozzle attached to pipes that jutted from the wall.

"Are you sure going to be able to do this, Lin?" asked my brother Mike. We had walked out onto a concrete porch that baked in the late summer sun; it spanned the front of the house. It was screened, in part, by a latticed wood pergola laced with vines of wisteria. Thick forest, dogwood, redbud, evergreen, maple, red and white oak, walnut, cherry, and sycamore trees surrounded us. Breezes rustled the leaves, which were crisping for fall. Across the dirt road in front of the house, a gas well hummed.

Mike's right hand propped open a weathered, hinged cover,

about thirty inches square, to a rainwater cistern built under the porch. He stared into the depths. "I think there are snakes swimming in the water," he said, amazed. My family crowded through the front door of the house to see. Dark strands moved in the water and rippled the surface. A shiver slid up my spine.

The house had a well, but the pocket wasn't big enough to supply water during the dry season in late summer. When the well "punked out," as we called it, we switched the plumbing to the cistern. Water in the cistern wasn't drinkable, so a large green glass dispenser in the kitchen for potable water had to be refilled in town. Among my family, there were murmurs of dismay and incredulity. "You wouldn't catch me living in a place like this," Ma said. She shuddered.

"I don't know, Ma, it's kinda cool," Mike said. He inhaled deep as he admired the forest that dwarfed the home. Visible between the trees to the left, a long, mowed meadow shimmered in the sun. "But it's a big change from what you're used to." His tone was a bit envious. Mike has a wild soul. I was grateful that he understood.

I wanted to pinch myself to make sure this was real. Jim and I couldn't believe our good fortune to live in this one-of-a-kind place, tucked close to nature. I felt something inside unwind. I knew I would love the nature and isolation.

We carted furniture and boxes into the house from the moving van the rest of the day and collapsed into bed around midnight. The house was filled with goodwill, banter, and teasing.

Around 2am my bladder called for a bathroom break. I climbed out of the loft in an annex to the main house, grabbed a flashlight and stepped into a drafty utility room. It smelled musty and woodsy; the concrete floor was cool.

The second step in bare feet landed on a firm, rounded object that moved! I swung my flashlight down and met the beady-eyed stare of a thick five-foot-long black snake. I jumped back, my heart pounded. I scanned the room for something to clobber the reptile. On a built-in workbench, I spotted a shiny axe with a sharp blade and oily wooden handle. I put down the flashlight, grabbed the axe and raised it above my head, but the snake had slithered off through a hole at the bottom of a wall.

What a picture I am, I thought. *I look like Lizzy Borden the axe murderer...about to do in a snake!* Both from seeing the humor and in a fit of uneasiness, I collapsed into giggles. *Good god! What had we done? We'd moved our daughter deep into the woods on a ridge into a very rustic home with no prior experience of living so close to nature and wildlife, with far fewer creature comforts than we were accustomed to. Would we manage? Was this even safe?*

We now nested on, what locals called, "hippy hill" or "granola hill" or even "Catholic hill" with two other families—including Denise, Larry and their son, Matt. The hill was a 200-acre farm of thick forest, pine groves, meadow, oil roads and working oil and natural gas wells co-owned by the families and the owners of the house we rented.

Two weeks after moving in, Laura and I took a break from unpacking and drove to Grantsville, the county seat, for the "Wood Festival"—the local summer fair.

"Heard y'all got new winders in your place today," the woman who sat next to me on the crumbled curb of Main Street said. "Y'all are living in the Franek house, right? The mid-day sun glared at my skin. Behind us towered a blackened squat county courthouse, built of thick cut sandstone. The stranger's well-worn jean cutoffs hid an ample frame with midriff rolls that pushed against the thin fabric of her plaid cotton blouse. Her brown hair, peppered with gray, was pulled back in a lazy ponytail, large strands escaped the wide red rubber band that fastened it.

"Excuse me?" I asked, not sure if she was talking to me. I saw furtive glances appraise us as strangers. My six-year-old daughter sat on my right; she fiddled with the button on the middle of a pink fabric flower at the top of her black-and-white striped shirt. Her pink jelly shoes cuddled up next to my leather sandals on the pot-holed asphalt street. "I bumped into the guy who installed the winders," the woman said. "He said they looked right nice."

Festive enthusiasm rippled among the several hundred men, women and children who lined the road of the small town and waited for the Wood Festival parade to begin. Their voices had a mountain accent that twanged like acapella bluegrass. Fire trucks, pick-up trucks, restored old cars and the high school band were queued up around the corner. The clothing of the spectators identified this place as one of mixed extremes in socio-economic status, simple and without pretense.

"I left home an hour ago," I said. "I don't know anything about new windows." We were surrounded by dilapidated buildings and empty storefronts. Old signage suggested that in a long gone past, the structures in this river town had thrived and some still did, housing a pharmacy, florists, and a well-kept bank, white brick with gold accents and a dark black sign: "Calhoun Bank." The smell of the muddy Little Kanawha [Can-Aw] River, which rolled behind the town, was captive in the humid, still heat.

"Honey," the woman swiveled to look at me and leveled a friendly gaze, accompanied by a chuckle, "Welcome to a place where almost everybody knows your business before you do."

Living here would take some getting used to.

CHAPTER 32

FIRE AND WATER

I TURNED ON the water tap in the kitchen. Nothing came out, not even a drip.

I pivoted to look above the windows in the living room. A bare yellow light bulb that jutted from the wall had switched on. The local water guy had created an ingenious system so that homeowners could be aware when their well pumps were running overly long. A lightbulb that went on and stayed on meant that the well was dry.

"Oh shoot," I muttered under my breath. *What was the sequence of things I needed to do to switch from the well to the cistern?* It was hot; we had moved in on the brink of the dry season in late summer and early fall.. The autumn sunlight was golden. Leaves danced on tender breezes that blew across the ridge and piled them, a thick gold and red carpet against our windows.

Laura watched her favorite movie, "Annie"—she knew every word of every song. She was on her tummy—her sneakers twiddled on a threadbare oval rag rug. Supper, stove-top barbecued chicken, and rice, simmered. I wiped my hands on a towel and hurried toward the porch. The large wooden screen door screeched and slammed behind me.

I knelt on the concrete porch and bent my head under the

rough wooden cabinet to manipulate the valves and switch from the well to the rainwater cistern system.

But the cistern was low, too. There had been little rain. "Laura, honey, it's time for your shower," I said to her later that night. She stood in the big tub encased in a wood frame stained and finished with polyurethane. "But we're going to take a different kind, an army shower." We turned the shower on, and she got wet. I soaped her little body up as fast as I could so she wouldn't get cold. We turned the water on to rinse her off.

"Mom, I don't like that kind of shower," she said, as I helped her pull on her pajamas. "I know, honey," I said, "it's different. We're learning that water is precious, a gift, and that here on the hill, we must use it wisely in the dry time of the year."

The next morning was a Saturday, and Jim took off early with Larry to cut wood on the hill. "I think we'll have enough wood for the winter," he said, when he came in for dinner. Jim's blue T-shirt, imprinted with sea turtles, was sweaty and speckled with sawdust. His face wore a wide grin as he stood next to the thick hand-built side door between the living space and the utility room. It was good to see him so relaxed and happy. Amidst the joy we had in our living situation, our conflicts had receded into the background. I don't remember asking myself why this was so. I was grateful and content.

We had purchased a chain saw and Jim was in seventh heaven as he mastered it. He took great care to clean and oil it after every use.

"You should have seen Lar and me, Lin. It was a hoot," he said. He'd gained a few pounds and his belly strained against his T-shirt. He wore suspenders to keep his pants up. "We sawed through huge chunks of dead wood and gave the logs a push to roll downhill. We used the farm pickup truck to stop them. That truck has a few more dents!" His laugh was hearty. Larry and Jim worked long hours to split enough wood to keep our wood supplied through long winters.

That first fall and winter, we mastered the skill of tending a fire.

I learned to build, bank, and monitor a blaze so that I could keep it steady through long winter nights and guard against overfiring or chimney fires. A nighttime bathroom break came to include a stop at the woodstove to poke the embers and toss in a log or two.

Against this backdrop of nature, I completed and defended my 350-page dissertation, *"Empathy and Self-Understanding in Seasoned Psychotherapists: A Qualitative Study,"*[12] and, in 1991, graduated with my doctoral degree.

Jim secured a job as an addiction counselor at Jackson General Hospital in Ripley, West Virginia, and Laura started the first grade at the same school where her Uncle Larry, Jim's sister Denise's husband, was now Principal! She thrived at school, made a best friend, a sweet, good-natured girl, Tia, who would become like a second daughter to us, as would Laura to her parents. Tia would accompany us on almost every vacation we took as a family, so that Laura had a companion.

To finish the requirements for licensure as a psychologist, I needed to complete a year of supervised clinical work, pass a national board exam, and sit for an oral exam with the West Virginia Board of Psychologists. Dr. Priscilla Leavitt, who operated a thriving private practice in Parkersburg, agreed to employ and supervise me. To get to her practice, then called the Center for Individual and Family Counseling, I had to drive sixty-eight miles one way to work and back across winding mountain roads.

At first, my body hurt from the constant back and forth as I navigated around sharp curves, sometimes hairpins. On one of my first treks homeward after a day at the office, as I rounded a curve on an isolated stretch of road in Calhoun County, a tire blew. I steered the car off the road, sat in silence and wondered if I could remember how to change it. I got out to look for the jack.

A white pickup truck rounded the bend and slowed to a stop. "You look like you need some help" the driver, a male in a baseball cap, said, his voice tinged with the familiar West Virginia drawl. He leaned out the window; forty-something; very good-looking.

It was pitch black; the sky twinkled with stars. The sounds of the Kanawha River and evening peepers rolled in the background. "I do," I said. I glanced, nervous, up and down the road. This was before cell phones. There probably aren't many women who would have found it comfortable to be alone with a male stranger on an isolated, dark road.

"Got a jack?" he said, after he had pulled his truck ahead and parked off the side of the road. He wore jeans, cowboy boots and a plaid shirt with silver buttons that reflected in the headlights. "This won't take long," he said, and got to work. He didn't say much, and, in a few minutes, the spare was on the wheel and the flat was in the trunk.

I reached into my car for my purse, extracted a twenty, and offered it to him.

"You aren't from these parts, are you?" he said, with a laugh, not unkind, but amused. "I just moved here," I said. He put his hand up to stop the movement of the money. "Neighbors here don't pay each other to do the decent thing." Embarrassed, I stashed the bill in my jacket pocket.

"Welcome to Calhoun County," he said. "I hope you love it here as much as I do."

We did! In short order, we were busy with wonderful, wildish life.

After two years, we were sure we wanted to be of this place and make it our home. We purchased a piece of property from Denise and Larry in a hollow just down the road from where we were living.

In the fall of 1993, we began construction on our dream home. We settled into Millstone; confident we would be there for a lifetime.

CHAPTER 33

HUMPTY DUMPTY

P EACH PAINT OOZED over the plywood subfloor, speckled the windows, and sloughed down the walls of my future office in the home that Jim and I were building in the hollow down the road from our rental. I was a tie-dyed mess, lying in a paint tray, nauseated with pain.

"Catch the drips!" I said to Jim, alarm in my voice. The late afternoon sun scowled. I'd gotten my legs tangled and lost my balance as I stepped off a ladder.

"I don't want to have to repaint that wall," I said. Jim picked up the roller and tried to smooth the gooey blobs.

It was New Year's Eve, 1993. We worked every minute we could squeak out of our job schedules to finish our dream house in the hollow. We'd torn down a 100-year-old cabin, dismantled a pig maternity hospital, and carted away a two-seater outhouse to prepare the land.

Jim had dowsed for a well. He'd unbent two hangers, crossed them with twine and carried them around the property until he found a place where the wires vibrated like crazy, even though he did his best to keep his hands still. The well driller, a local guy who went by his last name, "Shock" shook his head in skepticism and said it was as good a place as any to sink a well. He was surprised when we tapped sweet water, the best I've ever tasted, less than one hundred feet down.

A few months before, in late October, Jim, Laura and I had stood in the outlines of the foundation. "This will be your bedroom," I said to Laura, now age ten, at the front of the footings. She walked over to the area and looked around, a slender child in a puffy purple jacket, with glossy brown bangs and hair that fell below her shoulder. "Can we paint it purple, Mom?" she asked.

Jim and I had worked with the builder, our neighbor, to design a home that we hoped would be comfortable, practical, and beautiful. The architecture was a blend of a southern traditional and contemporary. Floor to ceiling windows around the entire house would drink in the beauty of the hollow, a two-acre flat of land cupped by a small creek, forests, and the soft contours of hills on all sides.

"Let's do our blessing," I said. We had driven down to the site to consecrate it before the base floor was laid. While drafting my dissertation, my mentor, Bob, had introduced me to a book of stories written by psychiatrist, Carl Hammerschlag, M.D., *Dancing Healers: A Doctor's Journey of Healing with Native Americans.*[13] I was deeply moved by the Jewish doctor's claim that he went to work with Indigenous peoples of the Southwest to "heal" them, but, instead, found himself healed by their spiritual wisdom. I had quoted his books in my dissertation and become an avid reader of Indigenous knowledge.

Jim pulled a bundle of sweetgrass and sage, a Native American smudge stick, out of his jacket pocket. I placed a large abalone shell in the dirt in the middle of the foundation footprint. I lit the sweet herbs; the pungent and fragrant smoke filled the air. I smudged half of the house, waving the smoldering stick back and forth in the air as I walked around the foundation; Jim smudged the other. We smudged ourselves and Laura. For Indigenous peoples, smudging purifies, brings clarity, and acknowledges the Creator's protection and blessings. We placed the smudge stick in the shell and held hands in a small circle.

"Bless this house, creator spirit," Jim said, "may it be a place of love and peace, a place of fun and happiness." His voice cracked. The dusk air was still, the hills watched us with benevolent quiet, an owl hooted and a whip-or-will sang. "Amen," we all said.

To control building costs, in the following months, through fall and early winter, Jim and I did all the finish work that didn't require a specialized skill. We were exhausted.

Jim emerged through the newly stained French doors, wiped his hands on a terry rag speckled with blue paint from his work in the master bedroom. He said he didn't feel well and needed to stop.

"I'm going to stay and finish this room," I said. The smell of sawdust, new lumber, and uncured plaster board shouted new house. My arms ached and my body wanted me to stop, but I was determined to soldier on. I was a little irritated that Jim had called it quits. And then, I fell off the ladder. Hard.

I tried, with Jim's assistance, to get up off the floor. The first step on my left leg was ok. The second, on my right, was not. Bone grated on bone in my right knee and sent shock waves into my ankle and hip. A rip of pain in my lower back followed.

The damage I'd done was considerable. The severe soft tissue injuries around my knee included torn cartilage. I'd blown out the L5S1 disk in my low back with such force that it looked like a mushroom cloud on a CT scan that I had much later.

I started the new year unaware that a two-year nightmare of severe continuous chronic pain had begun. I had become a real-life Humpty Dumpty, and it would take two major surgeries to put me back together again.

That New Year's Eve celebration was a blur of beauty blunted by the effects of pain and medication. A trip to the emergency room confirmed that I hadn't broken bones and that my injuries weren't urgent.

Jim and I drove straight from the hospital to Denise and Larry's home at the top of the hill to usher in 1994 with a sumptuous meal. Afterwards, we put our heads together over a jigsaw puzzle. I was in a not unpleasant opioid haze.

A fire crackled in the Vermont Castings wood stove and cast a warm glow on the reddish-brown concrete floor. A stack of firewood sat on the hearth. The scent of burning candles enveloped us in the beautiful cedar-sided rustic home with soaring front room windows. At midnight, we set off fireworks into the snow from the deck; the kids waved sparklers under our watchful eyes; this was how Jim and Denise's family celebrated midnight of the New Year.

1993 ended with a bang that would reverberate for the rest of my life. Pushing myself and my body would have permanent consequences.

CHAPTER 34

SNOW-CATION

F OUR DAYS AFTER my ladder accident, as I limped around on wooden crutches, nature added insult to my injuries. On January 4ᵀᴴ, we got a taste of what life was like for our ancestors before electricity was harnessed.

"Hey, Lin, something is odd," Jim said as he rolled over in bed and gave my shoulder a nudge. An eerie hush and murky darkness enveloped the house. The fire in the wood stove had died out and the house felt damp and chilly. "The power is out," I said. "I'll run upstairs and make sure Laura is covered up while you stoke the fire."

We stepped out into the living room and stopped; I leaned on my crutches. We couldn't see out the windows! Because of a breakdown in the polar vortex that normally kept frigid air in the Artic, over twenty inches of snow on the leading edge of a weather system had fallen overnight. The snow was so heavy; it toppled huge pine trees around the house so that their needled arms scratched our windows and snuffed out daylight. The temperatures had fallen below zero.

Laura was snug as a bug in a rug and from upstairs I heard Jim open the utility room and the side door and shout, "Holy Moly!"

A wall of drifted snow and pine branches blocked his ability to see or get out.

The gas stove worked, so I pulled out the small silver percolator pot we used for camping and brewed coffee. Laura padded downstairs and was pumped to go out into the snow. Jim fired up his chain saw to cut a path out the front door.

We slogged out into the winter wonderland. The white of it begged for sunglasses. It was brilliant! The world had become a tintype picture. Snow skirted the tree trunks and clothed every brown limb that raised its arm to an adoring blue-grey sky. Large clumps of snow, smacked by puffs of wind, fell to the ground, soundless.

That snowfall snapped or uprooted over one third of West Virginia's pine forests and brought down power lines. Power outages related to storms were common in the mountains and we were not overly concerned. We had plenty of wood stockpiled to keep the stove fired up, candles and batteries in storage for such occasions, and had purchased extra food supplies when forecasters had warned, several days ahead, that the storm could be heavy.

"Thank goodness we brought these five-gallon paint buckets up last night from the construction site," I said. I filled them with snow. Jim helped me drag them in the house and set them on towels next to the wood stove. The melted water would be used to flush toilets and clean dishes; it could be boiled and treated for drinking if the outage lasted long enough. We had stocked up on bottled water, too.

After twenty-four hours, we moved items from the silent refrigerator to a weather-beaten lobster trap that the owners of the house had nailed outside the front door as a decoration. The trap would prevent animals from accessing our food. Overflow items went to the large, blue plastic cooler set just underneath the trap. I cooked simple soups and dinners on top of the wood stove or on the green and beige Coleman camp stove; I kept several crates full of extra propane fuel tanks for just such occasions.

The road that snaked up the hill we lived on was temporarily impassable due to both the height of the snow and the pine trees that had fallen over it. We, along with our family neighbors, Denise, Larry, and Matt, settled in for an enforced break from routine. By this time, I had completed my licensure as a psychologist and had a thriving therapy practice serving adults and couples. Jim and I couldn't get to our clients, but they were also unable to get to our offices. The entire state of West Virginia ground to a halt. Laura, now in third grade, was happy to have "snow days," breaks from school routine.

The power outage ended six days later, on Monday, January 10TH; but normalcy would not last long. The red tip of the white plastic thermometer on the post outside our front window registered temperatures of twenty degrees below zero, even colder at night. The deep freeze kept schools closed and the roads were iced over.

Before the storm, we had been wise enough to leave one of our vehicles at the bottom of our hill road where it joined Sycamore, the asphalted "hard" road that connected to the main highway through Grantsville, the county seat. Grantsville was home to Calhoun County's single grocery store, Foodland. Our men walked down to the car, braved the icy roads for a grocery run and used a sled to haul provisions a mile up the hill.

"Lin, I think all the pipes in the house are frozen," Jim said one morning, after a trip to the bathroom. He threw on his down jacket and dug the snow out from around the wooden cupboard that housed our water pump on the porch. The insulation had not been enough to protect it from the cold; it froze, pipes burst, we were without a water supply. Many neighbors were in the exact same boat; the local "pump" guy put us on his service list, saying it could be weeks before he had parts and time to help us.

Jim and Larry made more runs into town and carted drinking water up the hill on the sled. Between January 14TH-16th, we lived through a bone-chilling, record-breaking cold snap.

Mother Nature decided to up the ante on January 17TH and dumped another twenty-one inch of snow in a second wide

Nor'easter; this was a lighter snow, but high winds whipped it into deep drifts, some over eight feet high across our road down the hill. The power was out, again. We could not even reach our neighbors, the Stinns, a quarter mile down the road. With over five feet of snow outside, we were truly "snowed in."

CHAPTER 35

RESCUE

T HE OLD ANALOG dial-phone buzzed; I leaned on my crutches against the kitchen counter, and I laid my hands on it. I moved with careful caution, to avoid bringing on stinging knee pain and uncomfortable shocks of pure anguish in my back and hip. We were on an antiquated party-line, shared with three families, which was still intact, despite the weather. The only way to know who the call was for was to press a hand against the phone and count the buzzes. Three short pulses. The call was for us. It was Larry.

"I'll shovel a twelve-inch swath out of the snow from our house down the road toward you," he suggested. "If Jim shovels the same toward us, we'll meet in the middle and at least be able to walk between our houses and share supplies. It could be a while before we get off the hill." Jim got on the phone and he and Larry agreed to start right away.

"Laura, could you put on your jacket and help me carry in some snow so we can bathe, and I can wash clothes?" I said. She sat on a rug in front of the wood stove, huddled over a drawing. At age ten, Laura was good at amusing herself and could get lost for hours in creative projects. Frost had built up on the living room windows. A macaroni goulash simmered on the Coleman stove and promised a simple, but tasty, dinner.

I was struck that life had slowed down and that the minutes were occupied with survival and household tasks. Except for evenings when the lack of light meant quiet, or an early bedtime, there wasn't much time to think. I marveled to realize that this is what life had been for our ancestors—perhaps they'd been happier because there had been less time to fret! A battery-driven radio, used for quick check-ins on the news and weather, sat on the kitchen table. "Mom, I'm getting a little bored with all this," Laura said.

That afternoon, I washed underwear, socks, and shirts out in the buckets of melted snow. I hung the clothes on a line strung across the living room. In the evening, I warmed two large canning pots on the wood stove, and we all bathed. We flushed commodes by filling their tanks by hand. We conserved by observing the rubric, "yellow is mellow, brown goes down."

I hadn't been able to leave the hill to get to Parkersburg, almost seventy miles away, to check in with specialists for diagnoses and treatment of the injuries from my fall, so I hobbled around with my knee swathed in compression bandages. It would be February 3RD before a trip to the city for medical care and a return to work was possible. Even though I was in terrible pain, the sheer amount of work it took to stay warm, keep fed, stay supplied and to deal with the snow didn't allow much time to focus on discomfort. Two additional ice storms in that month would complicate the area's recovery and further delay my treatment.

Toward the very end of the January, Denise phoned to invite us for lunch. We had been sharing meals together at one or the other's homes most days. "I've got a beef stew on the stove, and I baked fresh bread," she said, "come on down for dinner." The power was back on, but the road down the hill was still impassable. I had the ingredients, and time, to bake brownies from scratch for dessert. As I cracked eggs and measured cocoa and flour, I mused that the past month had been a high point of our time in West Virginia. Life had slowed down to essentials and family time, to the speed of love. We'd read books together, played games, and completed jigsaw puzzles. When the brownies were done, Laura, Jim and I walked single file through the quarter-mile snow tunnel that connected us to Denise, Larry, and Matt.

Denise's stew and home-made bread smelled delicious as we gathered around her table, set with white crockery, made colorful by winter-hued hunter green and steel blue placemats.

"I'm almost sorry that this month-long vacation will soon end," Larry said. The tiffany lamp with red tulips on a white background above the table showered its glow over our robust, but simple meal. He leaned back into the checked green cushion on one of the mismatched chairs around the table. We had spent hours at that table, bent over jigsaw puzzles and games of dominos, lit by kerosene lanterns and candles. There was connection and laughter, so much laughter. There were victories of ingenuity; in figuring out how to stretch supplies or invent from them, and in making do without when necessary. Jim leaned back, stretched his legs, and sighed with satisfaction.

"Me, too," he said, and he patted his belly, "though I think I've gained pounds from all the good eating," he said.

"Are you kidding?" asked Denise. "You and Larry have worked your buns off carting food up the hill on the sled, cutting trees and shoveling," she said. The music of John Denver played in the background. The Stinn's dogs snored from their places next to the wood stove. I looked around at my hill family and knew this was West-by-God-Virginia heaven. Conflicts with anyone, including Jim, were far from my mind.

"I don't want to go back to school," said Matt. A gangly twelve-year-old who loved the outdoors, he had helped Larry and Jim shovel snow and cut pine trees that had fallen over the road.

"Not me," said Laura, her ten-year-old frame swathed in overhauls and a sweatshirt. "I can't wait to see my friends. I mean, I love you guys, but there's only so much time with adults a girl can take." She reached for a brownie as we all laughed.

A loud mechanical sound, an engine, chugged outside and interrupted our peace. We raced to the porch and watched a massive bulldozer, run by an employee of the Department of Highways [DOH], make its way up the hill and driveway. Its giant yellow snowblade cut through the snow like a warm knife through butter. Normally, the DOH would not have serviced our private road, but exceptions were made to help stranded families. Our snow tunnel was no match for the big dozer; in a flash it fell to a flat swath of road.

We jumped up and down like children, hugged and high-fived. With a two-fisted thumbs-up, the driver acknowledged our shouts of "thank you" and a grin split his face from ear to ear. We were part of a community that had come through a challenging time. For an entire month, we had slowed down to the speed of love, reached inward for resourceful wisdom, and plumbed outer circumstances for hidden gems of togetherness and cooperation. We were better for it.

CHAPTER 36

SEPARATE ANGELS

B<small>UT OUR PEACE</small> did not endure as I moved through a haze of chronic pain after my ladder accident. I had surgery three months after my fall to repair the damage to my knee, but the physical therapy and rehabilitation were slow and painful. It would be eighteen months before my knee was pain free and I would never walk again without a slight limp.

The back and hip pain fluctuated, but at times, was unbearable. I was thankful it abated when I sat; I was able to maintain my psychology practice and tried to keep pace with the minutia of life, but I was miserable. Through the eyes of pain, life looked bleak.

The quality of my relationship with Jim plummeted to a new low. Jim did not like to see me in pain and felt helpless; he withdrew, not knowing what to do or how to help. His withdrawal upset me further. I wasn't good at asking for help and stuffed my feelings until the inside pressure erupted in criticism. I've heard it said that we take out our pain on the people we feel most safe with, and Jim was my emotional punching bag and sometimes Laura, too. I see-sawed between righteous indignation and deep shame at my poor coping.

We were involved in a local Catholic Church that was a source of community and shared religious practices, but I did not find it much of a spiritual comfort. I did not know how to think about a God who seemed silent and unavailable in times of great pain. I don't remember praying much or asking for help.

I was forty-two years old and traversing through a very dark time. Joan, the mother of Laura's best friend, Tia, had been stricken with cancer. Watching a dear friend move through the ravages of chemotherapy was painful. I have never known a person more steadfast in her belief and faith that God was with her. I was embarrassed that I did not seem to have Joan's ability to stay upbeat and in total trust of divine providence.

I was grateful to have work I was passionate about—when I sat in my therapy chair and cared about someone else, pain disappeared. Sitting may have eased the pressure on nerves and alleviated physical pain, but it never occurred to me to wonder where the emotional pain went.

"I just can't live like we've been living," I said to Jim as he walked, and I slow-limped along Sycamore Road. I'd asked him to get some exercise with me so that Laura would be out of earshot. It was late summer, and Sycamore Creek had ebbed to a trickle. My heart was like a mossy stone under water; what it wanted was slippery. The trees were brown around the edges. The mountains shaded us from the hot sun. Birds warbled.

"What do you mean?" he asked. Jim stopped in his tracks. The creases around his eyes wrinkled in dismay. Empty beer and pop bottles had been tossed on the side of the road. A small, dead snake flattened by a car, lay near his booted foot. "I want you to move out," I said. We stood at the foot of a clay-caked oil road. An old derrick rose above us. Rusted red pipes ran along the bank of the creek. I could hear the hiss of a leak and smelled gas.

"We're little more than roommates," I said, as my heart hammered. "Maybe some time apart will do us good." "If that's what you want, ok," he said. Jim's jaw was set in sadness and shock. "I also think we should get counseling." He was quiet as we resumed our walk. I wanted him to argue. I wanted him to stand up for us. I wanted him to have a say in it, not to defer to me.

I had three reasons for asking Jim for a separation. First, my state of mind was in turmoil. Second, and I thought that this was separate from my state of mind, our relationship had derailed again, and I had no idea how to fix it. At age forty-three, he sixty-three, the dearth of romantic intimacy was painful.

Finally, I believed there was an imbalance in the way we managed life, and I resented that. I was the chief cook and bottle washer. I had high standards for a clean, orderly home. I managed life, the minutia of doctors' appointments, childcare, and home maintenance. I paid the bills and did taxes. I thought I over-functioned in those arenas and Jim under-functioned.

I handled the discipline our daughter sometimes needed. I hated being the "bad guy." I worked full time in a busy private practice and commuted over three hours a day. I was overwhelmed. I wanted equity. That Jim worked full time, managed the property around our home, chopped wood for our fires and was a superb father to Laura, got lost in my haze of pain and resentment. I suspected that he was hurting, too, but he was loath to talk about it.

Jim and I initiated counseling in Charleston with a minister and social worker who we'd heard was insightful and competent. Our first visit was a disaster.

"What qualities attracted you to each other when you first met?" asked Skipper. His dark eyes searched our faces. I sat on a couch. Jim had elected not to sit beside me but had taken a side chair. I had put on some weight and was uncomfortable in a pair of too-tight jeans and a pullover summer blouse. Jim wore his trademark jeans, suspenders, and T-shirt. The counselor, who wore khakis and a blue polo shirt, sat beside a messy desk.

The counselor's office, in a church building, was spare and a loose composition of mismatched overstuffed furniture, worn end-tables and cheap lamps. "Linda, how about if you go first,"

Skipper said when both Jim and I met his question with stony silence.

I thought back to my early days with Jim. "I loved his kindness and gentleness," I said. "He was respectful and listened to me. He was tender and romantic and sent me lots of cards and notes. He was funny and sweet. He was adventurous. He opened my eyes to the beauty of nature. I thought he was handsome and sexy. I can't think of anything about him I didn't like."

"And you, Jim," prompted Skipper, "what attracted you to Linda?" Jim squirmed.

A clock on the bare wall ticked away a silent minute. "She was pretty," Jim said and paused. "She liked to ride the motorcycle with me." He stopped. "Anything else?" Skipper prompted. "Not that I can recall," said Jim.

I was mortified. I wanted the earth to swallow me; my shame was so great.

The rest of the session continued the pattern; I purged pain and distress; Jim sat in silence or gave cryptic answers.

We never went back to counseling. I couldn't bear a repeat performance of the shame and humiliation I'd felt during the first session. I looked at Jim sometimes, as he lay next to me in bed or sat next to me in his recliner and prayed to feel something more than affection.

I could not understand how the depth of love I'd felt for Jim had evaporated. Love could not be that capricious, that on-again, off-again. I looked for the beautiful feeling that had drawn us together and found emptiness.

Within months, we separated. I stayed in the home we had built. The house just a half mile up the hill that we first moved into when we journeyed to West Virginia from my internship site was still empty; Jim moved back to it. Laura was able to move as she wished between the two houses.

CHAPTER 37

THE BEAUTY WAY

NOT LONG AFTER Jim and I separated, about four months past that dismal therapy session, I was somewhere in a spacious house on the desert outside of Phoenix, Arizona in the mid-1990s, at a retreat offered by Carl Hammerschlag, MD, a Jewish psychiatrist, and two Indigenous healers.

Laura was safe with her dad in West Virginia. My sister, Carol, had jumped at the chance to join me at the retreat. Once we got there, I was thrilled to discover that a very dear friend, June, a psychologist, had also flown in for the retreat. It seemed like a marvelous synchronicity!

I sat cross-legged in a circle with twenty or so adults, men, and women, of all ages, dressed in jeans and casual shirts. The fragrance of a smudge stick—braided ceremonial herbs, sage, and sweet grass—perfumed the air; wisps of smoke drifted in shafts of sunlight. I wept and fingered a beaded Native American talking stick.

"I'm anxious most of the time," I told those in the circle. "I want to be free. I want to know and share my voice without fear. I want to be enough. I want to know what to do in my relationship with my husband. I can't seem to decide, and the limbo is painful. I want to understand where our love went. I am in terrible physical and emotional pain. I want it to stop." I wept, snot dripped from my nose, and the two traditional healers from the Pima tribe drummed louder as I sobbed harder.

During and after my training in counseling and psychology, I participated in many, many encounter groups and programs for personal development. This was my first experience of a retreat based on Indigenous spiritual understandings.

About two weeks before, I had finished reading *Theft of the Spirit: A Journey of Spiritual Healing.* [14] The author, Carl Hammerschlag, MD, a psychiatrist, told short, sweet stories about how he and native healers had helped themselves and others to connect with their Spirit, their soulful knowing, when they were lost and in terrible pain, or suffering with illness. I cried through the entire book. I felt like my spirit had been stolen, but by who? Or what? And why?

Could my pain be a sign that I was not listening to my soul? I had wondered. In one passage, the author suggested that most of us get stuck poring over, mourning and rationalizing about what he called our "inner garbage." In therapy, and in other personal development pursuits, we analyze and lament it to no end. He said a central life task for everyone is to let such garbage go and transcend it. *Was I lost in my own garbage and shoveling it around? If so, how could I discard it?*

On the internet, I found a phone number associated with the author; I thought it would connect me with his publisher or publicist.

Carl answered. "I can't believe YOU answered the phone," I said. There was a momentary pause on his end and a dry chuckle. "It was ringing," he replied. Embarrassed, I faltered, but managed to thank him for writing the book because so much of it rang true. Carl listened without commenting.

"I'm having a *Theft of the Spirit* retreat on the desert in two weeks," he said. "You should come." I registered on the spot. The Turtle Island Project sponsored the retreat, [15] a nonprofit organization founded by Hammerschlag and his native American colleagues, to blend the science of psychoneuroimmunology [mind/body/spirit medicine] with Indigenous wisdom and practices. Their aim was to facilitate physical healing by promoting mental well-being and conscious spiritual understanding.

Two weeks later, there I was holding a talking stick, sacred eagle feathers attached to a narrow wood totem, which had been passed around the circle to each retreatant. The floor belonged to whomever held the stick.

The medicine men drummed louder and louder as I shared my pain and stroked the feathers tied by leather strings to the talking stick. *Are they drowning me out?* I wondered. It got harder to keep my mind on my troubles because the drums were distracting.

With a sudden slashing motion of his hand, the lead medicine man signaled to stop the drums, and, in the abrupt, stony silence, he stared at me. The moment stretched. I was unnerved.

"Didn't you say you are a counselor?" he asked, his voice dry, marked by the subtle intonations of the Native American accent. His eyes were kind, his angular face with the high cheekbones of native peoples, was impassive. I couldn't read it. His sleek black hair was pulled back in a ponytail that fell to his mid-back.

"The Great Spirit has put you here as a healer," he said. His voice was kind, but clipped, like a rattle. "Do your painful experiences not force you to look inside for answers? A great gift, the gift of listening, is unfolding from these difficult experiences. *Forget about them!*" He paused and said, *"The gift is sacred."*

His words shook me. *Was I whining over garbage rather than putting it into service for myself and others? Perhaps the Great Spirit was using misfortunes to sculpt a gift? Was my brokenness revealing cracks in old ways of understanding through which new meaning could emerge?*

I stopped crying. *What are my experiences trying to help me to see?* I didn't have answers. But I had a sudden sense of peace...as though the decks had been cleared for a new, unwritten story. My thinking about everything seemed suspended. The gears in my mind that produced a constant stream of thought seemed jammed. The relief I felt was beyond words, beyond understanding. I felt washed clean. I drifted in a purity of mind. The inner quiet stayed with me through the rest of the retreat.

A sweat lodge culminated the program, a ritual meant to represent a return to the womb of Mother Earth to sweat away old beliefs and invite healing. The medicine men and Dr. Hammerschlag piled hot rocks that had been heated in a large fire in the open air, into a hole dug in the middle of a dome-shaped structure made of canvas stretched over bent tree limbs. This ritual was new to me. I was both hesitant and excited to experience it.

We crawled into the Lodge with the traditional healers and Dr. Hammerschlag. I was seated to the left of the medicine man who had spoken to me earlier. The heat was intense. A migraine headache bloomed.

I'm going to throw up. I know it, I thought. *This is awful; I'm embarrassed.* I leaned over to the medicine man and whispered, "I'm going to be sick. Can I leave?"

He whispered back, "Lean over. If you need to be sick, be sick. It's ok." Sitting cross-legged, I leaned over myself and pulled up into a crouched position, with my head in arms, crossed on the ground in front of the fire. I felt an arm, I'm not sure whose it was, on my back. It was a comfort. The heat intensified. Little by little, as I lay there, the urge to vomit and the headache subsided. I felt lighter and I sat up.

Songs emerged in a spontaneous way from the participants. Each praised the Great Spirit, God, in his or her own way. A man sang in Yiddish, but I could understand the words! I sang, "Holy God, We Praise Thy Name" a favorite Christian hymn since childhood. Although all the songs were different, the blend harmonized, a melody of awe and reverence. My heart swelled. The sweat lodge seemed to lift off and hurtle through space, spinning. It was an exhilarating sensation, like flying through a starry night, powered by love—an indescribable experience of "oneness."

I didn't want this exhilarating mystical journey to end, but the flaps at the end of the Lodge were lifted and I was relieved when cool air rushed in. We sat in silence as people crawled out. I started to curl my body into a crawl, but the medicine man beside me put his hand on my arm and indicated that he wanted to speak. He said something like this:

I want you to know that I too had to find my place in this wheel of life through pain. When I was a young man, I drank a lot. One night I got very drunk with some friends and somebody among us killed a man. I was accused of the murder, but I had no memory of whether I had done it or not. I was in a blackout. I was tried, convicted, and sent to prison on a life sentence.

I hated imprisonment. I was a bad dude. I spent many days in solitary confinement. By some grace, I met a Native brother who encouraged me to reclaim the Beauty Way, to live in harmony with all things. I found peace. I started to walk the Beauty Way and helped others. In time, someone else confessed to the murder and people began to take up my cause and got me released. I understood that my mission was to return to the reservation to help my people overcome substance abuse, which is the work I do now.

He ended his story with these words: *Look for the Beauty Way. It is your path.*

I had heard the term "beauty way" before connected to Indigenous spirituality, but I did not know in that moment that it pointed to finding beauty in everyone, everything, everywhere, without exception. I did not know that it pointed to living in total harmony with life as it unfolds. I did not know that I had found a deep, absolute Truth. But I felt the rightness of the healer's words and the sense of peace that had been with me since the talking circle settled even deeper.

The following morning, we gathered on the desert in a circle at sunrise for a final ritual of gratitude, praise, and closure. Coolish breezes wove around the tall Saguaro, purplish paddle cacti and mesquite trees; the dry smell of the desert was pungent, and a thin mistiness hung in the air.

The medicine man I had sat next to in the Sweat Lodge stood at the eastern doorway of the circle. He wore tribal gear, a cream-colored garment, with colorful embroidered accents. A blanket woven with Native symbols draped his shoulders. Head held up, eyes lifted to the sky, he played a haunting tune on a small flute.

The rising sun haloed his body. He looked mystical, substantial yet ethereal. I gasped at the utter beauty of the moment.

On the flight home from Arizona to West Virginia, I drifted in a reverie; my head rested on the steel frame of the plane next to a window. I was tired, but my heart was full. I whispered an internal prayer of gratitude for the forgiveness and peace I felt; the retreat had blessed me with many gifts.

I thought about my separation from Jim. I had no clarity about whether we should reconcile or divorce. *Was there something in our situation that held beauty for both of us? If our troubles indicated that I was way off the "Red Road," a Native American metaphor for a spiritual way of life, was I gathering "medicines," curative understandings, that would bless and help me? What should I do next?*

I was on the edge of sleep. A voice, neither male nor female, one of tenderness but potent authority, whispered into my mind.

"Relax. You are guided, always, by unseen hands. LOOK and SEE."

Life was about to gift me with lessons about BEING the Beauty Way.

CHAPTER 38

A PAINED LIFE

AFTER THE RETREAT, my back and hip pain escalated. For another year, I was in agony unless I was sitting. I pushed through pain and travelled the long distances to and from my office, to see clients, facilitate groups and offer programs.

I studied native American and Jungian thought and integrated the spiritual understanding I gleaned into my clinical work. My practice was busy. I became a speaker on psychological topics; as my reputation grew, I garnered national gigs.

I parented Laura, now a spirited pre-teen, attended her basketball and volleyball games, and kept up my home. Jim and I continued to live in separate homes on the hill in West Virginia; we were cordial and helped each other out whenever we could. I cooked him meals; he mowed the grass.

In the end, my back gave out after a six-hour round-trip excursion to Columbus to sit for another oral examination so that I could obtain a license to practice in Ohio. I made it home, took ibuprofen and laid down for a nap. When I woke up, I could not get out of bed. My legs would not respond, and my pain levels were out of control. I landed in the emergency room. I was confined to bed for two weeks of rest, and when that didn't alleviate the pain, underwent surgery.

Groggy and confused, I woke in summer 1996 to a dim surgical recovery room. I'd just had a laminectomy and diskectomy to address the damage to my L5S1 lumbar disk, ruptured after my fall. My mouth was a metallic desert, but I was alive. Relief surged from my head, swathed in a blue paper bonnet, to my feet covered in cheap brown no-skid socks.

Two angels, in green scrubs and face masks, stood on either side of me in the recovery room. One was Dr. Singh, an anesthesiologist, and the other, Dr. Lewis, the neurosurgeon who'd just closed a nine-inch incision in my back.

"The surgery was textbook perfect, Linda," said Dr. Lewis. His eyes above his blue surgical mask were kind. "Who is with you for me to talk to?" he asked. A beige and tan print curtain was drawn around the small space. An IV dripped fluid into my hand. I shivered under the heated blankets.

"There isn't anyone," I said. Tears leaked out of my eyes and down my temples. The doctors glanced at each other with raised eyebrows. Dr. Lewis grimaced. "I'm sorry to hear that," he said. "Don't worry, the nurses will take good care of you." He squeezed my arm and hurried away, brisk, his spine straight, his steps determined.

The morning of my surgery, I'd discovered that Jim, who had agreed to drive me to the hospital for the procedure, had forgotten to arrange childcare for Laura. She had been sick for a few days with a cold and couldn't go to school. Her after-school day care provider wasn't available. We both made calls to patch a solution together but came up empty-handed.

Larry's day at school was filled with meetings. Denise's day at the government agency she worked for was also packed. The only option we saw was for Jim to stay home with Laura. Denise dropped me off at the door of the hospital in Parkersburg, sixty-eight miles from home, on her way to work. I didn't feel like a priority to anyone. I felt guilty that I thought I should be—after all, I had asked for a separation from Jim. I wasn't his, or anyone's, responsibility. My extended family lived in Michigan.

I was terrified, even phobic about doctors and medical procedures. That I had to face a major surgery alone was my worst nightmare, a bottom in my life.

"I'll stay with you a bit longer," said Dr. Singh, a gentle man with olive skin and a warm, deep voice. He patted my hand. "You're a trooper," he said. "You're safe with Dr. Lewis. The nurses respect him. You can rest assured he'll leave detailed orders for your post-op care. Now rest." I slept until I was in my hospital room.

When I awoke, sunlight streamed through the steel-rimmed institutional windows. This was a Catholic hospital run by an order of nuns; a large wooden crucifix adorned the wall. As a therapist, I did employee assistance work for the hospital. Two of the technicians who had wheeled me into the operating room had been former therapy clients. They were caring and sympathetic.

"You're awake," a nurse said, as she entered my room. She was familiar—also a former client. Fluids dripped into my catheter from an IV line on a pole next to the bed. A morphine pump beeped and announced that another dose of painkillers had been delivered. She glanced at the empty blue vinyl recliner next to my bed. "I understand that you're by yourself," she said. I flushed bright red. I felt exposed and ashamed. "You'll be fine," she said, and patted my hand. "Call if you need anything." She left and I cried.

Friends and colleagues at the private practice where I worked were dismayed when they heard nobody was with me during the surgery. They were a wonderful bunch of psychologists, social workers, clinical nurse specialists, psychiatrists, nurses, pastoral counselors, mediators, and administrators. The practice owner, Priscilla, fostered a loving community of diverse helpers with a wide array of service specialties.

"Linda, I'd have been there in a heartbeat," said the practice administrator, Tammy, who was a dear friend. "We love you. Why didn't you call and give us a chance to help you?"

The short answer was that I was too proud to ask and didn't feel worthy.

The morning after the surgery, a physical therapist buckled a security belt around my waist and helped me out of bed to gimp down the hospital corridor. I hazarded a few hesitant steps and relief flooded through me. Beneath the surgical discomfort, the mind-bending, gut-shredding back and hip pain I'd endured for over two years was gone! I had my life back!

I felt a surge of gratitude that I'd been granted a second chance at an active, pain-free life. I couldn't waste that. It was time to resolve the ambivalence in my relationship with Jim and create a new life. *But what did I want it to look like?*

CHAPTER 39

A HEAVY HEART

A YEAR LATER, I woke up in my bed in Sylvania, Ohio, in a home I now shared with my friend June, the psychologist who had also shown up at the Turtle Island Project retreat.

Guilt and despair shot through me as I thought about my daughter, who I'd left behind in West Virginia. It was a grey, cloudy Saturday; thunder sounded in the distance and rain splotched against the curtained window. I stared at the white ceiling and beige walls and drew a hand through my short, curly hair.

Jim and I remained separated. I'd reconnected months earlier with Bob, my mentor from Siena Heights University. Bob, who loved Jim, was sad about our separation, but he'd been divorced once and knew well that relationships can be meant for a reason, a season, or a lifetime. When I told Bob that I wanted some space from Jim, he invited me to join his group private practice in nearby Toledo, where June also worked. June and I had rented a big enough house so each of us, and Laura, could have a separate bedroom.

I'd closed my therapy practice in Parkersburg and prepared Laura and I for the move. Jim would return to the house we'd built while we figured things out. Weeks before I was to move, a kaleidoscopic revelation shifted our plans.

"Mom, I want to stay with Dad," Laura said. "I don't want to move to Toledo. My friends are here. My school is here." My willowy daughter, thirteen, stood on a boulder at the edge of the Middle Fork River near Elkins, West Virginia. Denise and Larry owned property there, and we used it often for picnics and overnight campouts. Jim, Laura, and I had driven out in a burst of cabin fever.

Thunderstorms were about to roll in; the sky was heavy and gray. Under the sky, the river, high with a swift current in late spring, tumbled over rocks, a streak of muddied green water. Laura wore a purple and pink puff jacket. I stood below her on a shore littered with pebbles and rocks. "Honey," I said, "we've got this all planned out. I know it's hard but..." Laura interrupted me. She was a strong, expressive young girl. Her dark eyes flashed. Her jaw was set. "I'm not going with you, Mom. I'm staying with Dad," she said.

I felt stretched on a medieval rack. I wanted to rebuild my life. I wanted to resolve my impasse with Jim and move on. I wanted to explore more career terrain as a psychologist than seemed available to me in rural West Virginia. Everything in me strained to break free and grow. But I could not fathom leaving my daughter. *What kind of mother would do that? Was that degree of disruption necessary?*

Laura was rooted in West Virginia; she loved her father, and it would be difficult to pull her away from the deep connection she enjoyed with her best friend, Tia, and a host of others. I could not and would not force that.

In the end, after much soul-searching, I left. I reasoned that I could drive back to West Virginia every other weekend or more. I could call Laura every day. We could work out ways for her to join me in Toledo on holidays, and in the summer.

But I was heartsick. If I could turn back time, I would unmake that choice. The ache of being apart from her nagged deep, a far more pervasive chronic pain than any physical suffering I'd endured. I read everything I could get my hands on about the suffering and healing of mothers who are separated from their children by choice, divorce, imprisonment, or other life circumstances. My empathy for them knew no bounds. I also knew the separation was difficult for Laura, and my heart ached for her.

I sat up in bed and looked across the hallway to the room that would have been Laura's. It now served as my office, with a makeshift desk, a card table, set up next to the bed that was for her visits. Next Friday, I'd drive the 380 miles back to West Virginia to spend a long weekend with her. The house was still. June was working toward her doctoral degree and was away in Chicago taking classes. I switched on the lamp next to my bed. A thought, insistent and clear, bloomed in my mind: *"Go to the metaphysical bookstore."*

By this time, I was accustomed to intuition breaking into my mind and I trusted it to lead me to remarkable experiences and to solutions to problems. In fact, one of my biggest preoccupations was why intuition was so inconsistent. Sometimes it was loud and clear, at other times it was nonexistent. I named my solopreneur business, "WisdomSources," a nod to my perception that intuition, or wisdom, has all the answers but also a testament to my search to understand how it worked.

I had no reason that rainy day to go to the bookstore; I had limited discretionary funds. Yet, the bookstore had a diverse selection of books on spirituality, and I devoured that genre of reading in a desperate search for peace. I showered and headed out the door.

When I pushed through the glass door of the bookstore, I was greeted by a symphony of fragrances from essential oils, a warm, welcoming contrast to the chilly, wet weather. A lavender candle burned at the checkout counter. I sauntered around the bookshelves, tantric sex paraphernalia, crystals, and soaps. Nothing called out to me. *This trip was a waste,* I thought.

The bell above the door jingled; a tall, handsome Black man walked in.

He approached the checkout counter and spoke to the proprietor, a middle-aged woman with blond hair and large gold hoop earrings with turquoise beads at the bottom that swept her shoulders. "I want to consult an iridologist," he said. "Do you happen to know of one?" Her arms, each with a dragon tattoo, were akimbo on her hips. She shook her head. "What's an iridologist?" she asked.

I stepped toward the counter. "I have a business card for one," I said. I searched my jacket pocket for the card. Until two days before, I wouldn't have known what an iridologist was, either. But my friend, Maryann, had changed that.

"Linda, I did the coolest thing," Maryann said, as we downed breakfast in the booth of a pancake house. Blond hair fell over her forehead; her haircut was shorter and cute. "I consulted an iridologist." Maryann reached for her purse and extracted a large picture of the iris of her eye. "She analyzed the colors and inflammation markers in my iris and gave me lots of information about health and nutrition," Maryann said. "You should see her," she said, and she gave me the business card.

I extended the card to the man in the metaphysical store. He accepted it, said his thanks, and left. *I came all the way to this store to hand over a business card that I just got two days ago,* I thought, *that's crazy!* I shrugged my shoulders, pulled my coat tight, and headed into the rain.

At an intersection where I should have continued straight on, an insistent thought poked into my consciousness, *turn right; go to the shopping mall.* I wanted to go home, didn't need anything at the mall, and was in the wrong lane to make a right-hand turn. But I checked the traffic and made my turn. I reasoned that a trip to the mall would afford exercise on a rainy day and that a rich cup of aromatic coffee would pick me up.

At the mall, I blustered into the coffee shop and ran smack into the Black man to whom I'd given the iridologist's card. He spilled his coffee on his dark coat. "Clearly, we are meant to meet," he said. I grabbed a coffee, and we sat in the food court to talk.

Lonnie Hudspeth was a scholar and devotee of a cosmology

built around the story of Ma'at, an Egyptian goddess and an abstract set of principles.

"Ma'at is the principle of divine law, truth, righteousness, goodness, harmony and balance that governs all of creation and is *embodied in every human being's heart intelligence,"* Lonnie said.

Lonnie brought the story of Ma'at to life as we sat, for several hours, in the food court of the busy shopping mall. I was entranced—he was a passionate, vivid teacher. Mythology about Ma'at dates back several thousand years before Christ. Lonnie explained that when we listen to our heart-intelligence, it is Ma'at that informs us when we, someone, or something, is off-kilter. He acknowledged that heart intelligence could be hidden behind the noise of the body, emotions, feeling and thinking. He said this intelligence is always there, whether we know about it or not.

Ma'at, as a Goddess, is often depicted as having wings; she has a prominent ostrich feather tucked into her red head band. It is said that at death, a heart, lighter or equal to the feather of Ma'at weighed on a scale, signifies that its owner has lived a virtuous life, a life in harmony with Truth.

The image of the light heart, the product of living in harmony with spiritual truth and ethics, challenged me. *What was divine order in my situation? How could I return to a light heart? What was my heart-intelligence about my relationship with Jim?* If I could find answers to those questions, they would bring peace.

As I listened to Lonnie, my heart was not light. My separation from Laura and Jim weighed heavy. But I couldn't make Jim change and I wanted a more intimate marriage. I was stuck and saw no way out of the conundrum.

CHAPTER 40

DOCTOR OF WATER

T WO YEARS LATER, I remained very stuck. And I was in
physical pain again. For months, I'd had a searing discomfort in my left hip that was almost unbearable. I hoped against
hope that it would heal itself. After knee and back surgeries to
repair injuries from my fall off a ladder, I wasn't eager to go
through a barrage of imaging and doctor visits. When the pain
escalated; I had to do something.

One night, I had a vibrant dream—when I woke up I thought
what had happened was real. In the dream, my mentor, Sherry,
studied an X-ray of my left hip, backlit, on a huge screen. Her
manner was calm, dispassionate. "You need a Doctor of Water to
heal this, not a Doctor of Fire," she said. Sherry, who was the chair
of my dissertation committee, also had a passion for Jungian psychology.

I awoke from the dream in an upstairs bedroom at my
brother's house in Michigan in 1998. The therapist friend, June,
that I had previously shared a house with had completed her doctorate and moved to California. My brother, Jim, who lived alone,
invited me into his home on a lake in Michigan. My situation
with my husband, Jim, remained unresolved. We couldn't bring
ourselves to divorce.

I looked through the treetops at the shimmer of a lake that was visible just beyond them and thought about my dream. *What is a Doctor of Water? Sherry is one of the wisest women I know. What could her presence in my dream mean?*

I called my friend Grace, to seek her advice. "What comes to your mind when you think of a Doctor of Water?" I asked. I visualized her petite frame, lively eyes, and short, curly brown hair.

"Water is a symbol of intuitive and emotional healing," Grace said. "You might want to consult someone who works in that way. My friend Patty is an intuitive healer who does energy-based body work. Why don't you call her?"

I knew that energy work helped to balance, heal, and remove blockages in the body's life force, which dances through the cells of our bodies. Such healing modalities are based on the understanding that misaligned or blocked energy can result in pain, sickness, or disease.

I asked Grace what to expect. "Patty will do massage and position her hands on your body so that she can move energy between specific points," she explained. "Sometimes she gently rocks the body. It's comforting and I've found it helpful in dealing with pain." I was familiar with massage and body-work. I was eager to schedule a treatment session.

Patty's presence was kind and welcoming. Her shoulder-length brunette hair framed a face without makeup. She wore an embroidered tunic top over jeans; her feet were bare. She radiated a natural glow, a quiet and comforting presence.

I followed her into her basement treatment room, which was warm and pleasant. I was eager for pain relief, but nervous. I wondered what information my body would yield. Soft lighting cast a serene glow around Patty's treatment table, which was prepped with smooth, fresh soft linens and a blanket. I disrobed and slipped under them.

Patty moved to the bottom of the table, folded the sheet up and placed her palms on the bottoms of my feet; each finger touched each toe. *This is a strange way to begin a massage,* I thought. She explained that she was "reading" my long lines, energy currents that flow through the body. She closed her eyes and "read" for about five minutes.

"I can feel the breaks or blockages in your right knee, lower back and in your left hip," she said. I had filled out paperwork explaining the surgeries I'd had on my right knee and lower back and had told Patty that I was seeking relief from the pain in my left hip.

"The right side of the body is associated with masculine energy, the left with feminine energy," Patty said. I thought about that. My knee and back injuries had been the direct result of letting my masculine doing-ness energy get imbalanced, resulting in my chronic tendency to push myself too hard. *Could my left hip pain be connected to something related to being-ness, love, and compassion?*

For the next hour, Patty moved around my body with massage strokes, and connected trigger points via her hands. Sometimes her hands felt hot. I asked about this. She turned, picked up a book and opened it to a picture of two flattened hands, as though they had been pasted against the flatbed of a copier. The hands glowed bright white. "This is what healing touch looks like," she said. "My hands emit and work with light and energy."

During our time together, I explained to Patty that I was separated from my husband and felt stuck as I weighed how to move forward. She came to my left side and put her hand on the sheet, right above my heart; I could see the clock on the wall and knew our time was up.

"Your body will release toxins as this blockage clears." She was quiet for a moment. "Drink lots of water and rest," she said. "I suspect as you make your decision, you will see changes in your body. Forgiveness is the key you're looking for."

I thought: *Should I push through to divorce Jim? Should I acknowledge that I did not have the strength to divorce, reconcile with him, and return home to West Virginia? Could I forgive him? Could he forgive me?*

Late in the evening, hours after my treatment, nausea hit. I vomited several times, and I sobbed in great emotional suffering through the dark hours of the night. I wasn't sure if my symptoms were connected to the energy work or to eating something suspect. After a few hours of troubled sleep, I dozed, and woke early with a dull headache and a feeling of emptiness.

My hip was no better. I limped toward the coffee pot. I poured a cup, settled into a blue La-Z-Boy rocker recliner, and flipped the TV channel to the morning news. I opened the Ann Arbor News to the classified section and scanned for job openings that might ease my financial straits.

My thoughts drifted to the conflict I felt about my separation from Jim. *My heart knows the right answer,* I thought.

Three things happened; they were simultaneous. First, my heart responded, *I want to go home to Laura and Jim. Home to WEST VIRGINIA.* Tears flooded my eyes. Second, my gaze fell on an ad in the Ann Arbor News advertising positions for therapists in WEST VIRGINIA! Third, the news anchor on the television spoke the words WEST VIRGINIA, as he relayed a story on fracking for natural gas in the Mountain State.

The synchronicity of those events was unmistakable. A surge of energy shot through my body. I knew what I wanted to do. I picked up the phone and called Jim; my heart leapt to hear him. "Jim, I want to come home. I want to try again with you. I am so sorry for the pain this separation has caused you and Laura. Will you have me?"

I didn't have to wait for an answer. "Yes. Yes. Yes." Jim said. "Please come home."

We both cried. When he found his voice, it was thick with emotion. "I am so sorry for all the pain I've caused you, too," Jim said. "I didn't show much empathy for you and what you were going through. I am willing to do my best to be there for you, to heal us. I will listen when you are hurting Linda. Please come home."

The wall between us collapsed. It. Was. Just. That. Easy.

I could not believe my ears. Relief and joy, a sense of being heard and seen, a feeling that unconditional love had found a door and flooded around my bruised heart, brought me back to myself. It was as though my heart, soul, mind, and body, once again, were in harmony, whole. Jim had listened. Jim understood. Jim was going to be a partner in our healing.

The pain in my hip resolved fully within a day after making the decision to return to West Virginia. I set in motion all that needed to be done to close my therapy practices. My former employer in Parkersburg was delighted when she heard I was returning; I could reopen my practice as soon as I wanted. A new chapter clicked into place, fast and without effort.

Jim and Laura arrived a few weeks later in a rental truck. With my brother's aid, we loaded my belongings, and I returned to West Virginia.

The morning after I moved in, I sat on the couch with Laura; we folded towels. She was welcoming, but I sensed her uncertainty. I realized that I had inserted myself back into a life Jim and Laura had created over the past two years. I wanted to be sensitive to the rhythm they'd established. She was no longer a little girl; she was a precocious pre-teen. I had come back to a time when it was normal for a child to be stretching into independence. She didn't share much about her feelings. With good reason, I sensed that I'd lost her trust. I wasn't sure how or if I could rebuild that, but I wanted to. I hoped that with good will and sensitivity, I would find a way.

I looked over at Jim as he worked on a crossword puzzle, a favorite pasttime. The light from a lamp fell soft on his face as he bent over the newspaper, his square wire-rimmed glasses had slipped to the end of his nose. He was so familiar. This life was so familiar. West Virginia was so familiar. We were a family again, one that would need to heal, but that process could begin. Forgiveness and healing were in the air.

CHAPTER 41

ROSARY

A MONTH LATER, I stood with Jim and his family next to his father's hospital bed in Ann Arbor, Michigan. Grandpa Jim was dying.

"Ask my family to say the rosary for me, Lin, please," Grandpa Jim said. His lips had not moved; he was in a coma. But I heard him in my mind, his voice warmed by a slight Kentucky drawl. It was like he was right next to my ear, speaking to me. I wasn't startled, more apprehensive that he was asking *me* to bring the rosary to his family's attention.

"But I'm only an in-law," I said, speaking to him in my mind. "It's not my place to suggest that and I'm not sure how your family feels about me after my separation from your son." Grandpa Jim's family—children, spouses, grandchildren—clustered around the hospital bed. The stench of sickness clung to the air. No amount of disinfectant scrubbed it.

"Please, Lin," Grandpa Jim said, again as though he were in my mind speaking. "It's important. Ask them." The fluorescent light above the bed was dim. Except for the beep of the heart monitor, the room was quiet. A catheter dripped fluid into his age-spotted hand. No movement was discernable underneath his blue-specked gown; the ties around the neck were loose.

"It just wouldn't be right," I thought. My rosary, beads of ochre wood on a silver chain, was in the pocket of my sweater. Hours before, I'd closed the door of the car in the hospital parking lot, but a thought had said, *take your rosary,* so I'd reached back in to grab it. I kept it in the console, a talisman for safety on the road.

It didn't occur to me to ignore the thought. I had devoured books on intuition to understand my experiences, which suggested that there was an energy behind life that connected us to each other and that this force was guiding me. I was becoming more aware of how non-stop this guidance was.

"I want to hear the rosary one last time," Grandpa Jim said in my ear; even though his lips didn't move.

In the family's home, Saturday evening rosary had been a Catholic ritual. Grandpa's children would much rather have played outside until the streetlights blinked on. Over the years, I'd heard them rib him with affection about it. He chuckled, but without apology.

Grandpa Jim's heart rate zigged and zagged. He moaned. I drew up tight to my husband, the oldest of six, who stood next to the bed. He held his father's hand, limp, and pale, in his own, strong, and bronzed by sun.

I cupped my hand to his ear and said, "Jim, I think your dad would like you all to pray the rosary for him." Grandpa Jim's scratched eyeglasses and a frosty Styrofoam cup of ice chips rested on the bedside table, next to a spoon. My Jim raised his long fingers to shield his mouth and said, "I don't have my beads." His eyes were wet.

"I have mine," I said, and extracted them from my pocket. I reached around his shoulder to spill them into his outstretched hand.

I felt small, awkward, unprepared for the loss that loomed. I adored my father-in-law; he had a thoughtful way with everyone. I learned a lot from his deep kindness and small acts of service delivered without expectation of return and for the sheer pleasure of giving. Grandpa Jim didn't belong in this sterile place. He belonged to lilac breezes that wafted across his lazy Craftsman-style porch. He belonged to wild raspberries toasted in sunshine. He belonged to the rose-scented fragrance of drowsy Sunday afternoons. He belonged to the Hall of Fame for Dads and Grandpas.

Grandpa Jim moaned again, and one of his sons coughed out a sob. A nurse crept into the room on soft soles and turned off the heart monitor. The end was near.

"Would it be ok if we prayed the rosary," my husband said to his family. His voice was tender, hoarse. "Please." "Yes." "Of course!" came the chorus.

With the grace of a little boy slipping into a well-oiled family ritual, my Jim knelt on the floor and genuflected next to his father. I moved aside to make room for his jean-clad leg and signature black motorcycle boot. I put my hand on his shoulder.

The big wooden crucifix dangled from Jim's hands as he rubbed the beads and threaded them through his fingers at the end of the prayers, recited in groups of ten.

On the first "Hail Mary" of the second decade, Grandpa Jim expunged a long sigh. His last breath expressed from his lungs. I was shaken to the core. I had never seen anyone die, much less someone I had loved so much.

As if drawn by a current of energy, my body was pulled upwards. Grandpa Jim's spirit swept through me as it left the room. The hair on my arms stood in farewell. Our prayer grew more intense, a crescendo.

Much to my surprise, in that hospital room cathedral, I experienced death as mystical and as sacred as birth. Eyes closed, head bowed, I thanked Grandpa Jim for his love. I wished him God-speed to his destination.

As I left the room, I looked over my shoulder at him. His old body, slack-jawed, mouth open, lay pale, shrunk into the swath of white sheets. Framed by thin grey hair, his head lolled into the pillow. He was lifeless.

The essence of the man I loved was gone, the body left behind a crumpled costume left on the hospital bed. The stark contrast between what had been and what now was, shocked me. I understood in a new way that our bodies are a temporal home, a place enervated by a holy essence. *In the sudden absence of that essence, I glimpsed the nature of God, an energy without form. Intelligent. Wise. Alive. Breathing.*

There was nothing to do but wonder at the mystery of it all, get into a car and drive forward into the next moment, the next, and the next.

My husband, Jim stayed overnight at his parent's home to comfort his mom. We decided it was best that I take our teenaged daughter to spend the night at my parent's home. After I told my parents that Grandpa Jim had died, we made subdued small talk; there wasn't much to say in the shadow of such a loss. I went to bed and was soon asleep.

The digital clock beside my bed shone into the darkness and announced the time: 2:00 am.

I padded to the kitchen, feet bare, to get a glass of milk and home-made chocolate chip cookies, my way illuminated by the hood light on the stove. The night air was sultry, fragrant with fresh mowed grass and dew. I slipped into the screened Florida room at the back of the house and curled my feet under my legs on the couch.

My thoughts drifted back to the hospital. I wondered where Grandpa Jim's body was. It was incongruent to think of it in a morgue drawer, a cold space too ugly and clinical for such a warm, devoted, and tender life. I shivered at the unreality.

My musings were interrupted by a swirl of small, star-shaped lights that danced on the rolling lawn. They hovered, dipped, and spiraled, a gossamer, evanescent vortex.

Must be fireflies, I thought. I stood and walked closer to the large casement windows. I squinted to bring the whirlwind of twinkling lights into focus. *No, they're much bigger than fireflies and they're star shaped,* I thought, puzzled.

The apparition drew closer. Delicate and ephemeral, it was also very, very tangible. I did not question the reality of those dancing diamonds.

Grandpa Jim spoke one final time into the quiet of my mind. His voice verged on a gentle laugh. *"Lin, thank you,"* he said, *"for asking my family to say the rosary for me. It was a little bit easier to leave. I love you all so much. Good-bye."*

Riveted. Hushed. Breathless. The lights shimmered and vanished. As they withdrew, I had the sense that an energy had departed, the same sense that I'd had earlier in the hospital room, though the current was more subtle. Deep love and peace bloomed in my body as the echo of Grandpa Jim's good-bye faded.

I slipped my rosary out of the pocket of my robe, fingered the beads, and wept with grief and wonder. *Consciousness is eternal,* I thought. I didn't tell anyone but Jim about my experiences—I didn't want anyone to think I was odd.

There was not then, nor has there ever been, a shred of doubt that Grandpa Jim spoke to me from his deathbed and that he visited later, made visible in the tremble of fragile stars in the waltz of a spiral.

CHAPTER 42

STORY OF DEATH

J IM STOOD IN the warm light of the kitchen on December 22ND, 1999, less than six months after Grandpa Jim's death. "Can I read something to you, Linda?" he asked, his voice thick with emotion. I was touched to the core by his vulnerability. There was more of it since I had moved back home and since his father's death. He snapped the USA Today newspaper in the air to hold it taut.

At the kitchen island, I arranged bright red silk poinsettias and white tea candles around a copper candelabra, a Christmas decoration I planned to drop off at our church in the morning. We attended services most Sundays and enjoyed a connection to a small, tight-knit, and progressive community. Even though we wouldn't be there for Christmas services, I wanted to contribute.

"Of course," I said. I looked up at him and was grateful that tomorrow we would be in Michigan to celebrate Christmas with our extended family.

Jim cleared his throat. "This article is by a woman in hospice. At the end of the article, she quotes the poem, *Gone From My Sight*." [16] He read: "*just...when someone says, 'There, she is gone,' there are other eyes watching her coming, and other voices ready to take up the glad shout, 'Here she comes!'*" I assumed Jim was thinking of his father. Grief had shadowed his heart since his dad's death. He wrestled with what comes after death. He believed in a God, but what happened to personal consciousness? Was there an afterlife? He didn't know what to make of his father's "visitation" to me in the form of twinkling lights.

"That's comforting Jim," I said. "How does it speak to you?" It was early evening, two days after the Winter Solstice. It was dark outside. Laura, Jim, and I had settled into life again—our family felt whole.

The past six months had been peaceful, and we'd found a new rhythm. Laura had turned fifteen, and with that came the challenge of knowing when and how much to let go of an adolescent who wanted independence. She was a good kid—easy in so many ways—yet in those times when limits seemed required, I struggled. I didn't want to rock the boat and stress a relationship that was reknitting and seemed fragile.

But that night was a quiet, gentle one. A Christmas tree twinkled in the great room and a fire crackled in the wood stove. The air was scented with a tinge of smoke and the balsam and cedar candle that burned on the counter. A pile of presents lay under the tree, each with a hand-made bow. I loved making each present a thing of beauty.

We'd finished dinner but had not yet cleared the plates. A crumpled napkin lay on the floor at Jim's feet. "Dad saw his relatives in visions right before he died," Jim said. "It helps me to think he is happy somewhere with his mom and dad, with the people he loved. It lessens the sting of his dying."

Tears slid beneath his reading glasses down his face and dripped onto his flannel shirt and suspenders. He would celebrate his sixty-sixth birthday in January. His hair had greyed, but he was active, and loved to fell trees, split wood, mow grass, walk the hills and roller blade for exercise.

"It's a beautiful way to think about dying," I said. I was in my pink cotton pjs, robe and slippers, we had settled in for the night. Laura and I planned to leave the next morning to make the 400-mile drive to Michigan.

Jim was on call to the addiction treatment center where he worked. He would drop his pager off and make the drive the morning of Christmas Eve. If we took two cars, Laura and I would be able to stay longer for the Sandel Women's "shop 'til you drop" day, the annual shop-a-thon we did with Mom, my sisters, and their daughters the day after Christmas.

"Should we open our presents tonight or wait until we get home?" I asked Jim and Laura. The family vote was to wait, so we settled in for an evening of television, Laura flat on the couch; Jim and I in our recliners.

True to his word, since my return home, Jim listened with greater presence and respect as I shared my perceptions of our life together. He paid more attention to my feelings, hopes and dreams. I was gentler with him and felt far less judgment. I had decided to return, and the commitment settled my mind. I was so grateful to be free of the relentless debate in my head about living apart from Laura and Jim. No career opportunities or freedom to explore other relationships seemed worth the price of the excruciating internal rift I felt when I was out of kilter with my deepest values—family and love.

Our relationship wasn't perfect—we struggled to reconnect physically and talking honestly about feelings still wasn't Jim's forte' but we felt a comfort and rightness about being together again and hoped that, in time, our relationship would knit even deeper.

The next morning dawned bitter cold. Jim drew on his down parka, settled a brown tweed flat cap on his head and headed out to work. I kissed him and watched from the screen door in the garage as he moved to his car. He'd started it to warm it earlier, it idled in the driveway.

"Wait, Jim," I said. The desire to kiss him again was urgent. He stood next to the open door of his small red Chevelle, with a quizzical look. The car's exhaust formed a cloud in the frigid air.

"I want another kiss," I said. I wrapped my arms around his winter-clothed bulk, and he gave me a quick kiss on the lips.

"No, I want a big one," I said. He stopped, laughed, hugged me hard and we lingered over a long kiss. "That's better," I said, and watched as he pulled out of the drive. In an hour or so, Laura and I set off for Michigan. On the way out of town, I stopped at church and left my Christmas decoration on the altar.

We were greeted, eight hours later, at my parent's home near Ann Arbor, by the fragrance of Christmas Eve dinner in the making. The sweetness of fresh-baked Macintosh Apple pies spiced with cinnamon was a back note in the house.

The next morning, I was up early to help Mom cook. We ladled the Golumpki she'd made earlier in the week into a roasting pan and set it to warm. The aroma of cabbage and tomato sauce peppered the air. We finished prep of the pierogi and kielbasa that would be cooked at dinner time. Ma's favorite Christmas CD, songs sung in Polish, played on the stereo. The Christmas tree was decorated with her beloved collection of glass ornaments.

Ma had already cut up the Oplatek, the thin pink and white wafers that we would share tomorrow, after Dad blessed them, among all family members. I loved that we had continued this ritual after Grandma Sandel died.

It had snowed overnight. I was torn over whether Jim should make the trip. I wanted him with us for Christmas, but he'd been through a hernia procedure two weeks before, and still felt a bit fatigued. We talked on the phone. In West Virginia, the accumulation was less than an inch, and he thought he'd be ok. He considered whether to borrow his sister's four-wheel-drive vehicle but decided that was over-cautious.

"Be careful," I said. "I love you."

CHAPTER 43

THE GIFT OF SNOW DIAMONDS

Two hours later, the phone rang in Michigan. Ma called me from the sunny kitchen to say it was my sister-in-law, Denise. I took the call in the guest bedroom. Denise's voice seemed strangled, as though her throat was narrowed by emotion.

"Lin, I've got bad news," she said. I pictured my mother-in-law, Lil; she was eighty-six and ailing. *God, it would be terrible for my husband, Jim, and his family to lose their mom at Christmas,* I thought. I stood next to the bed. "Is it Lil?" I asked. Her pause hung heavy in the air.

"No, Lin, it's Jim. He's been in an accident." I was sucker punched; all the breath expelled from my lungs. "Is he ok?" I asked, alarmed. "It was a bad accident," she said. My arm holding the phone felt like lead. *Jim? Accident? How bad?* I clutched a white waffle towel in my right hand; I'd been drying dishes. I registered that there was a gold crucifix on the wall, a remembrance from a dead grandparent's casket. I looked at myself in the mirror of the dresser, face frozen in dismay, eyes wide. I braced myself "He didn't make it," Denise said. Her voice was compassionate and mirrored my disbelief.

I slammed the phone into the cradle. *She must be joking. That's cruel.* Seconds passed. Ice sluiced through my veins, and I felt light-headed. I thought I might faint. My mind was jumbled; my body numb and disoriented. *This is a mistake. It simply can't be true. I spoke to Jim a couple of hours ago. He was alive and fine.*

When the phone rang again, I picked the receiver up as though it were poison. As I expected, it was Denise, "Lin, this is so hard. I'm so sorry," she said.

"What happened?" I asked. My voice sounded far away, like it belonged to someone else. The accident was senseless. Jim's car had slid on black ice on a fifty-mile-per-hour curve; his speed was about thirty. Denise knew this because Officer Parsons, the sheriff of the little town we lived in, was in the car behind him and was first on the scene. Parsons and his wife were on their way to finish Christmas shopping and saw the accident occur.

Parsons thought as he tramped through the icy leaves behind the car that it was a minor accident. He looked through the broken driver's side window and was devastated to discover Jim was the victim and that his injuries were grave. Jim was alive but held onto consciousness by a thread. The sheriff radioed for a life flight helicopter.

Parsons knew Denise and Larry. He called them, and they left for Charleston, where Jim would be airlifted. Jim died of his injuries en route to the trauma center.

I listened as best I could to Denise, but the details were jigsaw puzzle pieces that floated in the air and would not coalesce into a picture that made sense. I hung up and curled over the edge of the bed. A deep, eerie, gut-wrenching sound keened from my body. NO. NOT. THIS. NO.

The next hour was surreal. I fielded a call from the state police. "Why did Jim have a thousand dollars in his pocket?" a police officer asked. "Because of Y2K," I answered.

We were on the brink of the turn of the millennium from the nineties to the two thousands. Much had been made of the fact that the change in the date at midnight on New Year's Eve could crash the world's computer network and close the banks. We had agreed that Jim would cash his paycheck and carry the money with him so that we would have ready access to funds.

"Who was the woman with him?" the officer asked. "A woman? That's not possible," I said. The officer let the question dangle in the air. Only later would everyone put all the facts together and realize that a good Samaritan had heard the crash and run out from her home across the road to the site of the accident.

The organ donor foundation called to confirm their desire to harvest Jim's eyes. Stump's funeral home called to confirm that I wanted Jim buried from Grantsville, the county seat near our home. The hospital called to confirm an autopsy had been ordered and to ask for my permission to release Jim's body to the medical examiner. "Did you want to see him first?" the nurse asked. I could not, being four hundred miles away. I sobbed.

There are moments in every life that we wish we could do over. For me, one such moment occurred when I told my fifteen-year-old daughter, still in her pajamas, nose buried in a book, that her father had died. I failed to find some way to cushion the dreadful blow. I wasn't composed. I was too blunt. My actions felt wooden; my voice was mechanical. "Laura" I half said, half sobbed, "Dad was in a bad accident. He, he...died."

When my words registered, she screamed. My father, who rarely wept, stood helpless and sobbed in the doorway as I held her. When Laura's sobs subsided, she fell into a deep sleep that would last until morning. I have never felt more powerless. There was no comfort, no protection from the pain of what had happened that I could offer her. *How would she get through this? How would I?*

The house was tomblike; hushed. I retreated to the bedroom where Laura slept, pulled a blanket around her, and sat at the foot of the bed. I stared out at the snow that had fallen overnight. I was in the worst possible bad dream. The sky had drizzled ice after the snowfall. The white lawn was studded with a glaze of crystals that reflected prisms in the bright winter sunlight. *It's a blanket of snow diamonds,* I thought. I caught my breath in a moment of pure wonder.

A wave of guilt washed over me. *The man I love and have shared my life with for twenty-five years with, the father of my beloved daughter, has died.* I thought. *Yet, for a moment I thought about snow diamonds, thought about beauty? What kind of person was I? I must be flat-out crazy!*

My next thought was crazier still, "*Linda, you will spend the rest of your life unwrapping the gift you have just seen. Beauty IS everywhere. Loss is no exception. Look for beauty, care about beauty. This will help you to go on...*

Never in a million years could I have conjured that thought; I just wasn't capable of it. I saw it as a communication from the spiritual realm, from God.

That night, my family did its best to create our traditional Christmas Eve for the kids. But nobody's heart was in it. Subdued and lost, we went through the motions; we ate, we opened presents, my dad did the much-awaited money toss and scramble for the little ones.

My mom had asked me what we should do about the food and the gathering, and I was the one who said, "Let's try to keep things normal." It was my way of denying reality so I could absorb the shock a bit at a time. Laura slept through the subdued festivities; I sat in my mom's blue recliner and shook. My teeth chattered and I was numb with cold, even though I was wrapped in a thick quilt. I was terrified that I couldn't stop the shaking. My friend Peggy, a psychologist, drove over from Ann Arbor to comfort me. It helped when she told me my shaking was the body's way of dealing with shock.

My brother Jim, a Teddy Bear of a guy with a heart of pure gold, stepped up to drive Laura and I back to West Virginia. I was so grateful to him because I was in no condition to drive. The next day, we settled in gritty silence for the long trip home in my purple Saturn. Laura slept most of the eight-hour drive.

I remember feeling closed out of everything. It was Christmas and all the stores and restaurants were shuttered for the holiday. We had trouble finding open gas stations. I was obsessed that I couldn't feel Jim's presence—it was like his sudden vanishing had created a vacuum of emptiness that had sucked me into a terrifying black hole.

Late Christmas day, we pulled into the long, snow-covered gravel driveway of our home. In the garage, I twisted the knob of the door to the kitchen. It was locked. I climbed the porch to the front door. It was locked. I checked the sliding glass doors off the wood deck on the back of the house. They were locked. We NEVER locked our doors; we felt so safe in the forests of West Virginia. I'm not sure why Jim felt compelled to lock them. I will never know.

I stood in sub-zero cold, numbed inside and out, and shook like a leaf. I felt terrified that I could not get into our home. I stood at the front door and tried to make sense of what was happening. I was locked out of the life I had known. Of all the memories I have of that time, this one is the most visceral and dark. It had begun to break through that nothing would ever be the same.

My brother Jim drove me up the hill and I retrieved an extra key we kept with my sister-in-law, Denise. Denise, Jim's sister, and her husband Larry met me with tear-stained faces. We cried and held each other. The enormity of their loss, of my loss, hit me with a fresh wave of shock and pain. They wanted Laura and I, and my brother, Jim, to stay with them for a while, but we wanted to collapse at home. I had not slept at all the previous night and was exhausted.

Denise handed me her key, and a box of personal effects the state police had given her from Jim's car. On the top was a small, wrapped Christmas present for Laura.

CHAPTER 44

ALONE IN DEATH

M Y HUSBAND HAD died alone. A man who loved bear hugs, laughed without reserve, and had given uncommon warmth died with no one familiar to hold his hand.

We had been robbed of the chance to say, "thank you," "I love you," and "good-bye." I had been robbed of a partner, a lover, a motorcycle buddy, the joy of growing old together, a future. Laura had been robbed of a doting father, a bringer of sunshine, a consummate hallelujah chorus, and a walk down the aisle. I was appalled that a God could let this happen. It was unthinkable, unfair, and stone cold.

The shrill ring of the phone interrupted my crying. I didn't recognize the tear-choked voice on the line.

"Are you the wife of the man who was in an accident on Route 33 outside of Ripley?" a woman asked. I stood at the kitchen counter. With my shoulder holding the phone against my ear, I buttered my toast. Bright sunlight reflected into the white and peach kitchen off the snowy hillside beside the house. Tears blurred my vision.

Jim's body was in Charleston sixty miles away. His accident had occurred on Christmas Eve and the medical examiner, like everyone, had taken a holiday with family. My hair stood on end after tossing and turning during a sleepless night. Members of my family who had driven from Michigan to attend his funeral were still asleep. The aroma of coffee, a hint of normal in a time that was anything but, hung in the air.

"Yes, I am," I said, on guard. Others had called to inquire about the nature of Jim's injuries. These calls baffled me. I had not wanted to know, nor do I know to this day, about his broken body. I thought the details would crush me.

"Is he ok?" she asked. "I was at the scene of his accident."

"He didn't make it," I said. "He died." The caller erupted in sobs. "I'm so sorry," she said, "Oh my God, I'm so sorry." For a few moments, she could not speak. I was puzzled, not sure whether to listen further or hang up. I wondered how she had gotten my phone number, but I didn't ask. In the small towns of West Virginia, information traveled fast.

When she regained composure, the caller explained that the accident had occurred across the road from her small bungalow next to a creek. She had come to Jim's aid. She explained that my husband was shivering, so she'd covered him with a blanket from the back seat. She explained that she'd noticed the simple gold band on his left hand. She'd asked him if he had family and he said that he had a wife and daughter.

She explained that she had asked if she could pray for him. "Please pray for my wife and daughter," he said. She told me that his breathing slowed as she prayed. Jim drifted into an unconscious state, with love for us on his mind and in his heart.

CHAPTER 45

GRAVE MATTERS

"WE'VE COME TO dig your husband's grave," said the man I recognized as a neighbor. He stood on my front porch with seven or eight others, a brotherhood of solemnity and respect.

The cadre of men wore the work uniform of the mountains, crusty overhauls bunched up over scuffed, heavy boots. Their jackets hugged them like down bunting drawn over their plaid flannel shirts, which were visible at the neck. Most had hoods pulled over baseball or stocking caps. Most were bearded. Some wore gloves. They gripped shovels, rusty, well-used, caked with mud. It was cold, below zero, and their breath vaporized in the frigid air.

Moments before, I had heard heavy footfalls clump up the wood steps of the porch. The muffled thuds jarred the quiet of the house and jolted me out of the miasma of grief. The interruption to my slow-motion existence wrenched me away from unanswerable questions. *Why? Why this? Why now?* I had peered, unsteady and cautious, through the long thin windowpane, the sidelight, beside the door.

Behind the men, it looked as if leaden grey paint had been poured over the sky. It dripped thick and heavy over the flat of land midway up the isolated hollow in West Virginia, where our house stood. The trees, stick figures on the hills, wore their stark winter nakedness. Snow and ice mixed with frozen mud pretended to be a driveway.

When I look back now, I remember the men on the porch in tintype, muted shades of service brown. I remember them as remnants of an age when death was less sanitized, less removed, and more collective. I remember them as simple kindness.

I recognized the man who'd spoken, but not the others. He lived in the tidy, small cottage painted periwinkle blue about a half mile down Sycamore, the winding hard road at the bottom of our hill.

Cold poured in through the open door, where I stood in my wool socks on the peach marble tile. The white doorway was still festooned with holiday garland. Three electric candles glowed in the semi-circle window above the door. A small red velvet Christmas bow had fallen off the garland and lay in the corner, disregarded, its wire fastening frayed at the edges.

"I don't understand," I said to the men, my brain in a fog. "We're your neighbors," he said. "This is what we do in these parts. We bury our dead."

Our dead, he had said. We were of this place. We were of these mountains. We had been outsiders from the city, but we belonged. We shared the pain of this loss.

When I found my voice, I explained that the grave was a mile up the hill. My brother-in-law and his son had begun to dig it the day before. Two shovelfuls in, they hit a hibernating turtle.

We took this as a message from Jim: *yes, bury me here, here on this ridge. Let my bones join the land that made its home in my soul.*

Setting the turtle aside with care, my family members continued to dig. They hit rock. Glaciers had pushed rocks around Appalachia like pebbles and left them everywhere. The funeral home sent someone to bust the rock out with dynamite.

I explained to the men on my porch holding their shovels that the grave was almost completed.

"We'll finish the digging, Ma'am" their leader said. The others said not a word. They tipped their shovels. They tipped the beaks of their hats. They tipped their hearts. I watched them walk down the driveway, turn, and climb the hill to a holy place.

CHAPTER 46

EULOGY

I WANTED TO write Jim's eulogy. I sat at his office desk just after midnight the day before his Mass of the Resurrection; a pile of crumpled paper spoke to failed attempts.

My entire family of origin slept in beds and sleeping bags around the house. I buried my head in my arms and cried. *I can't find words to share the feeling you were, the feeling of you, Jim.* I thought, and I prayed. *Help me.*

I heard his voice in my head; *"Keep it simple, Lin. Tell them about the lessons I learned."* I picked up my pen. These words tumbled out:

Jim's life blessed all who knew him. These were the lessons he learned and left.

Lesson #1

When you come across a turtle on the road, even when it is inconvenient, stop your car and move him out of harm's way. Try to figure out which way he was heading so you don't accidentally move him further from the family he was trying to reach. Remember that turtles are God's creatures. All creatures large and small are worthy of your service and tenderness. You are here to serve.

Lesson #2

Whenever you can, ride a motorcycle. If that scares you too much, find some other way to celebrate your senses. Look at everything carefully. Notice every leaf on every tree. Praise the intense colors in a sunset. Delight in the wind and sun on your skin. Go outside at dusk when nature is most fragrant and breathe deeply. Nature is a sacred trust. Work to preserve it.

Lesson #3

Whether on a motorcycle or not, lean into curves. Don't fight the flow of life. Go with it. It's a little scary sometimes, but it makes for a sweet ride.

Lesson #4

Clown around. Calling ground hogs "earth piggies" is a way to make you and everyone else laugh. Try wearing a dot on the end of your nose and walking into a fast-food restaurant. It will help you to loosen up.

Lesson #5

Little rituals are important. Kiss and hug your loved ones every time they walk out the door.

Lesson #6

"Pother mot." This is a special lesson for Denise, Larry, Laura, Linda, and Matt. Please remember me and keep me in your hearts. Say our special words every time you start on a new leg of your journey. I will be with you. I will never leave you.

Lesson #7

When you ride a motorcycle and you have your friend, lover, or daughter along, find some way to keep them on the bike and upright because people who trust your driving get so relaxed, they fall asleep. It is your responsibility to protect those who travel with you on a journey.

Lesson #8

Listen to others. Sometimes listening seems like such a small thing, but more often than you know, you are saving a life.

Lesson #9

It is much better to listen than to give advice. This lesson applies to everyone you love but is especially true if the person who is speaking is your wife.

Lesson #10

If God blesses you with a child, give her your heart every single day of your life. Keep her close. When she is little, carry her in a backpack as often as you can. When she outgrows her backpack, drive her where she needs to go. When she starts to grow beyond you, let her go gently: not too slow and not too fast.

Lesson #11

Wear suspenders. As your belly gets rounder and your hips disappear, suspenders are a Godsend. Self-love asks that you accept yourself and not be afraid to develop your own style.

Lesson #12

Remember: free people, free people. When you are spontaneous, open, and honest with others, you invite them to be the same way with you. That is how lasting relationships are created.

Lesson #13

If you like chain saws, REALLY get into chain saws. Don't do anything halfway: there is nothing worth doing that is not worth at least trying to do well and with gusto.

Lesson #14

Go places. Stretch as much as you can to visit this wonderful planet and its many peoples. You will discover that we are all one.

Lesson #15

Play fair and stand for what is right and just. Protest the exploitation of women, children, and the poor. Do anything in your power to protect them.

Lesson #16

Be happy. The time we have in this beautiful world is too short and precious to waste on anything negative.

* * *

After the Mass of the Resurrection, we processed to the top of the hill we lived on. I wished as we stood at the grave and said our final goodbyes, that I'd thought to bury Jim swaddled tight in a soft, warm blanket. As its threads rotted, his ashes, flesh, and bones could have crept into the blades of grass, blossomed into flowers, and built rings in the trees.

Instead, I had forever shut him away clad in a soft brown plaid shirt and gold suspenders in a cement locker and a metal box lined with ivory satin.

We had not talked about how we wanted to be sent off. It had not occurred to us.

CHAPTER 47

GRATITUDE

M Y RAGE BOILED over, and I raised my fist. "How dare you leave me!" I shouted. I hoped Jim could hear me. It was weeks after his death.

Thick split logs were curled in my other arm. For an hour I'd tramped back and forth through ice-crusted, crunchy snow between the woodpile next to the hill and the woodbin on the slippery deck off the back of the house. Snakes dwelled in woodpiles in the summertime, so Jim had located ours at a safe distance. Replenishment of the bin was his job, not mine.

Laura was spending a lot of time away from home with her best friend, Tia, and Tia's mom, Joan. I sensed that Joan could comfort her in a way that I could not. I also sensed that Laura didn't want to burden me with her grief—she is sensitive and caring, and I knew she saw that I struggled. She also had a new boyfriend who stepped up and wonderful friends who surrounded her with love. I was grateful for the community we lived in for supporting her. We were still receiving casseroles on the porch and notes of prayer.

My heavy down parka was unzipped; the job had made me sweat. Sawdust and splinters clung to the coat's puffy mauve sleeves. My dirty jeans were soaked to the knees. In my fur-lined boots, my feet were frozen, and my beige mittens were soddened. My head itched under my stocking cap and strands of hair stuck out like Medusa's snakes. Snot dripped from my nose. "What were you thinking?" I asked Jim. "This isn't fair!" I was exhausted.

I doubled over and dropped to my knees in the snow. "God help me," I said, in a prayer mottled by sobs. "I'm not going to make it through this." I grieved hard; I was angry and heartbroken. From time to time, I had an uncanny sensation that at any moment, I would wake up from this nightmare and discover that Jim had never left, that his absence was a bad dream. It was tough to manage our big house, in an isolated rural area, alone.

Spent with choking tears, I lurched to my feet. I caught my breath and looked around at the winter stillness. I had a sense of being enveloped by quiet. I was rooted into the snow; it felt like a force, love, moved my head and eyes. *LOOK! SEE!*

My heartbeat slowed and I breathed in cold, fresh mountain air. *How had I come to live in such a beautiful, beautiful place?*

Against the blue-grey sky, the bleached white trunks of the gnarled sycamore trees were brilliant and stood apart from the dense thicket of thousands of brownish-grey tree limbs. Sycamores are symbols of strength and divine protection. Wrapped in grief, I'd been blind to their beauty and now, I noticed it.

The sun played peek-a-boo through the clouds and teased the small creek that splashed behind the house with sparkling light. Wrapped in grief, I'd been deaf to the sound and now, I noticed it. Birds chattered around the feeders Jim had strung in the trees. Wrapped in grief, I'd been deaf to their warbling music and now, I noticed it.

I noticed this sudden shift in my emotions. Grief and anger had faded to the background, replaced by awe and thanksgiving for the splendor of nature. I felt uplifted. *I seem to shift from grief to gratitude when I focus on beauty,* I thought and felt awe at my awareness of this truth.

But I wasn't sure how to feel about the shift. *Was it disloyal* to Jim to see beauty and feel happy and grateful? Did seeing beauty mean that I didn't care about him? Which feelings were more appropriate—the grief and pain or the love and gratitude? Were both ok?

As I reflected, I realized that it felt much better to be grateful. *I chose which state I live in,* I thought. *Jim would not want my memory of him paired with grief and anger.*

This insight felt huge—I'd seen a light switch that had been hidden. From that moment, when grief surged, I did my best to look for beauty and gratitude.

CHAPTER 48

TURTLE ROAD

I T WAS MY first birthday as a widow; I was forty-seven. Jim had made twenty-five of my birthdays special. On this one, there would be no rose, no funny card, and no lame excuse for not baking me a cake. Sadness blanketed my vision; the world looked lonely.

"*Happy Birthday, Linda,*" Jim said, his voice cheerful and warm as I heard it in my mind. "*I'm nearby.*" He'd been dead for eleven months. A frisson, a strong chill moved through my body. I had a sensation of heightened alertness.

The exact instant I heard his voice, a lightbulb exploded on the garage ceiling. Sparks showered around me and bounced to the damp concrete floor.

I had just lugged a five-gallon white bucket filled with bird seed across a muddy path around the side of the house. Jim loved to watch birds nibble at feeders. He had hung two of them from a tall, bleached sycamore toward the back of the house.

It was now my job to tend the feeders. Sometimes this was just one more chore on my plate, an instigator of loneliness and grief. Sometimes it was a comfort; it connected me to Jim and pulled me forward into my new life, one task at a time.

I'd topped off the seed and shrugged my shoulders to ease the kink created by the weight of the bucket. I paused to listen to the silence, broken only by the soft rustle of a small animal in the dropped leaves and the cry of a raven who circled dead meat, a deer felled by a bobcat. I glanced up at the road on the hill above the house, renamed "Turtle Road" after Jim's death.

Smoke from the fire that smoldered in the wood stove wafted on the air. I felt grateful that Jim and I had found our way to this isolated, wild place.

I slid the muddy eight feet down the hill and headed for the garage. That's when I'd heard him, his presence announced by the shattered lightbulb.

I hated ladders, having broken my body in my fall from one seven years ago, but nobody else was going to change that light. Resigned, I retrieved a replacement bulb, hefted the clumsy ladder off the wall where it hung and climbed toward the blackened fixture. The blow out and Jim's voice had been simultaneous. *Are they connected?* I wondered.

The job was done. I dismounted and rehung the ladder and made my way to the door of the laundry room. The hum of the dryer soothed me as I moved toward the kitchen, shadowed with dusk.

I flipped on a light switch to the breakfast nook. The bulb in the sconce fixture on the far left flashed, popped, and went dark. Two trains of thought competed for my attention: *Jim is present here; I can feel him,* and *the wiring has malfunctioned. I'll have to call the electrician.*

This is a "flashbulb" memory, a moment so charged that I remember it with crystal clarity. The Microsoft screen saver lit the screen on the computer screen perched on the desk in front of the window. A half-drunk cup of tea sat next to it in a mug lettered "MOM" in bright orange, a gift from Jim on my first Mother's Day after Laura's birth. A Lipton tea bag was plastered to the inside of the mug and the string and label dangled outside. I had the sense that I wasn't alone in the house, though, in fact, I was. I was a little afraid, the feeling was so intense. I felt short of breath.

I retrieved another light bulb and screwed it into the fixture. I tested the light to be sure it worked and walked toward the darkened living room so that I could stoke the fire in the wood stove. I flipped the three-way switch to turn on a lamp. The bulb in the swirled ceramic-based table lamp blew out with such force that sparks cascaded to the parquet oak table supporting it.

Jim's voice rang out in my mind, emphatic, *I AM nearby, Linda. I love you. I will always be with you.* I was incredulous.

I approached the lamp with caution and peered over the edge of the shade. The blackened bulb had blown with such intensity that the metal neck around it had melted. They were fused. The lamp was useless.

JP, I've got it, I thought, *You ARE here.* Astonishment eradicated my apprehension. I chuckled and said aloud, "Honey, amp it down a bit! I'm on my last light bulb!"

Jim's laughter rippled in my mind; the heightened energy in the room dissolved. Colors returned to normal hue. Sounds became less distinct. The subtle sense of vibration in my body vanished. The house felt empty and still, but friendly. I was shaken. I felt torn between thoughts that Jim's spirit had been in the house and thoughts that I'd just experienced a random electrical phenomenon. His voice and presence had felt so real!

I decided to check out the house's electrical wiring. Several days later, Art, the tousle-haired electrician with the age-crinkled face who had wired the house, arrived to explore whether a malfunction had caused three bulbs to blow out in quick succession. He found nothing. Poised above the melted lamp, he scratched his head and drawled unpretentious wisdom: "Who knows why that happened?" he shrugged. "There's nothing amiss with the wiring. Some things are mysteries."

Months after my husband died, I befriended a Native American medicine woman of the Crow tribe, who had moved into Parkersburg. I enjoyed learning from her First Nation wisdom, and she was funny. Thanks to her, I experienced group drumming, spontaneous dancing and came to claim my "snake" energy: the power to help myself and others through transformation, times of shedding one skin for another.

One evening, over a steak she had grilled on a flatiron in her kitchen, she said to me, "Linda, Jim hovers near you and your daughter. You are spinning tops that wobble. He cups his hands around you both, to steady you."

The overhead light in the small dining room was dimmed and we sat at a rectangle table covered in a white lace cloth placed in front of a large window, beyond which dusk fell. A dreamcatcher hung in the window; cascades of red and yellow beads fell from the woven circle in the middle.

My teacher put down her steak knife and cupped her hands around a space to demonstrate what she meant. She paused and looked into my eyes. "Once you are righted, he will move on," she said. "He has important work to do in another level of reality." Her words settled into my chest with soft resonance; I felt faith in their truth.

As she spoke, the flame of a candle on the table elongated and flickered. The exaggerated movement drew our attention. My friend smiled. "Hmmm, yes." She was silent for a moment. "His love for you is unlimited. He is here. You are never alone—there are guides around you, always," she said. "He wants you and Laura to drop sadness and *live*."

CHAPTER 49

PREMONITIONS

For a long while after Jim's death, I grappled with anxiety. My body felt alert, vigilant to threats. I had a heightened sense that anything could go wrong anytime, that life could blindside me again.

Anxiety gnawed at the edges of awareness; sometimes it strung me wakeful and rigid through the nights. I was grateful that a psychiatrist I worked with in my private practice sensed my struggle and offered me a low-dose prescription for Xanax, which I took at night. It saved me in my desperate moments.

One dawn in early July, eighteen months after Jim's death, a dream premonition jerked me out of a restless sleep. In the dream, the phone rang. The caller was Joan, the mother of Laura's best friend, Tia. Her voice was urgent. "Laura has been in a car accident," she said. "She's banged up, but ok. It happened in Williams..." I couldn't catch the last part. I lay in bed in a sweaty heap, the rose and white tulip coverlet tangled around me. Anxiety prickled the hair on my skin and tightened my muscles. My blue bedroom was bright with a fresh risen sun. It would be a beautiful day in the mountains. But my inside experience was obsidian horror. I felt nauseated.

I swung my legs out of bed. Laura's bedroom door was shut,

and her room was quiet. I knew she'd stayed up late watching TV. I worried about her. She didn't talk about her father; her grief was private. She had developed asthma after Jim died. She now required an inhaler when she played basketball and volleyball. At times, from the sidelines, I could see her gasp for breath. The doctor we'd consulted had said reactive airway disease was common in the young who grieve. I felt like a failure, helpless as a mother because I could not take her pain away.

As my feet bit into the blue carpet, I looked up at the tulip border Jim and I had installed near the ceiling of our bedroom. *What should I do with the information in that dream?* I wondered. *Was that a premonition or just a nightmare?* Laura was a new driver. She was careful, but we lived in an area where sharp curves and steep elevations were the norm. Deer were plentiful in West Virginia; I'd lost count of the number of strikes and expensive repairs I'd had to make through the years.

And I hadn't been able to catch the last part of Joan's warning about "Williams." Williamson? Williamstown? Both of those were hamlets where Laura played sports.

Later, I decided to warn Laura. "Honey, I had a quirky dream last night about some road danger in Williamstown or Williamson," I said. She was propped up on a pillow on the dark teal and coral print This End Up couch in the living room. Typical for her, she was reading. A conscientious student, she excelled in literature, writing and art. One of her creations, a wine bottle she'd painted with lush iris flowers, sat on the oak parquet end table behind her. "Next time you're in those towns, drive a little extra careful." She glanced up and rolled her eyes. "Sheesh, Mom," she said. Her tone was exasperated; she didn't cotton to my intuitive nature and spiritual interests. "That's just a little weird." I left it alone.

Several days later, on July 3rd, I woke to an empty house; it was a Saturday and Laura had spent the night at Tia's house. I poured coffee into a mug and carried it, steaming, out to the front porch. It was a pleasant day to sit in shorts and a t-shirt on the wooden steps. The cedar siding house trim was fragrant, soaked with morning dew. The half-acre of grass that stretched in front of the house needed a mow. I made a mental note to get to it that weekend. It was tough to keep up with the care of the house; all of Jim's chores were now mine. Both of our dogs, part Collie, part German Shepherd, lay at my feet, panting in the warmth. The bitter scent of Marigolds, which I'd planted in the front landscaping to ward off wasps, wrinkled my nose.

Three hawks flew near the porch and circled. I watched them with dread. There was nothing dead in the near vicinity that I could see. Were they an omen? Their caws sent my ever-present anxiety into a full-blown panic attack. I doubled over until I could breathe again.

When I'd recovered, I spent the rest of the day cleaning house, a sense of foreboding curled in my stomach.

Night fell; the crickets were loud. I paced; I left my recliner to go to the front door. *When would the headlights of the car appear over the crest of the hill at the bottom of the driveway? When would Laura get home? When?* I had given her permission to be out until 11pm, her curfew. Restless, I was unable to concentrate on reading or on TV.

At about half-past ten, the phone rang. It was Tia's mom, Joan. "Linda, stay calm. Laura's been in a bad car accident," she said. I listened in shock, paralyzed with what might come next. "She's banged up, but OK. They've taken her to Minnie Hamilton Health Care Center. It happened in front of the *Williams* residence on Route 5."

I couldn't speak. I sobbed. "I know this is hard, Linda," Joan said. Her voice was steady and full of love. "But Laura *is* ok. I heard about the accident on my radio scanner and went over right away. I saw her. She crawled out of the car on her own. Can you call Denise and Larry to bring you to Minnie Hamilton? I don't think you should drive."

I called Denise and Larry and sobbed out the story. They flew into high gear—within minutes, the headlights of their car bounced up the rutted driveway and we were on our way to the hospital, about ten minutes away. I rocked in the backseat and held myself. *"She's banged up, but ok. She's banged up, but ok."* I was grateful my dream gave me that mantra as I faced the unknown extent of her injuries.

By some miracle, Laura suffered minor cuts and bruises. She'd lost control of our Toyota 4Runner when she swerved to avoid a deer on a downhill curve. The car had flipped over multiple times and slid down the road on its roof several hundred feet. There was a deep gash in the asphalt road that haunted me every time I passed it on my way to work. Laura had crawled out of the back window of the car between the pancaked roof and the seats. She remembered only that she saw sparks as the car slid. The car was a total loss; only the driver's cab, where Laura sat, remained intact.

She had a new trauma to deal with; my anxiety went off the charts. I didn't sleep for days. My insides buzzed all the time. I couldn't think straight. On the outside I went about my routines—kept the house, made meals, drove to work, went to church. But inside, I felt utterly paralyzed. The only time I felt normal was when I forgot myself and got present to the people I counseled. Presence to them, compassion and caring, kept the demons at bay. I prayed for help. *Where are you God? You gotta get me through this. I can't take it anymore. Why would you load my life with more grief and misery?* I wasn't hearing any answers. I decided I couldn't pray to God, but I could pray to Jim. I KNEW he was around me.

Early one morning around 5am, a couple of weeks after Laura's accident, I slipped out of the house with a bottle of water that I'd asked our parish priest to bless. In my pocket was a silver turtle bracelet that Jim's sister, Ann, had given me after Jim's death. I drove to the stretch of road where the car had slid.

I walked to the end of the gash that marked the spot where the car had stopped. I knelt in the gravel on the berm. Enigmatic fog blanketed the mountains, the rays of a just risen sun pierced it like a faceted diamond. Purple and yellow wildflowers created a serene watercolor along the ditch line. I shivered in my shorts and knit shirt, even though the temperature promised the day would be a humid sizzler.

I pulled the bracelet from my pocket, fingered the small metal turtles, and prayed. "*Jim, I could have lost Laura. There would have been no reason for me to go on. Thank you for protecting her. Thank you for her life. Please help me to live without dread. This is no way to live.*"

I laid the bracelet on the ground and sprinkled several hundred feet of road with the holy water.

That night, desperate for sleep, I followed my Native American' friend's suggestion that I invoke archangels to protect my rest. She had shown up in my life out of the blue and her Indigenous wisdom had great appeal for me. Her belief in Spirit was strong.

I couldn't figure out who God was anymore, but I did FEEL the presence of formless beings, including Jim. I had to look up the names of the archangels and I invited them to protect the four corners of my bed. "*Michael, who is as God, please protect us. Raphael the healer, please protect us. Gabriel, God's strength, please protect us. Ariel, Lion of God, please protect us.*"

My intuition and premonitions suggested there were mysteries beyond visible life that I might never understand, but that could be trusted. I put my faith in the angels.

CHAPTER 50

HEARTWOOD

"**R**ELAX THE MUSCLES in your face," Jude Binder said. That wasn't easy—I was locked in perpetual tension. Jude, artist, and dancer was creating a plaster cast of my face for a mask-making class at her beautiful arts center, Heartwood in the Hills,[17] embedded in the mountains and rural communities of Calhoun County, West Virginia.

The white plaster gauze strips that Jude had just crisscrossed over my entire face were warm. An oily, moist film of petroleum jelly had been layered between my skin and the strips. I had chosen to make a mask of Nepthys, the Egyptian goddess of death, destruction, and a magician of healing.

Beads of moisture seeped down my neck. They dripped onto the oversized, stained shirt I wore to protect my clothing. I felt warm water trickle into my hair, along my scalp. "Breathe, Linda, breathe from your belly," Jude said. She was a petite woman, crowned by a curly mane of dark hair laced with silver, an intense creative who radiated an extraordinary grace and strength.

I hadn't breathed deeply since Jim's death. Life had punched me in the stomach, hard a year before, and I walked through my days haunted and guarded, braced for another blow. I worried day and night about my daughter; her pale and drawn face wore the strain of a deep and private grief that I could not take away. I worried about making ends meet. I worried that life would never, ever, again, feel safe, humming along without effort.

The God of my childhood was not a comfort. The Jesus of liberation theology was not a comfort. The Great Spirit I had been introduced to in my Indigenous studies was not a comfort. I existed in a sea of unending sorrow, lightened only when I could find my way to gratitude and the appreciation of beauty. Desperate for relief, I turned to the Great Mother, the Divine Feminine, to Nepthys, a Black Madonna.

I had found a picture of her on, of all places, a Goddess calendar. Her ebony face was beautiful and inscrutable. It radiated strength and power. She wore a spiked crown of thin gold tines and a golden gown that flowed in rich folds. In her hand she carried an Ankh, the key to life. I studied her image, willing into my bones her grace in the face of death and destruction.

I had mixed feelings about taking the mask-making class. I was afraid I lacked the artistic skills needed to sculpt and paint. Jude assured me that I did not.

Once the cast dried on my face, Jude popped it off. Together, we poured thick plaster into the mold and left it to dry. Once the plaster had set, I cut off the cast. It was a curious sensation to look upon the plaster sculpture of my face. I was sad. I was silent. I was beautiful.

For weeks, I bent over that sculpture and used clay to mold the Egyptian features of Nepthys onto my own face. As I warmed the clay in my fingers and smoothed it onto the sculpture, I sorrowed and often wept.

Jude noted this, but let it be. On one pass by me, she squeezed my shoulder. The air in the warm light of the studio tasted of plaster and paint. Sequins, fabric, ribbons, gems, beads, the craft items the class would use to decorate their masks, spilled into the room in boxes. My curly hair, showing streaks of grey, was tucked behind my ears. I was surprised that despite my inexperience with artmaking, Nepthys was taking form. I could no longer tell where her face began and mine ended. We were inseparable; one. I massaged tiny beads of malleable, soft white clay into the bridge of her eye.

This mask-making is my healing story. Grief is reshaping me in untold ways. Will the day come when I am re-formed in a more powerful way of being where the old and the new are indistinguishable in a new creation? Is this suffering a thing of beauty? Something not to be judged or hurried, but to be accepted, embraced with tenderness, and moved through?

Concurrent with the class, I had been reading again the book, *Women Who Run with the Wolves: Myths and Stories of the Wild Woman Archetype* by Dr. Clarissa Pinkola Estés, [18] a Jungian analyst and storyteller. That book is about many things, but one essential theme is that the wildish nature of the feminine *knows, bone deep, intuitively, how to ride the life-death-life cycle embedded in nature.*

As I formed the features of the Goddess Nepthys on my own face, I was remade. I had experienced life in an exquisite, fragile, and fraught human relationship. I had died with him when our story ended. In the dark cave of my liminal time in the mystic land between life and death, a Goddess molded me as I molded her. Her dark beauty, her love and strength in the face of life's impermanence, was becoming my own. It was time for life to begin again.

CHAPTER 51

KAHUNA

A BOUT A YEAR after his death, Jim visited me in a dream. "I want you to move on and love again," he said.

In the dream, Jim wore jeans and a cream-colored tunic, embroidered in bright yarns—crimson, gold, royal blue—around the neck and long sleeves. He had brought several like it back from the Philippines and had worn them early in our relationship. He looked tanned, healthy, younger, as he was when we met.

What stood out most was that he looked relaxed and happy. He lounged next to a motorcycle. He was so real that I felt alarmed and confused. *Had I been mistaken about his death? Was that a dream? Was he alive and well?* "Go to Hawaii," he said. "That's where your new life begins."

Since Jim's death, premonitions, foretelling dreams, and strong intuitive hunches had picked up speed. The veil that separated the natural and spiritual worlds had thinned; that is how I perceived it, and guidance slipped through to help me with small and large decisions.

I devoured books about spirituality of diverse cultures, especially shamanism, and the wisdom of Indigenous peoples. These cosmologies spoke in a direct way about intuitive phenomenon and spiritual wisdom found via inward contemplation.

Whenever I could, I integrated diverse spiritual understandings into my work with therapy clients. I worked in bible-belt Appalachia, and I understood and respected the Christian framework of many of my client's religious beliefs. I devoured the mystical works of Thomas Merton, Thomas Keating, Richard Rohr, and Pierre Teilhard de Chardin and others so that I could better point to the potency of inner wisdom.

I was more aware of the limitations of cognitive and cognitive-behavioral approaches to helping. To me, they left out the spiritual—a profound and fundamental dimension of human life. It seemed like clients who wanted to go deeper into that realm showed up. Our explorations were creative and exhilarating.

I stumbled across and was captivated by the book, *Medicinemaker: Mystic Encounters on the Shaman's Path*[19] by Dr. Hank Wesselman, an anthropologist who entered spontaneous altered states of consciousness without the aid of drugs or spiritual practices, during which he had conversations with a descendent, 5,000 years ahead in time. Wesselman introduced me to the term "kahuna"—a Hawaiian word for an expert in a skill or knowledge. When Wesselman used the word, he referred to wise healers.

As I read *Medicinemaker,* which integrated spiritual understandings from the Polynesian and Hawaiian Islands, I felt waves of energy in my body and a sense that many of the lessons spoken of in the books were rooted in spiritual truth.

Jim's life insurance settlement for his accidental death provided the funds to follow the dream and take a two-week vacation in Hawaii. I planned the trip, which would include my daughter, Laura, her best friend, Tia, Tia's mother, Joan, as well as my mother, Caroline, and my father Marion. We decided to book most of our stay at a Marriott resort in Ka'anapali on Maui.

However, while planning the trip, my attention was drawn to an ecotourism resort on the island of Molokai, sometimes referred to as Moloka'i Nui A Hina — *of the Goddess, Hina.* Hina is the strong, independent feminine principle in Hawaiian spirituality, a creator Goddess.

If we booked at the Molokai Ranch we would stay in fancy tents, yurts, complete with queen size beds and luxurious bedding, which made the prospect of outdoor toilets less weird and formidable. I was able to convince my parents and daughter that this would not be a rustic camping experience and they agreed to humor me.

A couple of weeks before our trip's departure, I felt drowsy in the warm afternoon sun that streamed into my home office. I loaded a recording of Shamanic drumming into my CD player, settled into my bright rust, green and gold futon and drifted into a half-asleep state. A thought jarred me awake: *"While in Hawaii, you will meet a kahuna."*

My rational mind thought I had to create a plan for meeting a kahuna! How else could that happen? It occurred to me that the only person I was aware of who had met a kahuna was the author, Hank Wesselman. *Why not call him? I thought.* Although internet resources were rudimentary at that time, I searched and found a number for what I assumed would be Wesselman's publishing agent. I dialed the number.

"This is Hank Wesselman," the voice said, warm and lighthearted. A bit sheepish and chagrined at my boldness, I lapsed into shyness and stammered as I explained to the anthropologist author why I had called.

"I'd like to meet a kahuna while I'm in Hawaii," I said, and hesitated. "I know you have connections on the islands. Could you provide an introduction?"

Wesselman's laugh was spontaneous and hearty, but also warm. "Linda, it doesn't work that way," he said. The twist of the corded phone was in my hand. A hawk cawed in the distance. The scent of fresh-mowed green grass baked in a sweltering summer sun, filled the room. "If you are meant to meet a kahuna, you will!" he said. My heart quickened, but I was also disappointed, flattened really. The clothes dryer hummed in the laundry room. "Hold faith and love in your heart and perhaps it will happen," Wessel-mann said. With that advice, he rang off.

I figured my chances of meeting a Hawaiian spiritual teacher were slim to none. I breathed a heartfelt prayer that it might happen. And then let it go.

When the inter-island jet from Oahu braked to a halt on the runway of Molokai airport, kahunas were far from my mind.

CHAPTER 52

UNCLE MIKALA

"THE DRUMS KEPT me awake all night," Ma said. She was peeved; behind her glasses, her eyes looked puffy and tired. We were both out on a trail in the early morning and encountered each other coming from opposite directions. She wore a print knit top over her shorts and khaki walking shoes. The camp was quiet, hushed with sleep. Palm trees rustled in the breezes; the air was perfumed with tropical flowers.

"What drums?" I asked. Dawn washed us with soft brilliance. It had been a restless night, and I'd been awakened multiple times by the hoot of an owl, a Pueo, which traditional Hawaiians believe is an aumakua, or ancestor spirit, who guards and protects families. Salt seasoned the breezes and seagulls circled in the distance. Ma and I fell in beside each other. "You didn't hear them?" she asked. I felt the lead of jet lag in my body but was in wonder at the beauty around me and the fact that I was in Hawaii. "They were so loud, Lin," Ma said.

I had held my breath as my little travel group got its first look at our lodgings, A-framed yurts, "tentalos," whose canvas doors had been gathered back and opened into lovely rooms furnished with luxurious queen beds, plush chairs, and Island-themed art.

Ma raised her eyebrows a bit at the wood-framed outdoor toilets and showers.

I made a mental note to ask the camp staff about the drums. After showers and when our party was dressed, we made our way to the dining pavilion up on a hill where a sumptuous breakfast buffet was laid out. After our meal, Ma and I walked to the concierge's desk so that I could book an ocean kayaking adventure for Laura and Tia.

"Aloha, how can I assist you?" said a young Hawaiian woman with expressive brown eyes and thick brown-black hair that gleamed and fell to her waist. "Please have a seat," she said, and pointed to comfortable chairs in front of her, upholstered with bright yellow and pink flowers, plumeria, on a green leafed background.

The concierge exuded the gentle spirit that make the Hawaiian Islands so special. Her presence and kindness relaxed us into easy conversation as she booked the girls' excursion. Her belted muumuu fell in soft folds around her body. Around her supple neck, she wore a necklace of chocolate brown kukui nuts.

"My mother was kept awake last night by drumming," I said. The soft hubbub of the diners behind me hung in the fragrant Island air, perfumed by profuse white and pink plumeria encircling the pavilion. "Is there a drummer's circle on the island that we might visit?"

The young woman's eyes were puzzled. "I don't know of any," she said. Her head was tilted to the right. Her coral lips were pursed. "What time did you hear them?" she asked. I was tucked into the chair, relaxed and curious.

"All night!" said Ma, and then she added information she'd neglected to share with me. "I even heard them in my deaf ear!"

My mother had been deaf in one ear for more than twenty years. She slept on her hearing ear, so that her nights were quiet.

With her disclosure, the air hummed, as though the engine behind the universe slowed down enough to be in hearing range.

The feeling of a portal opening was as tangible as the prickled canvas fabric of my chair.

"Ma, you didn't mention you heard the drums in your deaf ear!" I said, incredulous, embarrassed. I sat forward and stared at her.

"Did *you* hear the drums?" the concierge asked me. "No, I didn't," I answered. "I heard an owl hooting the entire night, but no drums."

The impact of this information on our young Hawaiian tourism agent was electric. She looked alarmed and said, "Wait a minute!" She pulled out a clumsy registration book bound in a black cover and opened it. "Which tentalos are you in?" Her manicured finger, bright with coral nail polish, traced the page.

Moments later, a soft "ahhhhh" escaped her lips. "Just one moment, please," she said. She reached for a landline phone, made a call, and spoke in her native language.

After the conversation, she squared her shoulders, and said, "Molokai Ranch is a controversial development for Hawaiians. There is long-standing concern that some of the tentalos were built on *heiau,* small temples sacred to the Hawaiian people."

She looked at my mother, and continued, "The tentalo you and your husband are in was constructed on a *heiau.* You are the last guests in that tentalo, as it is soon to be moved."

"Your hearing of the drums was a spirit visitation," she said, her voice hushed. She was not apologetic about this; she was certain. My mother looked at me. Her eyebrows were raised, her lips pursed—the look was one of surprise, not disbelief.

"For your protection, you must visit with Uncle Mikala. Fortunately, he is on site this week and will be able to meet with your family tonight at 8pm." My ears perked up. I knew that kahunas were referred to by the Hawaiian people as "Uncle" or "Aunt."

"What does Uncle Mikala do at the Ranch?" I asked. I was on the edge of my seat.

"He is a kahuna who identifies *heiau* and supervises the movement of the tentalos," she explained. "Spirit visitations to our guests have occurred before. We make sure they understand them before they return home."

Thanks to my mother, I thought, *I am going to meet a kahuna.* I was incredulous.

At the appointed time, our travel party climbed the hill to the community pavilion for our visit with Uncle Mikala. Tiki torches cast soft, flickering halos of light on a small circle of chairs and hammocks that had been drawn together in the corner of the dark pavilion. The sound of ocean surf could be heard from the Camp's beach and gentle breezes whispered through the open-air structure.

Uncle Mikala appeared and welcomed us with reserved warmth. Bronzed skin layered his distinct Polynesian features and sculpted a face that was strong, placid, and powerful in a masculine way. That night, his long, glossy, almost black hair flowed free over his arms and shoulders. His movements were sensual, liquid.

Island trade winds fluttered the short sleeves of his Hawaiian shirt, printed in bright white flowers and deep green tropical leaves. There was a kindness about him, but also a no-nonsense charisma.

We selected our seats. Laura, Tia, Joan, and Dad fell asleep. I was curious about that. Ma and I remained alert and listened.

"It's not common for me to disclose to non-Hawaiians some of what I am going to tell you," Uncle Mikala said, "but I have been guided by my ancestors to share it. I don't know why."

"You," Uncle Mikala pointed to me, "heard our sacred Pueo. And you," he pointed to Ma, "heard drums. The veil between this world and the world of spirit thinned for both of you last night. Some might go crazy with fear about that kind of experience. It should not disturb you. That you saw the world beyond was *mana,* a gift."

From that point, Uncle Mikala shared knowledge about Hawaiian spirituality. I don't remember many specifics and did not understand much of what he said. His awe at the mystery of life and of what is at the source of life, which he described as a spiritual energy, was tangible. He spoke of life as a mystical dream and communicated total trust in this mystery, even when it is beyond analytical comprehension. I was mesmerized by his certainty.

I looked around at my sleeping companions. I looked at my Ma, who was listening to the Kahuna with rapt curiosity. The moment was special, mystical. I felt the beauty of Hawaii deep in my bones. I understood a little the gentle power of "aloha"—a way of being in the world full of kindness, grace, love, peace, and compassion—a way of living in harmony with all that is.

I thought, *if the power behind life is full of aloha and can open a path toward a kahuna, it could give me EVERYTHING I needed to feel safe.* As I sat across from Uncle Mikala, washed by ocean breezes, I felt the knot release in my stomach that had tied the moment I heard of my husband's death. The guardedness in my chest and shoulders softened. I felt the fear that life could slam me again, pop like a bubble and leave me.

I wanted to know more about this power the kahuna spoke of, how it worked and how it was connected to God.

CHAPTER 53

A TEACHER OF THOUGHT

T HE NEXT MORNING, gentle sea breezes fanned the tables under the thatched roof of the pavilion where our travel party ate breakfast. Uncle Mikala sat alone at a table across the large space. He caught my eye, crooked his finger, and beckoned for me to join him.

I approached. "Please sit," he said. His cupped hand welcomed me to the bench across from him. "I want to share something important with you." I climbed over the seat.

Uncle Mikala's glossy black hair was pulled into a ponytail, secured by a green rubber band. He wore a plain yellow t-shirt that morning. My denim jean shorts were topped with a flowered coral and olive-green blouse that cinched under the bodice and tied in the back. I wore the white plumeria lei a Hawaiian woman had placed around my shoulders at the airport. I had carried my coffee mug over; he held his, embossed with the name of Molokai Ranch. He sat hunched over the table and stared at me.

Uncle Mikala reached over the picnic table and thumped a spot on my forehead between my eyes. "The light that pours from your third eye is bright and strong," he said. "Others on the Island have noticed it."

I knew he referred to the energy center in the human body, just above and right between our physical eyes—which some spiritual traditions respect as the portal of intuition, wisdom, and psychic ability.

My inner experience of Uncle Mikala's words was bifurcated. On the one hand, my intellect thought *what the hell is he talking about and which people?* On the other, my heart, a quiet, certain observer without pride, nodded to his words; *yes, I know this.* I had a sense that the moment heralded something new, but I didn't know what.

Radiant sunlight danced around the thatched-roof building. Island breezes whipped the aroma of sausages, bacon, and seasoned potatoes from the breakfast buffet where mouth-watering bright yellow pineapples and orange papaya tumbled over the edges of white crockery. Toothpicks in a small crystal container had been placed next to the salt and pepper shakers. A clear plastic straw had fallen to the floor.

We both wore sandals. It was hot. Sweat beaded Uncle Mikala's brow.

I was relieved when he broke the silence. "You do not claim your full potential to help others heal. You hold it close," he said, and put his hand over his heart. His dark eyes were wells of the unknown, deep, penetrating. "You are asleep to your Self."

Again, there was a strange experience of my mind wanting to defend itself; *who the hell do you think you are?* and my heart simply nodding, *yes, you are right.*

"You are here in this life to bring ancient wisdom forward," he said. My head thought, *I'm lucky to have enough wisdom to make it through life day to day. What does he mean by ancient wisdom?* My heart thought, *"Yes, I know this."* My head was baffled by my heart's acknowledgment. To my intellectual mind, the heart's certainty and clarity seemed arrogant and unfounded. Uncle Mikala watched in silence as this inner war unfolded. He glanced away, as though listening to or for something. His gaze swiveled back and locked my eyes.

"Listen Up!" he said. He barked, as though to cut through my inner chatter. His tone was emphatic. "My ancestors have asked me to tell you that you will soon meet a powerful teacher of THOUGHT." Uncle Mikala emphasized the word, THOUGHT, and then paused. I had the sense he pointed to something beyond and before the thoughts that were like a ticker tape in my mind. His certainty had brought me into the present with him. "The depth of this teacher's wisdom has rarely walked the earth. Pay attention to him. He KNOWS."

I was puzzled. What was a *teacher of THOUGHT*? *What does he KNOW?* Those were odd turns of phrase. I wanted to ask questions, but Uncle Mikala silenced me with the wave of his hand. "Pay attention," he said again, with authority.

Uncle Mikala nodded, lifted his long legs over the picnic table bench, and strode off toward the ocean. I watched his back retreat toward the sea until he disappeared from my view. I felt an intense curiosity about the "teacher of THOUGHT." The reverence with which Uncle Mikala had spoken of "THOUGHT" puzzled me — I resolved to do everything I could to figure out what it was.

In the distance, I heard a Pueo. A small feather rested near my sandaled feet.

CHAPTER 54

PREDICTIONS

IT WAS A year after I had met the kahuna on Molokai. I was absorbed with my busy psychology practice and keeping up with my daughter's sports schedule—she played both basketball and volleyball. I hadn't made any progress in understanding what a "teacher of THOUGHT" was, even though I had scoured books on Hawaiian spirituality. This reading had accelerated my interest in the relationship between spirituality and health, which had unfolded the curved path that brought me to Ellen, the palm reader who sat across from me.

If palm readers wore purple robes and ruby-crowned turbans, the lady in the booth with me at the restaurant did not fit the mold. Ellen Bone looked ordinary.

A petite, compact woman, Ellen wore a pink blouse, pressed black slacks, and ballet flats. Her short blonde hair was styled around a pretty face. Ellen's brilliant turquoise eyes sparkled as she watched me.

The restaurant, a Bob Evans in Marietta, bustled with servers and hummed with robust lunch traffic.

"May I look at your left palm?" Ellen asked. She cupped my hand in hers and studied the lines. A Wildfire Chicken Salad sat in front of me; my right hand rested next to a white tureen holding the piquant barbecue dressing. Ellen had ordered the same salad. Mugs of tea sat on the table. Two slices of banana bread rested on a white plate; their aroma was mouth-watering. Buoyant chatter among the lunch crowd in the restaurant subsided into the background. My thoughts slowed down, and I felt an inner stillness.

Ellen recounted events that were close to my heart, one of them known only to me. Her psychic insights touched the realms of childhood, family, health, and wealth; their accuracy sealed her credibility. "This is uncanny," I said. "How long have you known of your gifts?"

Ellen explained that she was from a devout Catholic family and that all but one of her ten brothers and sisters had psychic gifts. She loved helping people and preferred a quiet lifestyle, close to nature. Her clients were CEOs seeking profitability, police departments seeking help with solving crimes, and people like me, seeking clues about next steps.

Ellen first introduced herself to me in 2002 after a meeting of the Healing Arts Practitioner's Circle, an organization I'd co-founded with a group of holistic healers in Parkersburg, West Virginia. Our mission was to introduce practitioners of traditional medicine to the power of alternative or complementary healing practices. Polarity Therapy, bodywork, had released my energy, resolved my ambivalence, and helped me decide to return to Jim and Laura—perhaps it could help my clients make choices in line with their wisdom.

The Healing Arts Practitioner's Circle was a diverse group of healers from: massage, Healing Touch, Reiki, Polarity Therapy, Neurolinguistic Programming [NLP], Emotional Freedom Technique [EFT], Eye Movement Desensitization and Reprocessing [EMDR], hypnotherapy and psychotherapy. Some modalities had become mainstream, some more controversial.

Palmistry, I thought, was too far out. Ellen's presence in the group might cause my colleagues to think I had gone off the deep end and dry up referrals to my practice.

When Ellen had approached me to introduce herself, she said, "Linda, I'd love to be a part of what you're doing here." Her voice radiated goodwill. "But some people will not respect my gifts and my presence will hurt your efforts. I'll stay away."

I was relieved, but also touched by her selflessness. There was no resentment in her voice. Ellen smiled and said, "I'd like to show you how I work. Would you have lunch with me?" I was curious about her story. "Yes," I had said, without a second thought.

As I sipped my tea and absorbed all that Ellen had shared, a thought crossed my mind: *I wonder if I should ask her if there will be another man in my life?*

"So, you want to know about relationships?" Ellen said, her face crinkled in amusement. *She must have read my mind!* I thought. A frisson, a sudden thrill like an electric current, surged through my body. Something extraordinary was in the offing.

Two years had stretched past since Jim died. I missed male companionship. It would be sweet to enjoy dinner or a movie with a friend. My libido had awakened, too. But, at age forty-eight, the chance of romance seemed slim.

"May I peek at your other hand, the right one?" Ellen asked. She studied it and pursed her lips. "Psychic impressions came last night as I thought about our meeting," she said. Emptied half and half cups were piled up on the table. "It's just as I thought," she said. Snow whitened winter light oozed through nearby window-panes. An empty Bob Evans matchbook lay tented under the table next to us.

"Two men, both doctors, will soon appear. Both will work out-side the mainstream of medicine. You will find both attractive," she said. There was no mistaking her conviction. I felt a mix of emotions: excitement that she was right and doubt. Ellen's humil-ity, coupled with her certainty, swung my inner pendulum in the direction of believing her. The aroma of the half-eaten banana bread on my plate grounded me.

"Two doctors; you mean physicians?" I said, no, blurted.

Ellen laughed. "Yes, physicians! I double-checked that with

my guides. You'll meet them within six months," she said, as she released my hand and reached for her tea. A mischievous grin played her mouth. She let me stew in the juice of wonder.

A wide smile creased her face and her eyes danced. "The man who's right for you will be the one you can't wait to get into bed," she said.

I choked on the tea I'd just sipped. We doubled over our salads and chortled.

I was reluctant when our lunch ended. I enjoyed being with Ellen. My heart told me she was a gifted psychic and a good person. I left our meeting with a lighter heart. Faith in possibility had tapped my shoulder. Life was about to shift.

Ellen Bone's gifts as a psychic medium, clairaudient, clairvoyant, palmist came enfolded in light-hearted love and powerful knowing. Meeting her was an exclamation point to my experience that love provided the right people at the right time to move us along. Spiritual truth, the invisible power and flow behind life, could come in many guises. There were many paths up the mountain of enlightenment, and I would disregard none.

"Would a God of love put us in the world without a map?" Ellen said, as she explained her psychic practice of palmistry. "Maybe our maps are in the palms of our hands."

Within six months, I encountered two brilliant physicians, one an internist in integrative medicine and the other, a psychiatrist who shared a radical new paradigm in mental health. Ellen was spot on.

CHAPTER 55

VALENTINE SHAKEUP
1

O N THE MORNING of Valentine's Day 2003, there were no
roses, no sexy or romantic cards. Jim's death was three years
in the rear-view mirror. I had compelling questions about what
would come next for me.

"Mom, this storm that's coming is a monster!" my now eighteen-year-old daughter said. She held a can of Diet Coke in her
hand as she stood at the refrigerator in the spacious taupe and
white kitchen. How I'd birthed a child who didn't like coffee was
beyond me. She was barefoot and wore shorts and an oversized
Calhoun County High School sleep shirt.

"Are you sure you want to drive to Morgantown?" she asked.
Long brown sleep-tousled hair cascaded around her shoulders;
her eyes were muddy with doubt. I held an oversized Navajo-
decorated turquoise and rust-colored coffee mug Jim and I had
bought on our honeymoon trip through Arizona. "I wish I didn't
have to," I said, "but I don't want to cancel my presentations."

I was scheduled to give two talks that day up in Morgantown
at West Virginia University, a 240-mile round trip. One presentation, a Grand Rounds *The Power of Unconditional Love in Heal-*

ing" had been booked by Dr. Greg Juckett, the head of the medical school's Department of Integrative Medicine. The other, a smaller academic colloquium *"Intuition, Dreams and Synchronicity in Psychotherapy—Toward a Transpersonal [Spiritual] Psychology,"* was scheduled for the Department of Counseling Psychology by my mentor and dissertation chair, Dr. Sherry Cormier. As I thought about the drive ahead of me, I was a ball of nerves. Since Jim's accident, my fear of driving on bad roads was a five-alarm fire.

The Weather Channel droned in the background from the TV in the great room. The projected snow and ice totals for the coming nor'easter grew by the hour. Framed by the wide floor-to-ceiling windows in the breakfast nook, the sky was opaque, shades of darkened gray.

"Well, be careful," Laura said. She sized up my black pants-suit, rust, brown and gold striped knit sweater and gold jewelry and black ankle boots. I read approval in her eyes. "I think I'll head down to Tia's. Her house has a generator," she said. It calmed me that Laura would be with the Satterfield family; she was like a second daughter to them. If the storm made it impossible for me to get home, she would be in loving company.

Laura hadn't seen her best friend, Tia, in over a week. Just yesterday, we'd returned from Michigan, where we'd attended Jim's mom's funeral. We'd left the funeral luncheon early to make sure we covered the 400 miles home to West Virginia ahead of the storm. I had phoned Drs. Juckett and Cormier to ask if they wanted to cancel both events as a precaution. Neither did; both expected a strong attendance. It's just a thing in the professional speaking world that speakers booked for an event move heaven and earth to show up.

On the 125-mile trip up to West Virginia University in Morgantown, I considered my future. Managing a house alone in rural West Virginia was tough. I thought about moving back to Michigan nearer to my parents and siblings. I could buy a small cottage on a lake. I could find a male dinner companion, or a lover. I doubted I could commit to marriage—too risky; I didn't want to suffer a shattered heart ever again.

My daughter, brilliant and beautiful, would soon start college and was considering options around the country. She was ripe for independence, and an empty nest loomed. I could not imagine daily life without her.

As I drove, I also thought about my career, which had shifted in new directions. About a year before, I had chanced upon a book, *The 12 Secrets of Highly Creative Women: A Portable Mentor*,[20] by Gail McMeekin, a creativity coach. The book was a qualitative analysis of wide-ranging interviews with creative women across a spectrum of pursuits. To my astonishment, I identified with them and could relate to the twelve secrets! Up to that point, I hadn't thought of myself as creative.

Coaching was brand new, and I didn't know much about it. The internet was expanding, though, and it had been easy to find Gail's website, where she described her services. I called and asked her to take me on as a client. We talked about my situation. "It's serendipitous that you called today," she said, her voice on the phone light and warm. "This morning, a long-standing client let me know she was ready to complete our work. I'm booked solid, but I have an unexpected opening."

I continued my drive and thought about Priscilla Leavitt, owner of the practice where I worked in Parkersburg, who had opened a beautiful retreat center just down the street from our offices. I had begun running workshops there based on Gail's book and referred my interested clients into them. Much to my amazement, when clients shifted their focus away from problems toward creative self-expression, their mental well-being skyrocketed! I wasn't sure what to make of that, but I was intrigued.

Guided by Gail's expert mentorship, I led creativity circles for women that morphed into a community in the mid-Ohio Valley area called "Diana's Circle", after the Greek Goddess. I found new joy and satisfaction in my work. I considered closing my psychotherapy practice so that I could shift to a solopreneur business as a life coach.

My musings ended and I breathed a sigh of relief as I pulled my beige 4-wheel-drive Toyota 4Runner up to the parking guard of the sprawling medical center complex. The storm was slow moving—I might be able to make it home without incident.

I finished my talk on unconditional love on that Valentine's Day—to about two hundred physicians, professors, essential workers and students of medicine, nursing, and pharmacy—with a guided imagery exercise. I wanted to show my listeners the power of thought to induce relaxation, not just tell them about it. A small rush of people approached the podium to share insights and questions.

One of them wore a knee-length starched white lab coat that identified him as a physician. As he stepped toward me, I stepped back. His energy was confident and potent—I was sure he was going to give me grief. Guided imagery was not a practice allopathic medical professionals took a shine to. Most thought of it as an unscientific New Age practice, despite considerable supportive research in the burgeoning field of psychoneuroimmunology, which studies the interaction between the human nervous and immune systems.

"I can tell that you love people and your work," he said. I liked his voice right away. It was husky, honeyed, and sexy! The dark blue letters embroidered on his coat identified him as Dr. William F. Pettit, Jr., the Medical Director of the Sydney Banks Institute for Innate Health, whatever that was. "I enjoyed your talk," he said. "We have a lot in common." His hands were solid and warm; his handshake was firm. I felt a sweep of compassionate energy as I looked into his translucent green eyes. I relaxed.

"You *know* that people do not care what you know until they know that you care. I'm touched," he said. The large amphitheater bustled as people exited my talk. Muted recessed lighting played on Dr. Pettit's thick brown hair. Through the glass wall of the conference center, I saw the skies had darkened and the wind had picked up. Dr. Pettit had not let go of my hand. I resisted the urge to pull away.

"I'd love to have dinner with you," he said. Behind his wire-rimmed glasses, his eyes twinkled, sincere and direct. "You mentioned living 125-miles south of here, but I'd be willing split the distance with you."

I was glad that my nails were manicured, and that I'd lost a chunk of the weight I'd gained after Jim's death.

"I'd enjoy dinner," I said. Other attendees who'd approached the podium to speak with me waited in line. "The half-way mark would be either Clarksburg or Bridgeport, an easy hour's commute from my office in Parkersburg."

He hesitated. "You mentioned that you were widowed a couple of years ago," he said. I wondered if he was asking me out on a date. Excitement tickled my gut, with an edge of apprehension. If it were a date, it would be my first since Jim died. I was glad that I'd remembered to turn off the microphone fastened to my lapel. "I was widowed too, in 2000," he said. "My wife, Sue, died of cancer."

He reached into a pocket and extracted his business card from a well-worn, creased leather folder. He held up a thin, light blue book he carried, entitled *Coming Home,* by Sue Pettit.[21] "This is a book of poetry she wrote," he said. "It's a gift." He stuck his business card into the middle of the book.

I glanced at a clock on the wall behind Dr. Pettit. My second presentation was in a different campus building in less than an hour. I needed to move on.

"I picked up your business card from the table in the back," he said. I felt self-conscious and tongue-tied. A Sharpie permanent marker, red, rested on the wood chair next to me. "I'll be in touch. I have patients to see." He hustled out of the room.

Later, Dr. Pettit admitted that he had almost missed my talk. He'd been headed to lunch when he saw the poster promoting it with my picture on it.

"I weighed back and forth, lunch, unconditional love, lunch, unconditional love," he said, with a hearty laugh, and moved his hands up and down, like a scale.

He was hungry; it was a close call. "Love won, fifty-one to forty-nine!" he said.

CHAPTER 56

VALENTINE SHAKEUP
2

L IGHT, WET SNOW spit at my car wipers' futile attempt to
clear the windshield as I left the Medical Center and drove
the short distance to Allen Hall for my next talk on spiritual psychology. This topic was close to my heart, an opportunity to share
the fascinating intuitive journey I'd been on all my life, rich with
prophetic dreams and synchronicities, which had quickened since
Jim's death.

Colloquia events were most often small, I anticipated ten to
twelve in the audience.

"Linda I'm glad you're here," Sherry Cormier, my mentor said,
and hugged me. I was thrilled to see her; now that I had graduated
and was immersed in my career, I missed her warm friendship,
wisdom, and our shared love of Jungian psychology. Sherry wore a
sweater over a royal blue top that complemented her white-blond
hair.

Under a bank of fluorescent lights, the room buzzed with
energy. Close to sixty people filled the rows of wooden desks and
their conversations were animated. Some drank coffee and tea
from the vending machine outside the door. The room was chilly.

Many attendees kept their jackets on. "I'm so pleased with the turnout," Sherry said, and turned to survey the room.

The topic had garnered strong interest! Some of the faculty who'd taught me, including my former program advisor, were in the audience as were students who had graduated from the program in the same time-period I had.

Near the end of the talk, I had a mysterious experience. Something spoke through me. "Mark my words," I said, a ring, a strength, bursting into my voice. "Most current psychotherapies will pass away and be replaced by a new understanding."

The words charged into the air. I did not know what they meant. I was rooted, fixed to the floor in front of the large chalkboards on the wall behind me. A lanyard with a name tag lay on the empty desk in front of me. My throat was dry, my lips parched. "Many of our psychotherapies are iatrogenic," I said, and stopped, aghast.

Iatrogenic describes *illness* caused by a *treatment!* I thought.

I swear to God that up to that moment, I had never thought of *any* psychotherapy as harmful. But I had just said they could be. I was shaken by my words. Confused and shocked reactions dawned on the faces of my audience. The room was still, and then abuzz with reaction.

"How dare you say such a thing?" said my former advisor, who leapt from his seat and approached me as I concluded my talk. "Show me research to support your statement," he said.

If I could have dropped through a hole in the floor, I would have. What had motivated me to say such a thing? I didn't believe it, or did I?

My personal experience of and results with clients suggested that therapy was helpful, even transformative for some clients. I was, and remain, convinced of the healing power of deep listening and presence. But some techniques, especially those that focused heavily on the past, didn't seem to lead to deep and lasting change. I searched for ways of helping that were hopeful, positive, recognized resilience, and included spiritual understandings.

As the room emptied, I moved toward Dr. Cormier. "Your sharing was wonderful, and I was very moved by it, but that last statement didn't go over too well with some," she said. She had already put on her coat and slung her purse over her shoulder. "We should talk sometime about what you meant, but it's probably a good idea for both of us to get on our way before the storm moves in," she said, with a glance out the window. We hugged.

I hurried to my car. I had a four-wheel-drive vehicle, but weather reports now forecast over twenty inches of snow in Morgantown and up to an inch of ice to the south, where I lived. Not just because of the weather, my stomach churned. My thoughts raced and my anxiety built; I was afraid I might have a panic attack.

I didn't think of anything besides my strange comment about iatrogenic treatments on my two-hour return to Millstone. As I pulled to the one stoplight in Grantsville, the county seat just fifteen minutes from my home, sleet sluiced down the windshield. In minutes, the wipers couldn't clear it. My Toyota 4Runner's tires struggled for traction on the ride up the hill where I lived; the dirt and stone surface was glazed with ice. I put my head on the steering wheel in gratitude when I pulled into the garage.

My first stop in the house was to turn on the TV to listen to weather reports. The second was at the desk phone in the breakfast nook to call my daughter. "Honey, I'm home," I said. From the cozy warmth of the house, I could see that ice sheathed the trees. It wouldn't be long before the road up the hill was impassable. "I'm glad Mom," she said. "You might want to think about heading up to Denise's and Larry's house, so you won't be alone. You could be without power for a while." I assured her I would be o.k.

I ran water into the bathtub for toilet flushes and took care of pre-storm preparations. I gathered candles, flashlights, batteries, and the propane camp stove. I filled up water bottles and dragged-out blankets. As ice poured from the sky in buckets, I stocked plenty of wood next to the stove and re-supplied the wood bin on the deck from the wood pile.

The sleet crusted my winter jacket; I pulled off fur-lined boots as the electric power extinguished. The house was a soundless vacuum except for the ice that drummed on the roof and licked at the windows.

I was alone in the house, and without power, for the next week. The storm dropped inches of ice, decimated the electrical grid in the county, and split hundreds of trees like matchsticks over the roads. Morgantown, where Dr. Pettit lived, was paralyzed by a thirty-two-inch snowfall.

I pulled my chestnut-colored fabric recliner up to the crackling fire I'd built, my bed for the next week. I changed into warm pajamas and a thick robe, put a battery-powered miner's light around my forehead so I could read, and settled into a quilt. Limbs split from the tree, weighted by icy sleeves. Branches thudded on the roof through the night, and I prayed. The house was well-built. After each big crash, I toured to check, but none of the fallen branches had breached the ceiling.

Coming Home, the book Dr. Pettit had given me earlier by his late wife, Sue Pettit, [22] was next to me on an oak parquet table. I opened it to where he had put his business card. I looked at page 67, and saw, "WE STOPPED BY THE TURTLES." On the opposite page, the first lines of the poem read, *"The turtles were great big, and clumpy, and slow. They bobble their heads back and forth as they go."* It is a poem about the protection afforded by living in a beautiful feeling, a feeling of love.

I stared at the letters on the page; they swam. I was riveted by the synchronicity that I had opened the book to a poem that focused on *turtles*. I thought about my Jim's love of them. A ceramic turtle painted bright blue, yellow, red, and purple, in the colors and style of Guatemala's folk art, rested in front of me on the hearth. It was a gift my friend and mentor, Peggy, had given me at Jim's memorial service. Inside it was the five-strand puzzle ring from Jim that I'd worn until a year after his death.

Cuddled into the recliner in a peach and brown quilt that my mother had made me as a wedding gift, I started to cry. I was sure the turtle synchronicity was an auspicious intuitive signal.

The eyes of love had flown open again. *I don't know whether it will be professional or personal,* I thought, *but I know that I'm meant to have a relationship with Bill Pettit.*

CHAPTER 57

COFFEE WITH SALAD DRESSING

B ECAUSE THE HISTORIC storm took down phone and internet service, it was two weeks before I connected with Dr. Pettit.

He called and invited me to attend a seminar he was teaching with his colleague, Judy Sedgeman, the educational director of the Sydney Banks Institute for Innate Health. Dr. Pettit told me the workshop would explain the Institute's work.

I accepted his invitation on the spot. I was curious about his work, but far more intrigued about my intuitive sense that I was meant to have a relationship with him. I now had a deep trust in my intuitive hunches. The seminar was to be held at the Hotel Clarion, an historic hotel in downtown Morgantown. Despite the strain on my budget, I treated myself and made a reservation for the night between the two days of the event.

The drive to Morgantown took two hours, so I got up extra early to make a 9am start time.

I changed outfits twice but settled on a sedate navy-blue pant suit over a navy and white striped sweater. To be honest, I couldn't remember clearly what Dr. Pettit looked like—we'd only met for about ten minutes. But we'd exchanged emails and he seemed, well, interested and a bit flirtatious. I had tummy butterflies. It had been just over three years since Jim's death, and the prospect of dating was exciting and nerve-wracking. I was forty-nine, but I felt like an awkward adolescent.

I parked my car, entered the crystal-crusted hotel, and found my way to a windowless seminar room. "Linda, I'm so glad you're here," Dr. Pettit said; he smiled wide when he saw me.

About twenty people sat around long tables arranged in a U-shape. Dr. Pettit wore a coffee-colored suit over a light peach shirt, and a colorful abstract Jerry Garcia tie. I went weak-kneed and blushed to the roots of my red hair. I was mortified that he would notice. He was a psychiatrist, bound to be observant.

I said something lame like, "thank you for inviting me" to cover the fact that I was having the same rush of knowing I'd had the first time I met Jim. The draw to Dr. Pettit was tangible. My world was in slow motion.

Next to him, underneath muted lights, stood a classy, attractive woman with short greying dark brown hair cut in a stylish bob. "This is my colleague, Judy," Dr. Pettit said. Judy wore a black and white houndstooth-checked jacket over black slacks. Her elegant gold necklace was perfect for her outfit, a piece of jewelry I admired but wouldn't have been bold enough to wear. I felt intimidated; Judy exuded a poise I did not feel.

I took a seat and watched Dr. Pettit roll up his sleeves and expose strong, thick wrists, the left encircled by a gold watch with a worn brown leather band. The rapport between Dr. Pettit and Judy was evident; they often touched each other on the arm or shoulder. *Were they a couple?* I wondered. I struggled to keep my attention off my sensual interest in Dr. Pettit and on the content he and his colleague presented.

They taught an understanding that at the time was known as Innate Health, Psychology of Mind, or Health Realization. In time, it would come to be known as the 3 Principles. They described the 3 Principles—Mind, Thought and Consciousness—as universal, meaning that they applied to all human beings, in fact, to all of nature.

Dr. Pettit explained Mind as another name for God, Love, or Wisdom. He defined Mind as a *formless* intelligent spiritual [invisible] energy from which all of life is created. *This energy, therefore, is encapsulated within everything it forms.*

As a "form" we humans share this unbreakable, shared core, which is why the understanding he taught was named "innate health." I considered at a deeper level that God might be a *formless* energy of pure love, moving seamlessly from form to formless and back again. This resonated with me.

Dr. Pettit described Thought as the link between the spiritual and psychological. Thought is both a universal and impersonal Principle that creates us and all the natural world. It was also described as a *power* each of us is given, via the gift of life, to create our psychological experience, our reality. I had never heard Thought described as a spiritual power. I couldn't make sense of it.

Dr. Pettit described Consciousness as the gift of awareness that enables us to perceive both the intelligent energy of Mind and the creative energy of Thought. The more we realize that we are manifestations of this intelligent, conscious, and creative energy, the more we harmonize with *it* rather than with our *identities,* which we make up with gift of thought.

Dr. Pettit suggested that *clearer awareness of our source, our nature,* resulted effortlessly in greater mental well-being and often, enhanced physical health.

These notions were too much for me to get my arms around! Dr. Pettit and Judy repeated phrases like, *"we are creating our experience moment to moment"* and *"life is created from the inside out."* I was confused the entire morning. I tried to figure out how what they were sharing fit in with the psychological theories I'd spent much of my adult life learning about and teaching.

At lunch, I found my place tag at a chair between Judy and Dr. Pettit. "Linda, what do you think about Innate Health?" Judy asked. Smart and articulate, it was obvious that Judy was confident about what she taught. She held a buttered roll in one hand, a fork in the other, and was prepared to dig into the first course, a crisp salad.

"I'm not impressed so far, Judy," I said. "It sounds like a sophisticated cognitive psychology to me."

Judy and Dr. Pettit had shared that the 3 Principles understanding emerged from an enlightenment experience by their mentor, a Scottish fellow, Sydney Banks.

At age forty-three and while living and working as a master welder at a pulp mill on Vancouver Island, Sydney, or Syd, as Dr. Pettit and Judy called him, and his first wife, Barb, had attended a marriage enrichment seminar. They loved each other and wanted to stop bickering.

Syd and Barb had befriended another couple at the program; all four weren't buying the seminar's focus on "fighting fair." They wanted to stop fighting! Syd shared with Barb and their new friends that he had realized how insecure he was. The male partner of the other couple, a young psychologist, said to Syd, "You're not insecure. You just think you are."

That comment initiated Syd's enlightenment experience! In a moment of insight, Syd said he saw that "there is no such thing as insecurity, *it's only thought.* It hit me like a ton of bricks." [23] Syd described how his angst over a difficult childhood and his "poor Syd" story vanished, forever. He said that from that moment, he only "felt love for those who had been hurtful to me."

For the next three days, Syd had spontaneous spiritual insights. On the third day, while sitting in his living room with his wife and mother-in-law, he felt himself sucked down a tunnel, heard a buzzing sound and was enveloped in a white light. Of this experience, Syd said, "I saw what people call God is. I saw what life is, and I saw how the two were connected."

Syd's story intrigued me. I had studied enough theology to know that enlightenment experiences were sought after. For goodness' sake, enlightenment was acknowledged in the Bible!

Some, like the one Syd described, were instantaneous and deep; others were incremental and evolved over time.

Dr. Pettit and Judy described themselves as mentees of Sydney Banks. That was unique—two health care professionals, one a physician and one a public health educator, who called a master welder their teacher! It occurred to me, though, that my primary spiritual teacher to that point, Jesus, was a carpenter.

It was obvious to me that both Judy and Dr. Pettit were intelligent, thoughtful people and were convinced that Syd's insights had changed their professional and personal lives in radical ways, for the better.

"This isn't the first psychological theory to say that our thoughts and beliefs are more important than our circumstances or experience," I said to Judy over lunch. "All cognitive and cognitive-behavioral theories point in that direction."

I was irritated at something I perceived in her and Dr. Pettit, a smugness that they had an answer that other helpers did not have. They were so certain and grounded in what they taught; I interpreted that as arrogance. Judy was calm and thoughtful; she listened without interrupting. "This isn't a theory, Linda," she said, with quiet authority. "It explains *how* we create theories. To develop a theory, we must have a mind, we must think, and we must be conscious of what we're creating."

Dr. Pettit chimed in. "Syd said these universal Principles were irreducible truths, what he called 'FACTS' or natural powers. They explain the system behind our experiences. Because we are Mind in action, no matter what we have experienced, are experiencing, or will experience, we can keep creating, keep finding new thoughts and enjoy mental health and well-being," he said. "We are not limited by our pasts."

I was doubtful. What he had said flew in the face of my training, and a body of research, suggesting that the traumatic effects of past experiences were tough to reverse.

Dr. Pettit took a sip of water. His conviction about the truth of what he was saying was clear. "Most of us just don't realize we are using the gift of Thought to think ourselves away *from who we truly are, pure love and understanding,"* he said. Around our table, everyone listened in. It seemed that all but me were enthralled.

"Please pass the bread, Judy," Dr. Pettit said and continued, in a fluid way, to describe what was second nature to him.

"In other words, outside events do not create our experience of anything. We create experience with the 3 Principles from the inside-out. That's why two people can experience the exact same events and have a different reaction to it. We call that 'separate realities.' If we don't understand how the Principles work, we create needless suffering—and can manufacture chronic mental distress, or mental illness. It's innocent but unfortunate. We don't have to suffer as much as we do." I was about to burst at the seams with arguments, and I interrupted him.

"Dr. Pettit, I'm just not seeing how the 3 Principles are any different from the cognitive therapy I've been teaching for twenty years," I said.

"Linda, call me Bill," he said. His eyes twinkled. "Cognitive therapy tries to change thinking after the fact, after it's already out on the airwaves. It tries to manage or control our reaction to our thoughts. The 3 Principles point to a deeper truth. They show us that we create the airwaves so that we're less likely to have reactions in the first place. It takes the effort out of the system."

"Keep listening," said John, a young adult male, who piped up from across the round dining table; his fork in the air had speared a leaf of lettuce. His solid square face, topped with short blond hair, rested on a thick neck and a linebacker's build. He wasn't smiling.

John had introduced himself that morning as Bill's former client. His story staggered me. Diagnosed with bipolar disorder and severe ADHD, he'd been committed to a state psychiatric hospital after, in a fit of anger, he threw his mother at a plate-glass window. While in the hospital, as a side effect of psychiatric medications, he had ballooned to over 250-pounds.

Six months later, after working with Bill and exploring the

3 Principles, John had slimmed to 195-pounds, played semi-pro football, and enjoyed college courses while working full-time. The young man expressed anger that the treatments he'd sought before learning of the 3 Principles had worsened his symptoms.

"This understanding helped me see that I didn't have to believe or act on every thought I had," he said. "It's different from cognitive behavioral therapy. It focuses on showing us how the gift of thought works, not on what we do with it. I wish therapists like you would pay attention to this." Defensiveness curled in my chest. *Who is he to criticize a profession I've spent half my lifetime trying to master?* A flush burned my cheeks and crept toward my temples. *I forgot and did not consider* that just weeks before, some voice had come through me to describe some psychotherapies as innocently iatrogenic, or harmful!

"It's important to remember," said Bill, between munches of bread, his voice soothing and conciliatory, "that helping professionals are doing the best they know how. We can't do better until we see better."

My head and heart were in an uproar—mentally, I argued with much of what they shared.

I was also enthralled by Bill's extraordinary kindness and compassion. I had never heard a psychiatrist talk about patients with such tenderness. He teared up often as he described men and women, children, and adults he'd worked with who had recovered after long, complicated bouts of severe mental illness. It was obvious that he was sensitive and cared deeply about his patients—for me, that was compelling, admirable, inspiring, and sexy.

Bill's presence and deep feelings made it hard for me to dismiss out of hand this notion he called "innate health." I assumed we would have time together after the seminar to get to know each other and talk about it more; I couldn't wait.

"I have a suggestion, Linda," said Bill. Judy, on the other side of me, shifted to watch him. "You are listening with your analytical brain, which reconciles what it hears with information already stored," he said. His tawny eyes were direct, and he spoke with certainty. I felt defensive again. "Listen softly, like you would to music," he said. "Your mind will hear the wisdom we are pointing to."

My heart hammered too loud to get that, and lust made me squirm in my seat. I reached for the Ranch dressing, instead of cream, to lighten my coffee. Bill touched my hand. "I don't think that'll taste good," he said, and laughed as he handed me a pitcher of cream. His touch sent a charge of desire through my body.

After lunch was served, we got up to mill around and stretch our legs while we waited for dessert and coffee. Bill's eighteen-year-old daughter, Maggie, had flown in from South Dakota to attend the seminar. She sidled up to me as I stood at a window overlooking Morgantown. She was petite and an extraordinary beauty, with dark eyes and thick, long, dark brown hair. From comments she'd made during the morning session, I had sized her up as creative, funny, and intuitive.

"My dad is quite the Don Juan," she said, looking sideways at me. The florescent lighting did not hide my embarrassed blush. I felt outed, and I froze. Maggie was smiling, but her scrutiny was intense. "He has a woman in every port." She flipped her glossy hair over her shoulder and walked away. Chagrined that she had sensed my interest in her father, I felt forewarned.

At the end of the afternoon session, Bill gave me Sydney Banks' book, *The Missing Link*: *Reflections on Philosophy and Spirit* [24] to read. That night in my hotel room, I took it to the bathtub. Much of the writing seemed like common sense and wise; some of it was beyond my understanding. It didn't seem relevant to my therapeutic practice.

To my deep disappointment, Bill did not ask me to dinner, nor attempt to connect during the rest of the seminar. I didn't know what to make of that; maybe his invitation to the seminar had been a professional courtesy. I drove home convinced I'd wasted a couple of days.

So, I was puzzled when, in the ensuing weeks, after sharing flirtatious emails, Bill phoned and said, "Linda, I wanted to connect in a personal way to let you know that I'm involved with another woman."

I felt blindsided. I sat in front of my computer and watched the rain pour outside the kitchen window. It was early spring, and the trees were budded, the ground was muddy, white tree-leaved trillium had sprouted through the carpet of dead leaves. Surprise and disappointment were a bitter pill. I felt humiliated that I'd misread him. The print on the wall of big red poppies rendered by Georgia O'Keeffe, failed to cheer me. A cough drop wrapper was crumpled next to my coffee cup. "I want to be respectful to her, so I won't communicate with you further," Bill said. "I hope you understand."

Well, if this man is a player, as his daughter suggested, he's a kind, respectful one. I'll give him that!

CHAPTER 58

POPLITEAL FOSSA

Two weeks later, as I fixed my hair for work, I thought again about Dr. Pettit. "How could my intuition have been SO wrong?" I said aloud to the wide mirror above my make-up table.

I held a curling wand in my hand; my auburn hair clung to it. I had finished my make-up; an uncapped bottle of foundation and a compact of blush lay on the bright white table. I untangled my hair and thought about Ellen, the palm reader, who had suggested that two doctors would show up in my life. She had been right.

I met Bill. And, through my work in the Healing Arts Practitioner's Circle, I'd also met an integrative family physician who worked in New Orleans. He had asked me to sit on the board of a national organization for healing arts practitioners. He was very good-looking and charismatic, but I hadn't felt the intuitive sense of connection that I'd had when I met Bill. Both relationships were professional. Perhaps Ellen forgot to predict whether either man would have more than a professional interest in *me!*

I stared at myself in the mirror of my dressing table. I mulled over two small but puzzling experiences I'd had since attending Bill and Judy's innate health seminar. One was a near car accident; the second was a revelation at a pizza restaurant.

The near accident was terrifying. "Asshole!" I shouted at the driver whose bright red Dually pick-up truck had just swerved in front of my car on a stretch of six-lane road near the Parkersburg shopping mall in Vienna, West Virginia. I watched in slow-motion terror as cars careened around me, cattywampus. I had swerved to avoid a collision and set off a chain reaction of drivers who did their best to avoid a multiple car pile-up. Mercifully, there were no metal and glass crunches. In seconds, traffic righted itself. Adrenaline stood my hair on end and my extremities felt numb; my heart hammered.

"I'd like to Tawanda your butt," I yelled, unheard, to the dually's driver, a reference to a line from the movie *Fried Green Tomatoes* [25] where a middle-aged woman, with deliberate glee, smashes the car of a couple of young people who smirk at her after taking a parking spot she waited for.

I was shaking hard; I knew it was a good idea to pull off the road for a moment.

I spotted the yellow arches of McDonald's and turned into the parking lot. As I did so, I noticed a neon sign above the arches that said the outdoor temperature was 98 degrees!

My next thought was that I had enough calories in the diet I was on to have a frozen yogurt. With that thought, I smiled and headed for the drive-thru, but midway there, I was so struck by how *fast* my feelings had changed from utter rage to delight that I had to pull into a parking spot to think about what had just happened.

Less than sixty seconds ago, I wanted to smash into a truck to punish a driver, and now I'm all about the thought of an ice cream cone. My anger vanished!! How did that happen? Were Bill and Judy correct—did experience change moment to moment all the time depending on what we are thinking? Were the creation of suffering and the creation of delight that simple? Was it true that the life of a thought is only as long as we think it? Could Judy and Bill and their teacher Sydney Banks be right about Thought being a creative tool we use to play the game of life?

I shook my head as I put my make-up and hairbrush in the drawer of the dressing table. *Did that mean no psychological experience existed UNLESS we are thinking about it? But do we have any control over what we think about?* I sat back in my mahogany chair and reflected on the second strange experience I'd had a couple of weeks later.

On a lunch break from my client schedule, it occurred to me to go to Pizza Hut, which was rare for me to do, for a slice of pizza and a salad. As I bit into sausage and green pepper pizza, I noticed the client I'd seen before lunch was also in the restaurant with friends. Their peals of laughter rang throughout the busy eatery.

"Wow," I muttered under my breath. My client looked happy and absorbed in whatever the group was in stitches about. *Less than thirty minutes ago, she was sobbing her heart out in my office over a traumatic experience,* I thought and wondered, *Where is that trauma now? Does her trauma exist if she's not thinking about it? Which is the truth—the pain that she was in moments ago or the hilarity she's in right now?*

I can't quite convey how confused I was—like I was seeing something important through a fog that would clear and then mist over again.

Was there any objective reality? Were we making up life, moment to moment, one thought at a time? Was life a series of thoughts in a time-space continuum?

Events were real. Jim's death was real. But my experiences had shown me that my psychological experience of his passing had often shifted in a heartbeat—from grief to gratitude to love and back again. Were the 3 Principles the logic behind that? Could what Bill had said about the past being a memory carried through time, only alive as we were conscious of it and thinking about it, be right? In innocence, did we re-traumatize ourselves by reliving painful memories when we didn't have to?

I shook my head and I reached for my favorite perfume, *Aliage*. No matter how much I turned it over in my mind, I couldn't figure out why the innate health seminar had gotten under my skin.

It was time to get on with my day. As I spritzed myself with the fresh, green fragrance, I heard Bill Pettit's voice! I was confused and thought: *Is he in the house?*

I hurried out of the bedroom toward the direction of the sound and realized that his voice was booming from the answering machine. I hadn't heard the phone ring due to the hum of the hair dryer.

"Linda, I can't stop thinking about you," he said, as I listened to him leave a message. Sunlight bathed the kitchen. Windows cracked open let in the freshness of an early spring warmth. Dead leaves rustled in a pleasant breeze that carried the scent of grass coming alive. I was relieved—it was reassuring to know that my intuitive certainty that I was meant to be connected to Bill had not been off. But I was also hesitant—after all, he *had* said he was involved with another woman. *What was up with that?* As I listened to him talk to my answering machine, that question was answered.

Bill's voice was husky, self-assured. "I've explained to the woman I've been dating that I want to get to know you, to give a friendship with you a chance. Would you meet me for dinner?" he asked. I did not hesitate. I reached for the phone. "I'm here and the answer is yes," I said. A woodpecker drummed on a tree.

The next day, Bill cancelled our dinner; he said he was swamped in his work as a consultation-liaison psychiatrist for Ruby Memorial Hospital. I was crushed and suspected that he was weaseling out of a date. Maybe his daughter was right, and he wasn't trustworthy. I tried to put him out of my mind. Days later, he called to reschedule.

I felt close to my female colleagues in the administrative office of the practice I worked in and had told them about Bill. We had a lively debate about what I should wear to dinner; their teasing about my date brightened our conversation over the next few days. In the end, I settled on a black pantsuit, a cream-colored blouse, and a thick gold necklace. Pretty, but professional and not seductive.

Bill and I met at Olivero's Italian Ristorante in Bridgeport, and, in a secluded booth surrounded by scenes of Tuscany and mirrors, we talked three hours over lasagna and breadsticks, chased with wine.

Much of the dinner, Bill entertained me with stories from his medical training. Light-hearted, he had a big laugh and was a consummate storyteller. It was clear that he was passionate about his four children, medicine, his work as a psychiatrist, and his mentor, Sydney Banks.

Bill was interested in my life, my practice of psychology, my daughter, my hopes, and dreams. I was fascinated by the interplay of his strong masculine energy and his feminine energies of connection and compassion. The chemistry between us was sensual and beautiful. Something was waking up inside of me—passion, a longing for a partner, a sense of myself as a desirable woman. It was easy for both of us to speak of our love for our departed spouses, Sue, and Jim.

As we shared a Tiramisu for dessert, Bill reached under the table, caressed the back of my knee. My leg jerked as though he had thumped it with a reflex hammer. "You have a sensitive popliteal fossa," he said and winked, igniting an instant sexual fire.

As we left the restaurant, we stopped on the steps of a portico. Thousands of stars twinkled in the dark sky. Bill asked if he could kiss me. I swear I heard a symphony play during that one, long, slow kiss.

CHAPTER 59

STRIKING GOLD TWICE

"WILL YOU MARRY me?" Bill asked three months later, in May, under the soft light of a chandelier in the restaurant of an historic hotel high above Morgantown.

The lights of the town, nestled into mountains, twinkled, and reflected off the wide Monongahela River. We'd attended his daughter Mollie's high school show choir performance earlier, and Bill had seemed preoccupied. That was my first clue something was up, but I wasn't expecting a marriage proposal!

Once we were seated and had sampled wine and bread, Bill reached behind him into the inner pocket of a navy sports jacket draped over the back of his seat and retrieved a small box.

He flipped it open. We huddled over the ring box in a cozy alcove paneled in dark, antique wood. The flawless diamond caught the candlelight and flashed a deep, true, blue.

"Yes. Yes. Of course," I answered without hesitation. He was sixty-one and I was fifty, but our love felt fresh and young and full of promise. It had seemed unlikely that I would fall in love again, but there I was, head over heels about a man who was tender, romantic, compassionate, and so, so sexy. To boot, he was "eye candy."

"I don't want a long engagement," Bill said. "How soon would you be willing to get married?" It hit me then that we were talking about a wedding—a lifetime commitment! My head shouted "slow down" but my heart gave me a green light. My intuition signaled this was the next right step. Bill sat catty-corner to me, holding my hand, fingering the ring. "Wel-l-l, I'd like a wedding," I said, "and that will take a bit of planning. How do you feel about that?" He smiled. "I'd like that. Let's see when we can get the right venue and go from there."

I admired the beautiful diamond-studded gold ring. It was unlike the simple gold band I'd chosen and loved when I was first a bride, but somehow seemed right for this relationship. We decided I would not wear the ring right way, and that we would not announce our engagement until after my daughter's graduation from high school. We did not want to steal the thunder of her big day.

When I did tell Laura that I was engaged, she wasn't a happy camper. "Mom, it never occurred to me that you would replace Dad," she said, in tears. I was moved by her vulnerability. "Dad can't be replaced, and we share you; a bond that is only ours," I said. "I'm surprised, too, that I have fallen in love again."

Laura was quiet. "You hardly know Bill. It's going fast. Are you sure?" she asked. Bill's children would echo her concerns.

"Yes," I said, on a slow exhale. When my mind was calm, I knew I was meant to be with Bill. He had been married to Sue thirty-one years, I'd been married to Jim eighteen and in that relationship for twenty-five. This was not our first rodeo. Yet, my brain could go into overdrive. Laura was right; this was a whirlwind courtship and defied my thoughtful, conscientious nature.

Bill was a big personality, persuasive and charismatic. I was much quieter and more serious. *Would he overwhelm me? Would I disappear behind him? Would he dominate me? Could I stand independent and strong in the current of his energy?*

As the palm reader had predicted, the sexual attraction between us was urgent. Bill was a thoughtful lover, devoted to my pleasure. I was hungry for his strong, masculine sexuality. It wasn't long after we met that we became physically intimate.

"How committed are you to this relationship?" I'd asked, after we first made love, just months before our engagement. I faced Bill in bed, the rose-colored sheet pulled up around my breasts. My hair was tousled, my skin flushed with lovemaking. It felt odd to be in bed with a man in the house I'd built with Jim. Laura was staying overnight with a friend, and I felt guilty about bringing Bill into our home. I was relieved that I'd remembered how to make love and was thrilled by Bill's bold sensuality and passion. I'd met it with a deep hunger.

"I expect monogamy and if you can't promise that we need to slow down," I said. Bill looked back. The sun was about to set, to slide behind the trees on the mountain outside my bedroom window. A whip-o-will cried in the falling dusk. Naked on the comforter, Bill was propped on his elbow, and he faced me. I remember thinking he was like an Adonis, comfortable in his body. I wished I could be more like that. His expression registered dismay. "It's a bit quick for that," he said, and his head dropped back on the pillow. "I don't know if I'm ready."

I stroked his thick hair. "That's ok," I said, "I understand, but I'm not in for casual sex." I eyed Jim's picture, which sat on the bookshelf across from my bed. I wondered if I should put it away. My heart was skipping some beats. I didn't want to alienate Bill, but in my heart and mind, sexual intimacy was tied to committed love. I knew already that I was in love with him. "If you're not ready, you're not ready. Let's hold off until you know." He pulled me in close and whispered in my ear, "I'll reflect on that." We didn't say much more about it.

Bill left in the morning for a conference in Washington, DC, afterwards he flew to Minnesota to visit his children. He said he would use the break to decide whether he could give me a promise of monogamy and fidelity.

A week later, he called on his cell phone. "I am in for a commitment to fidelity," he said. "The decision is going well except for a few minor symptoms. However, Imitrex is mitigating the migraine headaches, Imodium is keeping the diarrhea under control, and Benadryl every four hours has made the hives bearable!" He laughed heartily. His humor was contagious, and I burst out laughing.

Over the next couple of months, I learned more about Bill and his family. His first wife, Sue, had died of cancer in October of 2000. People spoke in reverent tones about her gentle compassion. Often, they told me that when Sue Pettit had listened to them, they'd felt like the only person in the world—she was that present! I worried that I would be judged as second best.

Bill and Sue had parented four children. Ann, their oldest, had a heart of gold, was out on her own in Minneapolis, a single mother to an adorable four-year-old daughter. Dan, a gentle man, a talented drummer who played with a popular country band, was out on his own working by day as a carpenter, also in Minneapolis. Maggie, the funny, creative soul I'd met at the seminar in Morgantown, lived with family friends in Aberdeen, South Dakota. Mollie, independent and whip smart, lived with Bill. I had mild misgivings about becoming a stepmom to four children, just as my nest was about to empty. *Would they accept me? Could I welcome anyone but Laura into my heart as a son or daughter? How would this all work out?*

Bill also got to know Laura and our community in Calhoun County. He drove from Morgantown to meet Denise and Larry. On our way through Grantsville, the county seat, we stopped at the Wood Festival, the annual summer carnival, arts and crafts fair, food fest and parade. As we walked past the bingo tent, we heard someone ask, "Who's that with Laura's mom?" I pointed out the superintendent of schools, the loan officer at the bank, and the CEO of our small hospital. Behind us, we heard whispers, "who's that with Linda?" We chuckled at the gossip.

As we left the fair, I asked Bill whether he'd be willing to stop at Jim's grave on our way up the hill to my friends' home. "Of course," he said. No sooner had the words left his lips than we spotted a slow-moving turtle crossing the road.

"Stop the car!" Bill said. I pulled to the berm, and he hopped out of the passenger seat. As he scooted up the road, I stuck my head out the window and called after him, "Remember to point him in the direction he's headed." He gave me a thumbs up.

CHAPTER 60

MARRIAGE OF OPPOSITES

T HERE WERE NO sweaty palms, no second thoughts, no hic-
cups on our wedding day. "I do," I said with a full and light
heart on September 20TH, 2003.

This time, I walked up the aisle between my parents in a
Catholic church at the edge of West Virginia University's campus
in Morgantown. I wore a cathedral length veil that swept behind
me over an embroidered, crystal-crusted ivory satin dress and carried crimson roses and alstroemeria. Bill wore a tuxedo with a
crimson cummerbund. Our children and treasured friends composed our wedding party. "I do," Bill whispered in my ear, "you
feel like home to me." I felt like a queen, in rapture that life had
blessed me with a second BIG love.

Our nuptials were celebrated by a White Catholic priest and
blessed by a Black Baptist minister, a dear friend of Bill's, Rev.
Dr. Virgil Wood, who for ten years had worked alongside Martin
Luther King until his assassination.

A Gospel chorale from a local African American Episcopal
Church that Bill and his daughter, Mollie, attended from time to
time performed before the ceremony, including the songs, "Ave

Maria" and "All are Welcome in this Place." My sister, Carol, sang a beautiful rendition of "On this Day," a favorite of mine, a song that venerates the Divine Feminine in the form of Blessed Mary, as I carried a single rose to her altar. I felt so grateful to the Divine Mother for the wave of pure love that had carried me to this sacred marriage.

Bill and I acknowledged our first spouses, Jim, and Sue, in our church ceremony. Because of them, we knew we would be better able to love each other.

There were sharper differences between Bill and I than there had been with my late husband. Jim and I had shared quieter natures, a slower tempo, a self-effacing humor, and a deep appreciation of people that was balanced by a strong preference for solitude. Bill, by contrast, was a dynamo—an outgoing man who preferred being with people.

Two days into wedded bliss, we went to bed early. In the morning, we would fly to Kauai for our honeymoon. I was ecstatic that we were going back to the lush beauty of Hawaii. The week prior had been a whirlwind; Bill had worked full speed to the day of the wedding while taking care of legal changes to accommodate his newly married status. We were both tired.

In the middle of the night, a crash jolted me awake me, and I watched, not sure how to understand what I was seeing, as Bill careened from the bathroom to a wall in the bedroom. He fell into bed and lay still, moaning.

"What's the matter?" I asked, as I sat up straight, alarmed. We were in Bill's house in Morgantown. Moonlight lit the bedroom and his face, which grimaced in discomfort and nausea. "I'm having vertigo," he said. His voice was high and thin. He did not move a muscle, except for his chest, which heaved. "It's a stress alarm for me. If I move, I will vomit. I'll have to call in a prescription for mescaline, an anti-nausea medication."

I studied his face. "How do you know it's vertigo?" I asked. My anxiety went through the roof. His skin was clammy and pallid. *Was he having a heart attack? Was he dying?* The picture looked catastrophic. "Well, it's either vertigo or a cerebellar bleed that will kill me in a few minutes," he said, with a weak laugh.

"That's not funny!" I said, scared. "I guess not," he said, "but stay calm. I've been through this before. It's vertigo. I'll feel better in a couple of days to a week." He hesitated. "We'll have to cancel our honeymoon," he said. "What?" I asked, as he lay there, still. "I can't fly," he said, "I'll have to stay in bed until it resolves."

My emotions ricocheted from compassion to concern to disappointment, and back again. I had empathy for Bill's obvious physical distress. I wondered if it was wise for a doctor to diagnose himself. I could not believe our honeymoon trip was scuttled. I was taken aback that he could joke about dying three days after we were married.

Who was this man that I'd married? What had been so stressful about our wedding that he'd gotten sick? Was he having second thoughts?

Later, after I picked up his prescription from Kroger, I pulled the car door shut and sat, thinking. It was a beautiful fall day and shoppers pushed grocery carts through the parking lot. They loaded bags into their trunks. I had been married just over forty-eight hours and I was alone in a car next to a pharmacy bag rather than on a plane to Hawaii with my new husband. He was in bed unable to move, looked pasty and grey and was sick. The emotional bliss of our beautiful wedding had skidded to a halt. Bill had made a cavalier remark about dying. *I could lose him, too. Had I made a huge mistake in marrying again? I had trusted love, but what if Laura was right and I'd been too hasty?*

CHAPTER 61

MEETING THE
TEACHER OF
THOUGHT

WITHIN A WEEK, Bill recovered, and we took a short "ad hoc" honeymoon to Pensacola Florida and New Orleans. As we traveled, the differences in the way we navigated life became even more apparent. Bill wanted to visit friends on our honeymoon and share me with them.

All my life, I'd been shy and anxious about meeting new people; I craved alone time with my new partner. I went along, but I was outside my comfort zone. Comments made by his friends about Bill's late wife had me worried that I came up short. I struggled for years with a sense of not being enough or second best.

After our honeymoon, Bill returned to work at West Virginia University's medical center. I sold my beloved home in Millstone, West Virginia and moved into his home in Morgantown. Laura had moved into a dorm at West Virginia University with her friend, Tia. Laura wasn't thrilled that I would be living so close by at a time when she was all about leaving home. I remembered how much the freedom of going away to college had meant to me, and I resolved to give her space. I was glad, though, that the lure of our washing machine and free food brought her home for visits on the weekend.

I closed my practice of psychotherapy in Parkersburg and said goodbye to treasured colleagues and clients. I felt uprooted and on a roller coaster of change, grief, excitement, romance, and marital adjustment.

Unlike most people I knew, Bill navigated life with an uncommon compassion, light-heartedness, and equanimity. He wasn't perfect, for sure. He could be unyielding, stubborn; he moved at times with the speed of a tornado. But more than me at that time, he lived from a center that was calm, and generous with unconditional love. I was in awe of him. I thought this was his personality. I did not connect it with the psychospiritual understanding, the 3 Principles, that he taught and shared with clients.

After leaving my practice in Parkersburg, I took a break from doing therapy. My love of helping had faltered. I'd had a couple of tough clients in the months before our marriage, including one who had threatened my life, several who more than skirted suicide, and one who was homicidal. Inpatient resources for supporting people who lived in such shadowed places had dwindled to nothing, and it seemed I had few effective tools to help them.

It was 2004; the discipline of professional coaching was in its infancy, and I was curious about it. I trained as a life coach through an organization for licensed helpers called Mentor Coach[26]; the thorough and upbeat training allowed me as a psychologist to add coaching as a proficiency. The International Coaching Federation [ICF] now defines coaching as "partnering with clients in a thought-provoking and creative process that inspires them to maximize their personal and professional potential. The process of coaching often unlocks previously untapped sources of imagination, productivity, and leadership."[27]

It seemed to me that the skills of coaching—listening, reflecting, clarifying, goal-setting—were like those of therapy, but the clients were different. Coaching clients were less focused on finding basic mental health and more concerned about realizing their full potential. I began to offer telephone-based mentoring to creative women—writers, artists, photographers—and women transitioning through losses like widowhood, divorce, or illness—from an office in our home.

Bill was supportive of my decision to build a coaching business, and I was both grateful about that and uncomfortable. Except for a brief few months after Laura was born, I'd never allowed myself to be supported financially by a partner. When I was a young girl, my father had often admonished me, "be independent; don't depend on a man to take care of you." Bill reassured me that he wanted to be my safety net, but it was hard to trust that and feel worthy of it. I worked hard at learning the ropes of coaching and internet-based marketing and was soon earning an income.

Several months after we married, Bill joined me for dinner after working out on his stationary bike in the basement. "Babe, my teacher, Syd Banks, has invited us to Salt Spring Island to spend a week with him," he said. His eyes were merry and his smile mischievous. "I think he wants to check out my bride."

I was excited and curious about Syd. What Syd knew and taught had been deemed valuable enough for Bill's boss, Dr. Bob D'Allessandri, a vice president of West Virginia University and chancellor of the entire medical center complex of programs, to support and help establish an institute in Syd's name. The Institute was housed in the main lobby of the West Virginia University School of Medicine, an oil painting of Syd occupied a prominent place on the waiting room wall. Dr. D'Allessandri wanted to strengthen collegiality, collaboration, love and understanding in medicine and considered the institute's work integral to this mission.

"You might listen to Syd's audiotapes before we go," Bill said. He slid behind the dinner table in his t-shirt and exercise shorts. I stifled an instant surge of irritation. Bill's passion about the 3 Principles was unbounded, but for the life of me, I couldn't figure out the hullabaloo about it.

Unbeknownst to Bill, after he left the house for work, I tried, many times, to listen to Syd's lectures. Every single time, I fell asleep. Syd was Scottish and his brogue was heavy; I found his low, quiet voice monotonous. It didn't occur to me, then, that when I listened to Syd, my mind quieted and I succumbed to tiredness from pushing myself too hard. I just thought Syd was boring. "When I have time, I will," I said to Bill, noncommittal.

We made our travel plans. Salt Spring is the largest of the Gulf Islands between Vancouver and Vancouver Island in Canada's Pacific Northwest. Bill and his colleagues often spoke of the uncommon beauty of the island and the spiritual energy they felt when they visited. I had never been to that area of Canada and looked forward to the adventure and to meeting Syd.

The journey was long and expensive; we hopped from Morgantown to Pittsburg to Seattle to Vancouver, Canada, where we boarded a ferry to Salt Spring Island.

Bill and I leaned over the ferry railings in the chilly wind. "I never get tired of this trip," Bill said. My eyes smarted from the cold. I pulled my puffer jacket close. I watched pine-studded shoreline and cliffs, shrouded in mists, slip by. A mystical state enveloped me as we docked in Long Harbor. "This reminds me of the mythical journey to Avalon," I said. In the Camelot myths, Avalon is the island of the Goddesses. Legend has it that the island was shrouded in mists until someone worthy of approach could command them to part.

It was winter and a snowstorm had hit the Pacific Northwest. We were lodged in a compact A-frame cabin across from a channel of water, heated by a small wood stove. When we first arrived, the electric power was out. I remember being stone cold. I tried, in vain, to sleep at night in a small stiff chair pulled close to the miniscule black stove.

Before we arrived, Syd had dropped off a manuscript he was writing. In a phone call to Bill, he asked us to read it. Each chapter had been composed by one of a dozen or so mental health professionals and businesspeople who said that the understanding

Syd shared with them had changed their lives. Their stories were heart-felt and spoke of transformations that had freed them from physical illness, psychological distress, insecurities, and troubling marital problems.

On our first full day on the island, I expected to meet Syd. He phoned Bill. "I think the two of you are too tired to meet," he said. "Get some *rest*." I felt irritated, but his suggestion made common sense.

On our second day, I expected to meet Syd. He called Bill and said, "The two of you are still too tired to hear anything." He recommended we go sightseeing. We did.

We sat on a bench at Ruckle Provincial Park on the south end of the Island, a serene, north woods setting and watched birds fly by. We drove up to Mt. Maxwell Provincial Park and took in stunning views of Fulford Harbor and Burgoyne Bay. Against the backdrop of a pale winter sky, the towering pines and lapping steel-colored waters were magnificent. Tucked close to Bill, I enjoyed an intimate silence and was so in love with him. By the end of our day in nature, I was centered and felt as rested as I could be after sleeping upright in a chair for two nights.

On the third day, I expected to meet Syd. He called to say we were still too tired to meet and scheduled lunch for the following day with him and Judy, his wife. Syd's first wife, Barb, had passed away years earlier.

Bill was not even a little bit perturbed. He said that the quieter our minds were, the more we would take in of what Syd had to say. Of course, Bill was sleeping like a log! He said Syd had an uncanny sense of when people were best able to hear what he had to offer. I was baffled and irritated at Syd's behavior. I attended many continuing education programs. This experience was unlike anything I'd had before with a teacher or professional expert.

We had spent a lot of money to get Salt Spring. While Bill snoozed under the duvet that night, I wrapped myself in a blanket near the tiny stove and continued to read Syd's manuscript. My hair stood on end as I ran my fingers through it over and over.

From time to time, I'd quiet down inside as I read the beautiful stories, but then my mind would get to judging them, doubting them, arguing with them, and I'd get into an inner uproar again. My back ached from the cramp of the chair.

At the appointed time, we drove to a restaurant on the harbor. Bill stopped in the restroom, and I took a seat on an outside deck with tables. The weather was still crisp, but the sun was warm and melting the ubiquitous piles of snow.

"I would've known your smile anywhere," Syd said, his Scottish brogue thick, as he approached me on the deck of the restaurant. I recognized him from a picture on the back of his book, *Second Chance*.[28] Syd was trim, even a bit slight and a touch stooped. His longish brown and silver hair, thinned, framed a tanned, lined face. His beard was full and trim. He wore khaki-colored corduroys, a green shirt, and a chestnut brown winter jacket. There was nothing about his physical appearance that distinguished him as a mystic, an exceptional spiritual teacher—he looked like a normal, ordinary Joe—nonetheless, he radiated a deep calm.

The wood table I sat at was greyish brown, faded under hours of direct sun and days of salty spray from the gulf just below the deck. At the edge of the table, a saltshaker with a rusty silver cap leaned against the balustrade. Boats, sailboats, fishing boats, power boats and house boats bobbed on sun-dappled water that lapped, stirred by a slight breeze both, salty from the water and sweet with the smell of fresh pine. I shivered under my down jacket.

I stood and Syd offered a hug, which I stepped into. "I'm so glad to meet you," he said. "My wife, Judy, is parking the car, but she'll be up soon." It's hard to explain this, but I fell into a silence. All my irritation about Syd keeping us waiting vanished. I mean vanished. I searched inside for it, but I couldn't find it! Instead, I felt comforted and bathed in the unhurried, nonjudgmental presence, the quiet, understated, and calm energy that Syd radiated.

I do not remember if Syd shared anything about the 3 Principles understanding at lunch. The four of us, Bill and I, Syd, and

Judy, enjoyed a simple delicious seafood meal punctuated with light-heartedness. Bill told stories and Syd kidded him. Like me, Judy was a quiet woman. I took her in as thoughtful and kind. A peaceful feeling of companionship shrouded our lunch. All the questions I had wanted to ask Syd had evaporated. Somehow, they were insignificant. I couldn't explain this to myself.

The next day, we met again for a late lunch, this time in the quaint seaside town of Ganges, the hub of Salt Spring. The clam chowder I had was the best, the fish and chips the same. I felt inexplicably light and open. We were the only patrons in the restaurant on another grey, wintry day lit by a watery weak sunshine that managed to peek now and then through thick clouds.

Once our meals were served, Syd began to talk about the 3 Principles. As Bill had said during the first seminar I attended, Syd emphasized that the power and principle of Thought was the link between our spiritual nature and our psychological experiences.

He said that God, a formless energy, took form as the power of Thought, which we all use to think. I had become more comfortable, even excited about seeing God as a "formless energy," which Syd also spoke of as "Wisdom" and "Love." But this idea that God took form as the spiritual power of "Thought" given to us as part of the gift of life to *create all experience* still puzzled me. I couldn't remember coming across it ever in my wide exposure to spiritual and mystical texts, and it certainly wasn't in psychological theories.

Syd spoke of life as a great spiritual dream and said that all human beings, whether they knew it or not, searched for God through their experiences. We were all trying to find our way home—home to an understanding of ourselves as God in motion. He said it was from the "nothingness" of the invisible infinite that we create the "all-ness" and the "is-ness" of life using the paintbrush of *Thought.*

I was thunderstruck—Syd was the "teacher of *Thought*" that the Hawaiian Kahuna had predicted I would meet!

We decided to walk off a bit of our delicious meals with a

stroll around downtown Ganges. The harbor bustled with shoppers who moved in and out of the Thrifty Foods and Mouats Clothing stores. We stepped for a moment into Black Sheep Books, a nostalgic and intimate corner bookseller steeped in the scent of paper and bindings that housed a mix of classics, worn versions of well-loved stories, and modern paperbacks. We continued into the business district and enjoyed a handful of art galleries and soap shops.

On the way back, Syd and I fell behind Bill and Judy and strolled along a sidewalk that moved us away from the rustic harbor. I was curious about Syd, the human being.

"What's it like to be a spiritual teacher sought after by students from around the world?" I asked. Syd's hands were in the pockets of his jacket; he had pulled up his collar to ward off the chilly air. His shoulders kissed his ears. "Frankly dearie" he said, he used that endearment often, "it's boring!" I stopped in my tracks. His answer astonished me, and a snort of a laugh escaped my nose. He laughed, too.

"I keep saying the same thing over and over again," he said. "I tell people that the 3 Principles are a metaphor for love. *If you're not feeling love, you've wandered onto the rocky shores of your own thought system. That's it. That's Truth. When you understand the Principles, you hold the mystical key to love.* People get caught up in the metaphor of the Principles and they miss the message." I did not understand this, but I wanted to. I kept having this sense that a big truth, an answer I'd searched for, was flirting with my brain.

We continued along the sidewalk. Moments later, we stopped to look at a painting in the window of an art gallery. I don't remember the precise subject, but it was religious in nature. Syd turned to me and smiled. "There are many forms [meaning rituals and dogma] in religion," he said. He looked straight at me. I had the sense that he was speaking to something specifically for me.

"In the end, Linda, all forms will pass away," he said. "What will be left is Truth."

What I heard was that religious rituals and dogma are not

Truth They are mere echoes of it—human attempts, sometimes quite misguided—to point us toward it. Rituals and dogma can separate us, but Truth will always unify. I heard that Truth would thrive into eternity beyond all such separation. I heard that Truth, God, was Love—the only absolute and trustworthy guide. This was the God I ran to the day I sprinted from the confessional!

I was certain Syd was right. I had discerned a degree of that Truth on my own. My glimpse had allowed me to step beyond form, to follow love, and to marry my late husband, confident that no God would punish living from Truth. My glimpse had bypassed my internal arguments that I wouldn't be able to hold my own in a relationship with Bill, nor be comfortable in a larger family. The voice of love, that it would be o.k., that it would be good, had allowed me to step beyond my thinking.

I left Salt Spring convinced that Sydney Banks was a remarkable *spiritual* teacher, confirming my sense that the God behind life was Love in motion. But I was doubtful that his insights about Mind, Consciousness and Thought had anything to offer me as a *psychologist*.

CHAPTER 62

SEPARATE REALITIES

Bill REMEMBERS OUR first year of marriage as a long honeymoon. I remember it as a sometimes thrilling and sometimes downright scary roller coaster.

Sometimes I snuggled up and enjoyed the ride. Other times, I lost my stomach as we barreled downhill, out of synch, in conflict. Many of our disagreements centered on the 3 Principles understanding. When Bill brought them up and tried to soften my day-to-day life adjustment to our new marriage, I got riled up.

Bill saw no value in arguing about anything. He said, "If what you're going to say and the way you're going to say it doesn't stand a *ninety-eight percent* chance of improving our relationship, why go there?" It wasn't that he wanted to avoid hard conversations, he insisted they could be had from a place of love.

As I explored the fathomless depths of our differences, I asked new questions: *Can we ever know another human being? Was there any validity to the fact I often thought I was right, and others were wrong? Was there any way to bridge our different viewpoints by realizing that we all THINK differently?*

Is this what tripped up the couples I counseled in my practice of psychology—that we have separate realities, and we judge them? Had my lack of awareness of and understanding of unique separate

realities contributed to the difficulties in my marriage to Jim?
Underneath our judgment, had love been there, all along?

When I was upset and wanted to talk about it, Bill asked me to wait for a nicer feeling, a quieter mind, and a flow of fresh thinking, an intuitive way of understanding a situation from a new perspective. Now, his request makes common sense, but early on, I felt dismissed and that my concerns were trivialized.

There were things, real things, which caused upset—including him! I mean, the man left salt all over the kitchen counters I'd just cleaned when he seasoned his food. When I mentioned that, he'd say he was sorry that he had "in-salted me!" Funny, but *was* he sorry? He created piles of things all over the house and seemed oblivious to the amount of time I spent cleaning up after him.

It seemed to me that Bill had limited respect for my love of order. I felt anxious in disorder. Communicating from a place of anxiety led to reactivity and drama. For the life of me, I could not imagine that I could pare the *drama* away and still be heard and respected. I had learned that *drama* was needed to get results. The Principles, as I heard them, seemed to point to bypassing and negating my emotions.

Eventually, I would learn that when I communicated with Bill from a place of calm neutrality, free of judgment, it was easier for him to listen and *much* less likely that he would resist what I was asking for. In fact, it elicited cooperation and a feeling that we were a team pulling in the same direction. But this learning for me was hard won and long in coming. When I was in drama and upset, I also failed to notice the times when he *was* accommodating my preferences.

About a year into our marriage, we had an argument—or rather, I should say, I argued, and Bill listened—about the 3 Principles and I asked him never to mention Sydney Banks to me again. I even threatened a divorce if we could not leave the 3 Principles out of our marriage!

I stomped off to my downstairs office. I sat and seethed as I looked out the window over the hills and forests. We had moved from Morgantown to a rustic home on fourteen acres of wooded land crisscrossed by streams and trails, our private park. Our property line skirted the border, the so-called Mason-Dixon line between West Virginia and Pennsylvania. I loved the isolated quiet!

Spring was around the corner, and the thick snowpack had thawed, creating a patchwork of white. Afternoon sunlight heightened the shadows of the tall trees on the Laurel Highlands. As I looked over the land I loved, and saw the beauty of the natural world, I calmed down. Daffodil shoots, thick spurts of green, sprouted through the mix of dead leaves and snow. The crocuses outside my window had budded, deep purple with yellow centers.

I reached into my desk drawer for a financial file and opened it. On the top of a pile of receipts was a copy of page 154 from the *Tao of Pooh* by Benjamin Hoff.[29] I had not liked that book and had no clue how that excerpt got into my file. I read this passage:

"The masters of life know the Way, for they listen to the voice within them, the voice of wisdom and simplicity, the voice that reasons beyond Cleverness, and knows beyond Knowledge. That voice is not just the power and property of a few, but has been given to everyone. *Those who pay attention to it are too often treated as exceptions to a rule, rather than as examples of the rule in operation, a rule that can apply to anyone who makes use of it.*"

The last line hit me like a ton of bricks. *What if Bill, with his calm, compassionate and light-hearted ways, was not an exception to the rule, but the rule in operation? What if the 3 Principles had given him the key to the rule in operation? What if everyone, including me, could be as calm and happy as he was?*

In an instant, in that moment of grace, my resistance fell away, and I became a genuine student of the 3 Principles understanding.

CHAPTER 63

CREATING

WITH MY HEAD in my hands, I stared at the excerpt from the Tao of Pooh.

I flashed back to an experience that had occurred *weeks before* I met Bill, when I still lived at my own home in Millstone.

I remembered that I'd picked up a rumpled towel out of the basket of clean laundry, prepared to fold it the way my mother did. A fire crackled in the woodstove; it was bitter cold outside. Sunlight streamed through the wide windows in the great room and the patina of the white pine vaulted ceiling gleamed.

I sat with my back to the windows on a couch from This End Up, with the towel in my lap, on cushions upholstered in a swirl of hunter green, rose, and dark blue. I thought about how lonely I felt. Laura was about to go off to college and an empty life loomed. A large print of Georgia O'Keefe's Pink and Blue No. 1 was on the wall—I stared at the arch in the painting. I put the folded towel on the couch. *I don't know how much more sadness I can stand,* I thought.

In the next second, I had a curious sensation of sitting outside of my body as I watched myself fold laundry.

I thought about sadness and loneliness, and saw my mood go lower. Another thought came and I watched myself think it. *I will never find another man to love.* My mood sank more. *I will be lonely the rest of my life.* My mood dropped into the basement.

I switched the thought up. *Being alone is not so bad. I enjoy solitude and independence.* My mood lightened. *With Laura away in college, I'll be freer to pursue my own interests and make new friends.* My mood lightened more.

Goodness, I thought. *I'm CREATING depression and then UNCREATING it. Depression is not something that comes from outside and sits on me. I am an active participant in it. Thought creates my feelings. Outside experience does not!*

I remember thinking: *why hasn't psychology taught me this? I've been a counselor and psychologist for twenty years and nobody has spoken of thought as a creative power, a tool. Isn't that important for everyone to know?*

I had been taught that chemical imbalances created depressive thinking. *But what if it was the other way around—what if ruminating on depressed thinking caused the chemical imbalance? If that was true, then we had far more power over depression than we understood.* That could be a game changer!

Looking back, I'm amazed that I'd started to have spontaneous insights in the direction that the 3 Principles understanding Bill and others taught pointed toward. It was as if my intuition, love in motion, was preparing me for what was to come. But as I sat on the couch folding laundry, I didn't have a language for describing to myself or anyone else for that matter what I had glimpsed.

I stared at the excerpt from the Tao of Pooh. I wondered: *Could understanding three simple Principles change me? Change my clients? Change the world?*

I dropped my head into my hands. A Windows screen saver danced across the screen of my computer monitor. Our kitty, Misty, was curled up on the wide top of my mauve-colored desk chair; her tail was draped over my shoulder. Except for the hum of the dehumidifier and furnace, the long room was still. A flash drive lay on the taupe-colored carpet. My ever-present "Mom" mug was half-filled with cooled coffee. I reached for it.

A memory of another earlier experience flashed into my mind, one from the first conference on the 3 Principles I attended with Bill in San Jose, California. Bill was a speaker at that conference, so I sat in the audience by myself. There was a slight man sitting next to me, his hair was disheveled, his body odor was pungent, and he muttered to himself. "Excuse me," I said, thinking that he was talking to me. "I didn't hear what you said."

"Don't mind me," he said with a dry laugh; his lips twitched. "I have schizophrenia. I talk to the voices in my head. I'm a client of one of the speakers." I was thunderstruck. This was the first professional conference I'd been to where the audience was a mix of helpers and their clients! That was just the first revelation. Prisoners in orange jumpsuits and ex-cons had taken seats on the stage to teach the audience about the 3 Principles! *What??*

Later, Bill and I joined a group at an Ethiopian restaurant for lunch and sat across from two of the former felons, Wilson, a muscled, lean man with slick blond hair and a trim mustache, and his wife, Pauline, an attractive brunette with a wide smile and kind eyes. Both were dressed in casual clothes and seemed at ease among the helping professionals at the table.

Bill had introduced me to everyone as his girlfriend and mentioned I was new to the 3 Principles understanding.

"Can I tell you a story about how this understanding shifted my life in new directions?" asked Wilson. He leaned back in his chair, a picture of confidence. His left arm rested on Pauline's shoulder. He told me both had multiple convictions for drug-related offenses. Condensation on their glasses of iced water dripped to the table in the summer warmth. We sat outside, bathed in California's illuminating light. "Everything changed the day a 3 Principles teacher said to me 'just because you have a thought doesn't mean you have to act on it' and a lightbulb went off in my head."

He shared his story. "Pauline and I had violated our parole agreements and were high as kites," he said. "I got pissed at her and got a pair of manicure scissors from the bedroom. I had a big gut back then. I stabbed myself as hard as I could with the scissors and ran into the living room to Pauline."

His eyes danced with mirth. I was incredulous! Wilson continued: "Pauline," I said, "help me out. I'm stabbed," he chortled. "She pulled the scissors out of my belly. Do you know what I did? I called the cops and told them she stabbed me. The scissors had her fingerprints on them," he said.

"Was that crazy or what?" he said. Both he and Pauline were laughing. Inside, I recoiled. *That was more than crazy—it was insane!* I thought.

"We both ended up back in jail," Wilson continued, "but this time we were given the option to go to classes on the 3 Principles. I had no idea I had a choice to let a thought just pass through," Wilson said. "We haven't been back to prison since. Now we teach this understanding."

I was skeptical and I stared at him. *How could that thought have changed his life? It's common sense that none of us must act on a criminal thought! I know that and that's why I've never been to prison,* I thought. *How could he have been so blind to that FACT?*

A small voice whispered into my mind. *"Linda, but do you know that just because you have anxious thoughts, or angry thoughts, you do not have to take them seriously or act on them?"* I squirmed in my professional dressy casual slacks and blouse. *"No, I do NOT know that"* I thought, and felt deep humility.

I had never been behind physical bars, but in that instant I realized that I'd lived my life imprisoned by upset feelings—anxiety, fear, inadequacy, guilt, hurt, judgment, irritation, anger—of my own making. Maybe, the 3 Principles were the key to unlock the door and be free. The maybe began morphing toward certainty when l stumbled upon the Tao of Pooh excerpt in my financial file.

CHAPTER 64

BOATS ON A RIVER

ONTHS AFTER THE Tao of Pooh insight, I decided to reopen my practice of psychotherapy in Parkersburg and my colleagues welcomed me back. For over a year, I commuted the 120-miles there and back, staying overnight to devote two to three days a week to seeing clients and sharing the 3 Principles.

Syd Banks called our home one Sunday, and I mentioned that I was doing therapy again. He was delighted. "I'm not certain I know how to share the 3 Principles," I said to him, as he listened without interrupting. "I don't have the extensive stories that Bill, and other teachers have. My metaphors seem rudimentary by comparison. I'm also not sure the 3 Principles can help people, but I want to give the sharing a try." Syd didn't seem the least bit offended by my reticence.

"Tell me one of your metaphors," he said. I sat in a swing on the screened porch as fall breezes dropped leaves by the hundreds. I told Syd about a time when my dad bought his first small speed boat. I'd taken it out on the lake alone. I entered some choppy water caused by the wake of a passing water skier and punched the throttle to move the boat through it. But I had given the motor too much gas and the sudden forward thrust turned the boat sideways. The wake swamped the boat and I almost fell out. I had the bruises to prove that I'd hurt myself!

"I've begun to think of Thought as a river, and the thoughts I think as boats that are moving through it in a steady stream," I told Syd. "Sometimes I use the power of consciousness to jump from the safety of the shore, where I'm watching the thought boats, onto one of them. I give the thought boat so much gas that it starts turning in circles and the next thing I know, the entire river is jammed up and I'm drowning."

Syd, by then, was laughing outright, but his next words were so kind, I didn't feel offended. "That IS a rudimentary metaphor, dearie," he said. Then he added, with unmistakable fondness, "And it's YOURS. People will hear the truth in it because it comes from your knowing, your heart." I looked out on the carpet of red and gold leaves that covered the soft hills around me. I felt quiet inside; Syd's tone and words were comforting.

"Don't be surprised if, when you share your metaphors, people jump beyond you and see more than you do," he said. "That will happen. But if you stay humble, their insights will pull you along. It'll be like playing a game of leapfrog."

He was right. I shared the 3 Principles with every client I saw. I wanted to be sure this new way of doing therapy was helpful, so I asked my clients to fill out recognized self-report inventories like the Beck Depression, Anxiety and Obsessive-Compulsive scales, and the OQ-42—a comprehensive snapshot that measure symptom distress, interpersonal relations, and social functioning. I was super excited that in most cases, after three sessions, clients were doing markedly better. I had found a way to help that was far more efficient, faster, and positively affected my client's lives in global ways.

I played the game of leapfrog with the very first client I shared it with. I listened, first, to Melinda's story. She was in a conflicted relationship with her former husband. They'd been divorced for years and struggled to co-parent several children. She felt angry and stressed most of the time and it was affecting her job and her health.

Along with my best attempt to describe what Mind, Consciousness and Thought—the 3 Principles were, I shared my "thought as a river" metaphor and suggested to Melinda that her best bet to avoid stress and find common sense solutions to her very real dilemmas was to stay on the shore until a thought boat that took her in the direction of common sense, calm and love came through.

When I was done, she said, "Oh my God, I'm not a bad person and he's not a bad person. We are just two people who've been jamming up the river of life by giving the wrong thoughts too much gas! THAT is fixable!"

The downtrodden woman who'd come into my office looking like she carried the weight of the world on her shoulders left with a smile and a sense of excitement. I gave her one of Syd's books, *The Enlightened Gardener.*[30] Melinda returned two weeks later, bubbling with elation about the shift in the relationship with her ex-husband. They had both read Syd's book and it had helped them approach each other calmly and with more understanding.

"I told him about your thought boat thingy," she said, as she flipped her shoulder-length brunette hair behind her neck. "When one of us heats up, we remind each other that we're giving a thought boat too much gas and we let ourselves simmer down inside until the river is moving smoothly." She leaned back, crossed her legs, and smiled at me. "Dr. Pettit, it's like—POOF—all the hot air is gone from our relationship," she said.

"I mean, do you get it—how much has changed?" Melissa asked. "We saw that when we got upset and accidentally jumped on a thought boat, we missed solutions that were floating right by us on the river because we were preoccupied with our thought boat messes. We know that now. We laugh about it, and the tension disappears. Then we see the answers we need."

At the time, I did not see that Melinda had shown me how the intuitive way of love works—it was serving up solutions all the time, but I didn't notice them because I was too busy thinking!

CHAPTER 65

WISDOM SOURCES

W ELL BEFORE I met Bill and Syd, I knew intuition was an asset to the artistry and practice of psychotherapy. As I mentioned earlier, I named my psychology business "Wisdom-Sources" as a nod to my quest to understand, and to help others acknowledge, the wisdom within that guides us. But I wasn't sure how intuition worked, and this intrigued my science-practitioner side. An experience I had with a client I'll call Paul explains why I had such trust of intuition prior to hearing about the 3 Principles.

Paul was a mid-level executive who had been referred to me by the employee assistance program of a large international firm. His CEO was worried about him, concerned that depression was interfering with his work performance; he had become indecisive and was irritable with coworkers.

A stoic gentleman, Paul resented that he'd been sent to me for therapy as a condition of keeping his job. It was my third session with him, and I had gotten nowhere; engaging him in talk therapy was like pulling teeth.

An image, I guess you could call it a vision, of a grave marker with flames around flashed into my mind. I was puzzled and shook my head a bit, as if to ward off the strangeness of it. It came back, stronger, and clearer. It didn't seem to apply to me. I wondered, *could this image be a clue about what's going on with Paul?* I didn't share it at first; I didn't think Paul would cotton to talk about intuition. But the image was so insistent, I decided to take a risk. I wasn't getting anywhere with Paul anyway.

"This may sound a bit odd, Paul, but I keep seeing an image of a grave with flames around it in my mind," I said. "I can't make sense of it, can you?"

To my shock, Paul dropped his face into his hands and said, "Oh, my God." His shoulders shook. I was alarmed; I didn't know what had happened. "If you want to tell me about it, I'd love to know what you're going through," I said.

"How did you know?" he asked. A sun beam played through a nearby window, and I watched dust motes swirl in it. Paul, in an austere charcoal business suit, was hunched over his knees on my cream-colored couch. I stared at his short-cropped white hair. He rubbed roughened knuckles repeatedly. He could not make eye contact with me.

"My dearest friend, a golf buddy I've known since childhood, died six months ago," Paul said. "He had metastatic cancer and his husband told me that it swept through his body like fire. He was gone so fast I couldn't absorb it. I have not been myself since he died, but I did not connect that to what I have been going through at work."

My heart went out to him. Paul had grown up in a family where feelings were forbidden. He had not known what to do with the pain of his loss except to deny it.

I asked Paul to tell me about his love for his friend. Over the next few sessions, he shared pictures, letters, memories—we spiraled together through his grief, gratitude, and questions about death and his own mortality.

Paul asked big questions about life and loss and explored what he had regarded as off-limits—spirituality, eternity, what is after life, and love. Before long, he found more peace with his loss, his depression lifted and his work relationships not only stabilized, but they also improved. He relaxed and felt less guarded about sharing himself with others.

Where had the image of the "grave marker surrounded by a ring of fire" come from? Why did I sometimes get such clues and sometimes not? Was there a way to have more continuous access to intuitive guidance? I was on a quest to find a logical answer to these questions.

I had been influenced by the work of Carl Jung, which suggests that intuition is a personality trait, a way of motivating through life that differs among people in strength and preference. I wondered: *What accounted for such differences?*

When Bill and I travelled to Salt Spring Island so that Syd Banks and I could meet, on our second lunch date with him, I saw my opportunity to ask about intuition and I leapt on it when Bill excused himself to go to the bathroom. I hoped this enlightened man could shed light on questions that preoccupied my work

"Syd, I've had intuitive hunches, dreams and premonitions many times," I asked. "How do the 3 Principles explain those?" Syd cocked his head and gazed at me. His wife, Judy, sat close to him in the restaurant booth. His hand cupped a mug of tea. "Well dearie," Syd said. "I don't know." I sat up straight. I didn't know what answer to expect but that was not it! I was bewildered.

"Oh, Syd, you do, too, know," Judy said with a gentle laugh, and she elbowed Syd's side. Her kind face, framed by a soft bob, was turned toward his. He looked over his shoulder at her. I studied them, noting the playful and gentle quality of their exchange. Syd cocked his head, grinned, and said, "Well, Judy, what is it that I know?" He gestured toward me as if to say, "go ahead and tell Linda."

Judy looked across at me. "*Anyone* can see outside the boundaries of time, space and matter." Syd patted Judy's hand and looked at me. The sound of silverware being sorted clinked in the background. "That's right. It's not special, Linda," Syd said.

I felt equal mixes of deflated, curious, and excited. In a snippet of conversation, Syd and Judy had both leveled and elevated the playing field for intuition.

When Syd said intuition wasn't special, what I heard was that it was commonplace, normal, ordinary, and available to all! It wasn't a personality trait exclusive to anyone. Perhaps it didn't even need to be cultivated—*only noticed.*

I wasn't sure what Judy or Syd meant by the phrase "outside the boundaries of time, space and matter" but it sounded mystical, magical, and *powerful.* I wanted more of it!

Syd explained that intuitive wisdom—knowing what to do and when to do it—flows through our minds all the time. It is sourced in the mysterious force behind life that has been called many things—God, Love, Spirit, Creative Genuis, Supreme Intelligence, the Wisdom of the Ages. When we are in a beautiful feeling and our minds are calm, this intuitive knowing surfaces in a natural, easy way.

This is what I remember most about all my personal interactions with Syd—his gentle guidance toward the deep beautiful feeling at the heart of life—a feeling more easily found when the mind rests in the *now,* a state of quiet, a state of "no thought"

Over time, I realized that intuition was logical. The formless spiritual energy behind life is ever evolving us to higher order, to intelligence. When we are in harmony with that energy, we will see what to do. Only misguided personal thinking can create disharmony.

Insight—seeing something fresh and new is a funny thing. Sometimes it seems to happen, and I'm not even aware of something being different until I notice that I am thinking, well, in a softer, wiser way!

Somewhere along the way, I realized that I *understood* how it *seemed* I had lost the feeling of love for my precious late husband, Jim, and how it had *seemed to* come back. In truth, I had never lost it!!

Let me try to explain. I saw that Jim and I were love in motion, love in the form of two human beings intertwined in a partnership. We could not be separated from that love. But we did *THINK* ourselves away from it without knowing that was what we were doing! Love was like the sun—ever present, ever burning. We created overcast skies with our thinking, and it seemed to us that the sun had disappeared. When we let go of that thinking, the sun was once again visible. That's why forgiveness in our situation had been accomplished in a heartbeat!

Syd wrote in his book, *In Quest of the Pearl*[31] that "When the thought system is jammed with imperfect thoughts the system must create an imperfect reality." As soon as I let go of judgment of Jim, my jammed thought system, there love was again, and I saw a more perfect reality. If we'd understood this, Jim and I could have sidestepped so much suffering. Even if we had decided to go our separate ways, we could have done it in love and peace.

Conscious awareness of who I was at my core and an understanding of the logic of staying connected with it was enough to transform my life.

As the logic of love settled into my bones, I changed without *doing anything*. I felt more secure, less anxious. I was less reactive, more poised, and calmer. I was more intuitive and creative. I had found greater peace with myself.

CHAPTER 66

FLOURISHING

A NOTHER CLIENT, CECILIA, a cosmetologist, mid-forties, had done the deed and admitted it—committed a serious identity theft with far-ranging implications. Her attorney had recommended that she seek therapy while out on bond during the trial; it might soften the judge's mind as he considered length of imprisonment.

But Cecilia wanted far more than a lighter sentence. She wanted freedom from compulsive behavior and an inner peace that had eluded her.

I remembered the day she had called me to ask if she could schedule an appointment. By then, I had been sharing the 3 Principles understanding for several years.

"Dr. Pettit, your website says that everyone can find peace no matter what they have been through, are going through, or will go through," she said. A throat thickened with tears made her voice tremulous. Her pain was obvious, and I was alert, paying attention. I rubbed the twisted phone cord between my fingers. "Do you really believe that?" she asked.

"It's much deeper than a belief," I said, the phone cradled to my ear. Through the sliding reception window, I looked out on my practice waiting room which was decorated in soothing brown, teal and beige and tall lamps with crystal bases. I'd finished my last session for the day and was writing clinical notes in a stack of files nine inches tall. I'd kicked my pumps off and crossed nylon-stockinged feet under my work desk.

Thanks to my growing understanding of the 3 Principles, I felt deep, strong confidence that I could help Cecilia. All the anxiety I'd felt earlier in my career over whether I could help any client had vanished. I now understood how every single human being operated—I understood the *system*, the *logic* underneath all the flavors of ways that human beings behave. I sat forward in my office chair, closed my eyes, and willed this woman, this potential client, to hear the conviction I felt. "I know it in my soul," I said.

She exhaled. "I want that," she said. "How soon can I see you?"

"How did you find me?" I asked. I made note of referral sources. "My lawyer gave me a list of therapists and I left messages with several to call me back for an appointment. But while shopping on the internet, your advertisement on Therapist Directory popped up. When I saw your picture and read your ad, tears came to my eyes. Something inside said *this is the woman you need to see.* I trusted that."

When Cecilia walked into my office, I gasped inwardly. She was flat out a beautiful woman. Trim, fit, she had waist length auburn hair that curled around a pixy face, drained of color, and stressed. Her eyes were troubled—deep blue-green rivers fed by a sea of misery. As she clutched my pillow, she sobbed out her story—one I'd heard too many times over my career: severe childhood abuse, intergenerational family mental illness, and shame that drove compulsive dysfunctional behavior.

I sat across from Cecilia on my beige loveseat and did what I did in every first session—listened in stillness to her story and to the story beyond the story. Thanks to my exposure to the 3 Principles understanding, I was able to listen with empathy to her pain but also for the evidence, always there, that love guided her and showed up in her life in acts of kindness and compassion.

"I hear your shame and anger about what you've been

through," I said, with a tenderness I felt to my depth for the dev-astated woman. "And I hear the love you've given to your children and partner. In so many ways, your uncorrupted inner essence, your soul, has shone through. It's unstoppable. You are not bro-ken, even though you think you are. You simply get hoodwinked by your own thinking."

I could tell that Cecilia wasn't buying what I pointed to, but I also sensed she could tell I had zero judgment about her theft. Her next action confirmed her trust in me. She reached into a large handbag and pulled out a bulging journal.

"This is my writing and poetry about what a mess I am," she said. The cover stained with tears. "Would you read it before I return?"

I leaned forward to accept the journal and rifled through the lined pages, filled with entries and pictures. "Of course," I said, "but, in return, I'll invite you to read a book called *The Missing Link*[32]. You are pure love. Your experiences cannot and did not harm your spiritual essence, the intelligence that you are made of. Your personal thinking about them, which is ephemeral and changeable, has created suffering, but you have the freedom to create a new story." Cecilia was quiet, doubtful, but thoughtful.

I ushered her out the door and returned to my couch. I mar-veled that I'd just finished seeing nine clients, but I felt refreshed. My body was tired from sitting, but my heart felt light, and my mind was rested. Therapy, from the vantage point of the 3 Prin-ciples, had become a meditation, which Syd Banks had defined as a "mind at peace with itself." I was calm and very curious about what would happen for Cecilia as she read Syd's book. I took a minute to pray that she would experience grace.

Over the ensuing week, I read Cecilia's journal. That was tough. Her childhood pain and misery were made poignant and powerful by strong writing and a lyrical voice. I wept over the vic-timizing experiences through which she had lived. My husband, Bill Pettit, often said "hurt people, hurt people."

The minute Cecilia walked into my office for her next session,

I knew something profound had happened. She looked quite different—alive in a new way, much more rested and there was color in her high cheekbones. I was now accustomed to seeing transformations like this in clients—not all the time, but far more of the time than before I found the 3 Principles. She held a new journal in her hand with a colorful, hand-drawn cover.

"Did you read my journal?" she asked, straight away. This session, she had opted for the loveseat, so I sat in the tall purple chair. Her journal sat next to me on a round table that held a tall lamp with a purple glass base. "Yes, I've finished it," I said.

"Drat, I wish you had not," she said, and smiled. She extended a hand that held the journal she had carried in. Her manicure was a rosy color. "Writing has poured out of me this week," she said. "It's different. Would you read a couple of entries, now?"

I paged through and read aloud two or three entries. They were poems themed in hope, resilience, freedom, self-compassion, self-forgiveness, and love. The prose bubbled, like a clear, sweet stream.

"This Sydney Banks guy is a genius," she said. She flipped open her copy of *The Missing Link* to page 120, which was awash in yellow highlighter. She read, "To dwell on past trials and tribulations is to *deny* the moment. If you live in the past, you can never find happiness. *You are trying to live in a reality that no longer exists.*"[33]

She looked up at me. Her blue-green eyes glowed with light. "That's it. That's it," she said. "That's what I've done. I've kept alive a past that no longer exists and have punished myself for something that wasn't my fault in the first place!"

And that was just the beginning. The next hour, she shared multiple spiritual insights that had cracked the door of freedom open. I was still new at sharing the 3 Principles and was astonished by her rapid progress toward peace with her past. "This new journal," she said. "This is ME! This is what I will carry with me into prison."

She did go to prison and for years I did not hear from her, though from time to time I dropped her letters and quotes from

Syd that I hoped might uplift her. She was released early for good behavior and for inspiring her fellow female inmates.

Six months after her release, she called. "Thank you again for not judging me, for loving me, and for introducing me to the 3 Principles," she said. "I don't need therapy. I'm doing great." It's difficult after a felony conviction to find work. She now cleaned houses and buildings for a living and was proud of it—every bit of restitution for her crime seemed to scrub the dust off her confidence.

We met for lunch, and I asked Cecilia if she would join me to co-facilitate at a 3 Principles workshop. She sipped on a cup of coffee, held between two hands, and cast thoughtful eyes at me. "Do you think I can do it?" she asked. "What do I have to offer?" I leaned back in my chair at the Chinese restaurant and finished my bite of chicken with cashews.

"Your story," I said. "There is not a human being alive who will not relate to doing something stupid in a moment of upset thinking that cleared in the next minute. Our job is to help people stop obsessing about what's wrong with them and peek at what's right with them. We can show them it's possible to live in harmony with the logic of the human experience, the logic of love."

At the workshop, when Cecilia shared her story of finding psychological freedom and spiritual peace, a pin drop could, indeed, have been heard in the room.

I marveled that while the details of our stories were quite different, the underlying drama was the same.

We had both created mess-ups—hers a criminal offense with serious consequences and mine a relationship disaster that had hurt others — by paying attention to faulty thinking that tanked our moods, distorted our perceptions, and fueled hurtful behavior. We had both healed by remembering that a spiritual force, love, is always present underneath even the most aberrant thinking, and that it will guide us, always, to do the right thing, including sticking up for ourselves in common sense ways.

I marveled about how different the world would be if we all

knew we could trust love. I marveled that I was free from anxiety. I marveled at the degree of faith I had that a spiritual intelligence behind life guided me through every curve in life.

I marveled at how much Cecilia had lost—her childhood innocence, hours spent in shame and anger, the years spent in jail, her standing in the community—and how she had re-found beauty by leaning into curves and following spiritual guidance—including what drew her to me.

When the seminar was over, it was Cecilia who people gathered around. They wanted to thank her for inspiring them. And for bringing a message of hope.

CHAPTER 67

ENDINGS AND
BEGINNINGS

I T WAS 2010; Bill and I had been married seven years and many
signposts suggested that our time in West Virginia was about
to end.

A change in administration at West Virginia University's
Medical Center had brought a close to Bill's work as Director of
the Sydney Banks Institute for Innate Health. He'd taken a job
as a staff psychiatrist at a hospital in central West Virginia, about
two hours away from our home. The commute was grueling.

Our children were now scattered around the country. My
daughter, Laura, had finished her studies in Morgantown and
moved to Arizona to pursue a doctorate in literature. Bill's daughter, Mollie, had also graduated from WVU and begun a master's
program in hydrology at Stanford in California. Maggie was in
South Dakota; Dan and Ann were in Minnesota.

What was next for us? We considered many proposals and
travelled to check out numerous options—London, Hawaii,
North Carolina, Wisconsin, Minnesota, but nothing felt right.

Meanwhile, my dad, who had struggled with Parkinson's disease for sixteen years, was also nearing the end of his life. For a

year, I drove from West Virginia to Michigan every five weeks to help my Ma with his care. He grew weaker and qualified for in-home hospice assistance. I stayed in Michigan the last two weeks before he died.

My brother Jim had a beautiful home on a lake. One Saturday morning, he invited my brother, Michael, and me to go for a boat ride. I jumped at the chance to be out on the water and get a breather from the sadness of my dad's illness.

"Thanks for picking up 'Mickey D' breakfast, Lin," Jim said. He sat in the captain's chair of his blue and white pontoon boat in navy cargo shorts and a blue T-shirt. His beloved white Labrador, Cooper, or "Coop" for short, was curled up beneath his sneakered feet. Bro Mike sat in the bow of the boat, shirtless, shoeless and in blue shorts, munching a sausage and egg McMuffin. From where I sat in the back of the boat, with my feet up on a leather seat, it was a beautiful morning. The early sun had just begun to burn the morning mists off the water and shot shafts of light through the fog. There was no indication that the jigsaw puzzle piece that clarified Bill and my next chapter was about to slip into place.

The boat rounded a curve and Jim throttled down the engine so we could move into a canal, a "no wake zone" that connected two lakes. I saw a Mallard family—a mama duck and six ducklets moving single file behind her. I reached for my phone, snapped a photo, looked at it, and gasped. It was a stunning picture. The duck family was shrouded in a misty prism on sun-dappled water.

The picture, the smell of the lake water, the gentle rocking of the boat, the camaraderie with my brothers, coalesced in a sudden desire to return to Michigan to live. I felt the puzzle piece snap into place. But what would Bill think? Michigan had never come up between us as a place to move.

Later that day, Bill and I spoke on the phone. He had remained in West Virginia to work. "I had a sudden thought today about moving to Michigan," I said. "After Dad passes, Ma may need a little extra support."

Much to my surprise, Bill answered right away. His voice

thickened with tenderness. "How perfect," he said, "that feels right!"

Less than a week later, Dad slipped into a coma. He lay in a hospital bed in the room he shared with my Ma. It was early September and warm. I had just checked on him and noted that soft breezes were ruffling the curtain. He was comfortable but was not responsive. I walked back to the kitchen at the opposite end of the house where Ma was in conference with my sisters and a hospice nurse. The nurse wrote out instructions for Dad's nighttime morphine and left.

"Before he went unconscious, Dad asked me to prepare for a big party," Ma said. Her sleep-deprived face was pale; her eyes under her glasses, the frames edged in light purple, were sad, a dark patch of earth without flowers. She wore purple pedal-pushers and a cotton blouse. A Bic pen rested on the kitchen island where she sat.

A grandfather clock that Dad hand-made chimed the hour in the background. Dad's tiny blue Smurf, no bigger than a shot glass, rested on the edge of the lampshade next to his blue recliner. We kids gave it to him as a Christmas gift years ago. It has been at his side ever since. A calendar rested on the glass end table, put there to remind him of the day, year, and month, to keep him oriented to time.

"He said he wanted to wear a top hat," Ma said. Her look was quizzical. "That surprised me," she said. Cubes from the automatic ice maker in the refrigerator dropped into a bin. And then there was silence.

"We should get him a top hat," my sister, Laura, said. She ruffled a hand through her attractive, short-cropped hair. "But where would we find one?"

"Hey Siri," I said to my iPhone. "Find me a costume shop." Siri identified one about twenty miles away in Ypsilanti. "I can run over and rent one," I said. I was happy at the thought of a break, a reason to get into the sunshine, to do something other than wait for death.

I punched the number for the costume shop. "Yes, we have top hats," a clerk said. "What size will you need?"

With the phone lifted from my ear, I asked Ma, "What's Dad's hat size?"

From the other end of the house, my comatose father shouted, "Six and seven-eighths!" Ma, my sisters, and I stared at each other and bolted, simultaneously, toward his bedroom. Dad was unconscious.

Assured that he was comfortable, we returned to the kitchen. "How could he have heard us?" Ma asked. I did not say so, but I think that Dad had begun to leave his body and had been with us in the kitchen eavesdropping on our conversation.

When I returned from the costume store with the natty black top hat with a satin band around the rim, Ma took it into the bedroom and placed it on top of the maroon-colored family Bible. "We are ready for the party, Dad," she said.

Several days later, we walked as a family into the funeral parlor where Dad's body lay. At the door, a metal stand held a single red rose, his top hat, and a picture of him wearing one as a young man. Dad's favorite dance music, the polka, played through the room's overhead speakers.

I couldn't help but think that my first husband's dad had asked for a family rosary to help him die, my late husband had asked a good Samaritan to pray for his wife and daughter; my dad had asked for a party. Each man had conjured the thoughts needed to cross the threshold of death. I found this fact oddly comforting. I mused as I looked at my dad's top hat that I, too, would find whatever thought I needed to face the unknown beyond life. There was nothing to fear.

CHAPTER 68

CATHERINE OF SIENA

AFTER DAD'S FUNERAL, Bill and I got to work preparing for a move to Michigan. Right as it felt, the decision also meant that Bill would need to get a license to practice psychiatry in Michigan and I would need to re-activate my Michigan license in psychology; we would need jobs and a home! We would need to follow ethical and legal guidelines to prepare our clients for practice closures and facilitate smooth referrals to alternate providers of mental health services.

Bill and I were experts in moves—over our lifetimes, not counting changes in college dormitories or apartments, I had moved seventeen times; he had moved twenty-seven. The curve that was a move to Michigan wasn't easy, but we leaned deep into it and watched the road fly by with smooth rhythm.

Bill and I lived by the rubric "when things are right, they unfold with ease." This maxim was rooted in a story Syd Banks had shared with Bill during one of their phone mentoring conversations.

"Was there ever a time, Bill, when one of your children wanted to drive your car?" Syd asked. Bill acknowledged that his daughter, Ann, when she was four years old, had asked to drive and he'd taken her to an empty church parking lot. He put her on his lap, worked the gas and brake pedals and let her steer.

"At any time did she steer toward something that wasn't good for either of you?" Syd asked. Bill laughed and recalled that she'd guided the car toward a metal pole holding up a basketball hoop. "What did you do? Did you take over control of the steering wheel?" Syd asked. Bill explained that he'd applied pressure at the *bottom* of the steering wheel to move the car away from danger. It appeared to Ann that she was still in control, but it was becoming harder to run into the pole.

"That's what God does," Syd said. What Bill took from the story was that when life seems hard to do, it's best to stop, get still, and listen inside for what comes to mind, including a course correction.

If, in putting the gears in motion to move to Michigan, the way had been difficult, we would have recalibrated. But things fell into place with the speed of lightning.

I called my friends and mentors, Bob, and Linda Brewster, for recommendation letters to help in my job search. "I can't believe how perfect the timing is," Linda said. "I've decided to retire from my position as Director of Counselor Education at Siena Heights University. Bob and I think you would be perfect in that job."

The idea of being at the helm of my alma mater's counseling program thrilled me. Since earning my doctorate, I had taught psychology and counseling courses at the bachelor's, master's and doctoral levels and loved it. To mentor students and introduce them to the 3 Principles understanding was a perfect next step in my career. I applied for and earned the job. In short order, Bill secured a position as a psychiatrist at a community health clinic with a mental health program. Two years later, I was promoted to Dean of Siena's graduate college and enjoyed three rewarding years working in higher education administration.

I pinched myself over and over in those years. I could not believe I had come full circle and landed back in the place where

I'd completed my master's degree and spent so much time with Jim.

One day, I stood in the soaring lobby of Sacred Heart Hall, a 100-year-old brick Gothic building in the center of the older section of the campus which housed many administrative offices and the library. I paused next to a statue of Jesus, arms upraised, that the students called "touchdown Jesus" with great affection. Just down the hall to my right was the chapel where Jim had said Mass. Down the stairs and hall, to my left, was the Sage Counseling Laboratory, where I'd learned so much about the art of helping. I breathed a prayer of gratitude to Jesus for the opportunity to serve a university that had changed my life so much for the better.

I treasured the Adrian Dominican sisters who had founded and now sponsored Siena Heights. Their steadfast commitment to social justice, inclusion, and diversity—they lived from a knowing that there were many paths up the mountain to God—was a never-ending source of inspiration.

I no longer worshipped a God of form nor practiced most of the rituals of Catholicism, but I was comfortable working alongside powerful, clear-sighted women who did. As I now saw it, God was a formless energy, a spiritual intelligence, a truth, love, that takes form in many ways—in the thoughts we use to create separate realities, in our bodies, in nature, in the all-ness and is-ness of life.

That had been Catherine of Siena's knowing—that we were love in motion. She had said, "when you are who you are meant to be, you will set the world on fire."[34]

CHAPTER 69

THE BLACK MADONNA VISITS

A BRISK WIND, a dispassionate broom, swept across a barren wasteland of sand checkered with patches of withered grass. Chelmno, a Nazi death camp in the middle of Poland, a corpse of scorched earth beyond comprehension, lay in front of me.

There was no grand museum marking the site. No trees. No lush, flowered bushes. One large stone wall broke the field, humble metal markers had been hammered into it by the families of the dead. "Nothing grows here," said our dear friend Shaul, an Orthodox Jew and Rabbi.

Rabbi Shaul squatted, scratched the earth with a light touch and pulled up a yellow-white penny-sized rock, sun-bleached. "This is a human bone fragment," he said, "they are everywhere in this field." I looked down at the black kippa on his head. A tear hovered at the edge of his eye. I am ever in awe of Shaul's compassion, and in that moment, I felt the depth of his heart. "As the wind erodes the field, the millions of fragments rise to the surface," he said. "I wish I could do something about it, but there is nothing to do."

We stood on a mass grave of the bodies of Jewish people, where

Hitler's Nazis pitched and bull-dozed them under. We stood on an unspeakable chapter in history. We stood on the bones of human beings. I was appalled that there was no way to step around what was left of hundreds of thousands of men, women, and children.

Bill and I had travelled to Europe to offer classes on the 3 Principles understanding in Denmark, Norway, and the United Kingdom. We had decided to make a personal trip to Poland, so that I could trace my roots, the homes of my four grandparents, who had emigrated to the United States through Ellis Island.

Rabbi Shaul, his wife Chana, a woman of depth and grace, his son, daughter, and a small group of friends had offered to accompany us on part of the trip so that they could show us aspects of Jewish and Holocaust history we might not otherwise be aware of or able to find—a hidden synagogue in a crumbling brick house, a quiet Jewish cemetery, the gravesite of a heroic Jewish woman. We had jumped at the chance to be with such beautiful souls, people who lived from a deep feeling of love. Our plan was to tour with them and then make our way to visit the Black Madonna, the Lady of Czestochowa.

Our motley crew was of different religions and of different minds about Jesus, the central figure of Catholicism. For Bill and me, both raised Catholic, Jesus is an enlightened man, a revered spiritual teacher who we had been taught was the son of God. Our Orthodox friends did not regard Jesus as a prophet.

Nevertheless, our understanding of the 3 Principles created common ground—an awareness that under all our rituals and beliefs, which are created by humans, byproducts of the power of Thought, we are one, formed of the same love. The love and respect between us were evident throughout our lighthearted travel—even to the most difficult of places.

We journeyed to the Auschwitz-Birkenau Memorial and Museum in Oświęcim, Poland, which documents the horror of the concentration and extermination camp located there, where about 1.1 million people were killed, the overwhelming majority

Jewish. Some 70,000 were Polish people and others that the Nazis thought of as "sub-human." The far-flung grounds felt peaceful, quiet. I had expected shadows and difficult energy and had approached the concentration camp with dread. But it was as if the place had made peace with itself.

As we toured the grounds, I felt quiet, contemplative, a sense of being connected to all human beings before me who have experienced tragedy and faced imminent death—until I came upon an enormous mountain of baby shoes, footwear stripped from tiny children before they were gassed. I ran and sucked air behind a building; my guts heaved.

"I don't know what to say, Shaul. What is it like for you and your family to visit these places?" I said, when we returned to our van. Shaul twisted around in the driver's seat. "No matter how many times I come here, it doesn't get easier," he said, "But your witness to it and the way it affects you, reminds me that this is a tragedy for everyone—a scar on the surface of humanity."

I was grateful for his gentle words and kindness. I had a deeper, clearer sense of how the power of thought can be used to create good, or unfathomable evil. We also toured the Birkenau camp, where gigantic gas chambers were built that could exterminate two thousand human beings at a time. I was horrified by these buildings.

I have family who were interned by Russian or Nazi forces during the Holocaust. I had been aware of this before our trip, but as we visited the camps, I felt more connected to them and the enormity of their suffering. I was much more aware of, and grateful for, the blessings of freedom I've enjoyed in my life.

While in Poland, Bill and I also visited the Carpathian Mountain region, where most of my relatives had lived, and made a pilgrimage to the Black Madonna at Czestochowa. I wanted to fulfill the promise I'd made as a child to my Grandma Sandel. I also wanted to honor the Black Goddess. For me, she now was a meaningful, ancient symbol of a Divine wisdom which remains steadfast, loving, in the face of human suffering and sorrow. I wanted to thank her for pointing me toward love and showing me how to restore divine order, meaning, during a time in my life when I had felt so broken, so alone.

We drove through breathtaking mountains, lush with the green of summer, and dotted with pristine, bright blue, lime green, coral, and butter yellow bungalows; many displayed statues of the Blessed Mother, Jesus, or Pope John Paul, who is revered by Poles as a fellow countryman.

We arrived in Czestochowa in the evening and got a good rest at our Airbnb. In the morning, we paused for coffee and a light breakfast midway up the hill to the Jasna Gore Monastery, where the icon of the Black Madonna is housed. We joined a throng of pilgrims and tourists who surged toward her chapel. It was a while before we passed through the ornate stone arch into the massive monastery, white brick blackened with time. Men and women who wore the garbs of nuns and priests seemed to be everywhere.

I felt disquieted. I hadn't expected the churning crowds, and the way people jostled each other. Years before, when I had visited the Black Madonna in Monserrat, Spain, I'd had to wait in a lengthy line, but the queue to get a glimpse of the Lady had been reverent and ordered, a quiet contrast to this tourist attraction.

A sharp cramp doubled me over. It may have been our breakfast or the culmination of days of eating heavier foods. I was about to be ill. "Bill, honey, I have to get to a restroom," I said. Sweat broke on my forehead. Another cramp twisted my gut and bile rose in my throat. "I'll ask for directions," Bill said. He was concerned and galvanized into action; he ran interference to a restroom in a brick courtyard. I burst through the door into the stench of urine and a long wall of women who waited in silence to use a few toilets.

"Please, I'm sick," I said, and motioned that I needed to go to the head of the queue. Eyes turned toward me. I read lack of comprehension, perhaps because of language differences, and suspicion. No one moved or responded. "Please, I'm sick," I said again. "I need to get to the toilet now."

A Black woman stepped out of the line and took charge. "Ladies, this woman is ill," she said. I don't know if the waiting women understood her English, but her gestures made quite clear her intention to get me to a stall that had just been vacated. Swathed in a dark print dress, her frame was generous. Her ankles spilled over thick-heeled shoes. Short, braided dreadlocks tied with purple beads draped her head and grazed her shoulders. She put a protective arm around me, steered me to an open stall, and closed the door behind me. Just in time.

"You ok, honey?" she said after a bit. Her fingers gripped the door of the stall at the top. They wore plum-colored nail polish. She was my guardian angel. Her voice was compassionate. "I am," I said, between waves of cramps. "Can you let my husband know I'm going to be a while." My voice was weak and hoarse. "He's wearing a blue jacket with a logo for Siena Heights University. He's right outside the door." "I can," she said. Her sturdy shoes clip-clopped out the door. "Thank you," I called after her.

Twenty minutes seemed like an eternity before my stomach calmed, and I was able to reconnect with Bill. We made our way to the famous icon of the Black Madonna, a picture in an ornate frame above an altar heavy with candle tapers and flowers. I couldn't get close due to the throngs of people, and felt too weak to muscle in.

"Let's go," I said to Bill, disappointed that our much-anticipated visit had been spoiled. My gut rumbled as we exited the monastery. The lawns outside had been turned into a makeshift chapel; rows of chairs stood like soldiers under brilliant sunshine in front of steel scaffolding that served as an altar. A large reproduction of Our Lady of Czestochowa was framed on a brick wall. High above our heads, a priest was celebrating the Catholic Mass.

"How about if we sit for a bit?" I said to Bill. We clutched frosted bottles of water that Bill had bought inside the shrine. Both of us felt tired. I watched the priest move through the rituals of the liturgy via a massive television screen above the scaffolding. I surveyed the throngs of people who listened. I joined hands with others to pray the "Our Father." The scene and ritual felt impersonal.

So many of us are drawn to this icon of a woman who sorrows and suffers with us and offers healing. I thought. *She is the seat, the soul through which the word of God burst into the world. I'm so surprised I didn't experience her in a meaningful way today.*

And then an insight cantered in on a wave of gratitude and reverence. I had indeed met the Black Madonna. When we are our true Selves, at our best, she is everywoman, everyman, everywhere.

That day, the Madonna wasn't dressed in royal blue and gold filagree. She wore a dark print dress, chunky-heeled shoes, plum nail polish, and purple-studded dreadlocks.

CHAPTER 70

DESERT GIFTS

"Mama, Craig and I are going to have a baby," my daughter, Laura, said over the cellular network that connected Tipton, Michigan and Phoenix, Arizona. Her voice was happy and excited.

Laura had married Craig, a handsome, talented, and kind lawyer, a solid, good man, seven years before; she worked as a marketing executive in health care. She has her father's cocoa-colored eyes, and, in that moment, I imagined the shine of motherhood in them. The couple had a lovely home in north central Phoenix—I pictured her looking out on their beautiful landscaping filled with roses, cacti, red and orange bougainvillea, and palm trees. "Give me a minute, honey," I said. "I can't speak."

"Me, too, Mom," she said. Bill and I enjoyed eight grandchildren who ranged in age from two to nineteen. Laura and Craig hadn't spoken of having children, and it had seemed disrespectful to ask. They'd been married seven years, so I'd assumed they had decided on a lifestyle that didn't include becoming parents, which was fine with me.

"When are you due?" I asked. The window in my taupe-colored office looked out on a snowy November day. The trees were bare, so I could see Sand Lake sparkle beyond the road behind our home. Golden rays played on the carpet; our sweet calico kitty, Misty, stretched out on a patch of sunlight. I had left Siena Heights nine months before and had decided to take some time off to recover from the demanding pace of my job but had taken on a consulting project for the university. An accreditation report covered my large all-in-one computer screen. I'd made a pumpkin pie that day and there was a hint of savory spices in the air. "In early June," Laura said. "You guys should come at Christmas time for a visit."

And so, we did. The beauty of their Christmas tree, the gentle feeling between my daughter and her husband, and the soft swell of Laura's belly, which we would learn sheltered a little boy, were gifts beyond measure. Jet lagged, I awakened early that Christmas Eve, made coffee, and sat on a couch in the living room. I posted a memorial to Laura's father, Jim, on social media. As always, as the anniversary hour of Jim's death approached, I closed my eyes and remembered.

At the exact moment of passing listed on Jim's death certificate, my cell phone buzzed on the seat beside me; the caller was from Ripley, West Virginia, the town right ahead of the scene of Jim's accident. When I picked up, the line was dead. That such a thing could happen still astonished me, but I no longer doubted that it was a message from beyond material life. I had seen and accepted that life was a seamless flow of energy back and forth across the veil between the formless and formed.

Jim, I know you're happy we're here with Laura, I thought. *And you know she's going to be a mother. Did you ever think you would be a grandpa?* The air was pregnant with love and happiness.

Later that day, over dinner, Bill and I told Laura and Craig we planned to move on from Michigan. My mother had decided to share a household with my brother, Jim. We considered moving closer to Bill's children in Minnesota or South Dakota, but the wintry weather and snow was a deterrent.

"Mom, Craig and I would like you to come here," Laura said. We had just finished a sumptuous meal; Laura is an excellent cook. We sat around a heavy wood dining table over dessert. I couldn't believe it was warm enough in December to have the patio door open to the night air—Phoenix was so different from the Midwest! I could pick up the vague odor of chlorine from their backyard pool. "It would be nice to have you closer with the baby coming and as you guys get older," she said.

I couldn't speak. Laura's move to Arizona ten years ago had been a loss I'd felt as keenly as her father's death. I had adjusted to her living so far away, but my grasp on peace over it was tenuous. At the thought of being close to her and her baby, I was overwhelmed with a crazy mixture of relief, love, excitement, and longing.

We weren't certain about a move, but Bill and I returned to Phoenix months later to get a better sense of the housing market.

After several days of visiting lackluster condominiums in our price range, we took a walk one March morning on the Bridle Path, a stretch of sand that meanders alongside Central Avenue through downtown, midtown, and uptown Phoenix. Back in Michigan, the temperatures were sub-zero, but there we were, walking coatless.

"This *is* so nice!" Bill said. The sky was overcast and the smell of rain on desert dryness made the air a touch acrid. High spring, the tree leaves were fresh budded and bright green. Bill was in shorts; I wore black spandex yoga pants, a coral-colored shirt and black sweatshirt. "You know, I'm done with snow," Bill said. "I could get used to this warmth." His tawny eyes were alive and warm; he smiled at me. "How about you?"

"Could we move here, honey?" I said and held my breath. He didn't hesitate. "Let's do it," he said, and we finished our walk, outlining all the steps we'd need to take to make a move happen—new licenses again, new jobs, a new home.

When we returned to Laura and Craig's home and told them we were ready to move closer, we also discussed that we hadn't seen anything that appealed to us on our condo-hunting expedition.

"Mom, there's a cute mid-Century modern complex just around the corner from us that Craig and I think would be perfect for you guys," she said. Excitement edged her voice. She picked up her phone. "A new listing there has just been posted and it's for a six-month rental. I'll call to ask if we can look at it," she said.

By the time we left Phoenix two days later, we had put a security deposit down on the beautiful art-filled condo owned by a couple who lived in Vancouver, Canada. They spent six months out of every year at their place in Phoenix. Our rental would begin in June and afford us time to look for a house. In the next few months, Bill and I hatched a plan to move to Phoenix and to secure some kind of place in Minnesota that would allow easy access to our northern-based children and grandchildren.

It was late afternoon and we'd been packing a truck for the move to Arizona for two days. "I can't believe I'm helping you move again, Sis," said my brother, Mike.

Mike wiped the sweat from his tanned forehead. He carried a box in his ropy, muscled arms. He had to push hard on it to stuff it into the bulging truck. Behind him, Shari, his wife, and I stood with brooms; we had swept the last bit of dust out of the garage of our Michigan home. Her curly brown hair and my short-cropped red hair were limp in the humidity. "We are going to miss you," Mike said. We had enjoyed six years in Michigan close to my mom and siblings, for that we were so grateful.

We shared big hugs with Mike and Shari and set off bound for the Southwest, Bill driving the truck and me behind in my burgundy Toyota Highlander.

Half mile down Highway US-12,, Bill braked and pulled off the road. He ran to the front of the truck, out of my line of sight. A minute later, he returned and came back to the car. "Guess what I just had to help across the road," he said. "No way," I said, "a turtle?" He nodded and his eyes filled with tears. "This is the right move," he said. "Jim is letting us know."

On June 4TH, 2017, we rolled along the Mogollon Rim in

northern Arizona. I was delighted to discover gorgeous mountain views, sweeping Ponderosa Pine forests and sparkling creeks just hours out of the city. We were enthralled to move through Saguaro stands on the snake-like Bee Line Highway, just before they gave way to our new home, the vast, sprawling city of eight million known as "The Valley of the Sun."

I couldn't have imagined that I would ever be a desert dweller. A new landscape invited us to explore and enjoy. I was determined to follow one of my cardinal rules to "bloom where I'm planted."

Four days later, Bill and I stood next to Laura's bed in St. Joseph's Hospital in downtown Phoenix.

"Do you want to hold him?" Laura said. Small freckles marched, little dots, across her nose against a face pale with exhaustion. Her labor had been long and tough. Pride, joy, and love imprinted her features. The little package in her arms squawked, a tiny bundle swathed in a white blanket embossed with orange elephants, a small face under an orange knitted cap.

"Yes, please," I said. Craig picked up my grandson with tender hands and placed him in my arms. Tears smarted my eyes as I held him close, a precious little boy, perfect tiny fingers enfolded and clasped tight across his chest. A silver tree of life pendant hung from my neck.

"Mom," Laura said, "meet our son, Luke James."

Laura looked straight into my eyes and nodded. The little one's middle name was in honor of her father. Two years later, Luke's brother, Alex Ean was born.

On the circle of life, in two tiny, perfect miracles, James Noel Pfeffer, love in motion, lives on...

EPILOGUE

TAKE ME HOME

I N AN AMAZING synchronicity, in February of 2022, I came to enjoy five blessed weeks of solitude, a writing retreat, in the 200-year-old farmhouse next to Sycamore Creek in my beloved West Virginia where Jim and I first came to visit Denise and Larry and I became "of a place."

I had an intuitive sense that the third round of book revisions was to happen in West Virginia. Denise and Larry, my dearest friends and family who still live there, suggested I contact the current owners of the farmhouse where I stayed the night I became of the mountains, to see if I might rent their home, which was empty because they were wintering in Florida. I crafted an email and hit send. Within minutes, Mimi McDonald phoned me.

"We would love to have an artist's energy in the house," she said. "The house will welcome you." I booked my flights.

Denise and Larry still lived a quarter mile down the road and up the hill. There, too, was the beautiful home that I built with Jim, now loved by another owner. There, too, was Jim's grave, in a private cemetery marked with a simple brown marble headstone inscribed, "Blessed are the Peacemakers."

On many evenings while there, I shared meals with Denise and Larry, and their adult foster-daughter, Janeen. Larry and Denise were remodeling their kitchen, so we ate at the portable butcher block island that is their workstation. I have shared meals with them at that table countless times over forty years.

"Denise, instead of putting our cooking equipment back on the top shelf near the ceiling, we ought to display your pottery," said Larry. His square, solid German face was butter soft. His kind eyes caressed his wife.

"We can't do that," Denise said. "They're not good enough to show." She ran her hands through her greying hair and laughed, but it was apologetic. "Let me get a few pieces to prove it." She bolted for the steps to the basement and retrieved two green-glazed dinner plates, and a taupe plant holder decorated with her signature blue brushstrokes. She brought back two additional vases and assembled the pieces on the butcher block table.

"I've always liked this one," Denise said. Her finger traced the green ridges of a grey dinner plate. "But it was an accident, a fault. The glaze crawled into these abstract lines." Janeen reached over to trace the lines with her. "This is my favorite," Janeen said.

"These are flawed," Denise said. "They're imperfect." The irregular grain of the new grey and white granite countertop gleamed in the dusky light. "Isn't that true beauty?" asked Janeen, "that everything is perfectly imperfect."

I thought about the Japanese art of Kintsugi where gold, silver or platinum dust and lacquer are used to repair broken pottery. The effect refines, enhances, and makes beautiful new art of accidents.

I mused that we are all artists of life; our paintbrush is the gift of THOUGHT which we use to think our way into all manner of accidents—dramas, traumas, conflicts, suffering. Yet, we use that same paintbrush to create beauty—stories of forgiveness, reconciliation, hope, peace, new life, and love. We choose how we paint, though the subject often seems dictated by life.

I never thought I would live anywhere else but my beloved Appalachian Mountains, but a curve in my road took me to Phoenix, a desert megalopolis of palm trees, stark brown mountains, and perpetual sunshine. I came here to be an intimate part of my daughter's village and for the exquisite joy of being a grandmother to two loving, energetic little boys. I was determined to lean into this new curve and bloom where I was planted, and I have.

My work with people who want to function at remarkably high levels of love, creativity and transformational service continues to unfold. I have been blessed to become an internationally recognized spiritual mentor to many intuitive-creative souls who have found a way to love beyond measure, forged and made stronger by personal hardships, losses, and transitions of many types. These beautiful souls come from all corners of the globe, every continent. It has been a powerful joy to watch my fascination for the intuitive way of love, for helping others and for writing come together.

I am grateful to my core that I found the 3 Principles understanding. It has cleared many of the cobwebs out of my inner house and molded a priceless helping hand onto my heart. And, of course, brought me the second love of my life, Bill.

When I stayed in the farmhouse in West Virginia, I asked Mimi for permission to go upstairs, into the bedroom where Jim and I slept on our visits to Denise and Larry, who rented this house while they built their own.

"Explore all you like," said my host. "The house will love to be loved." I felt the truth in her words, for the energy about the old place was solid, benevolent.

I felt quiet, reverent as I climbed the steps back into the past. I stood in the doorway of the bedroom and could see my younger lush, naked body in bed with Jim, my whiter limbs entwined with his, browned by years under jungle suns. The heat of the image was so aflame with love, I thought my heart might melt into nothingness. My husband, Bill, would arrive later in the week to enjoy with me my last few days there. His presence and the love I feel for him would be the punctuation that brought that round of revisions to a close.

I walked to the window where I had first looked out on Millstone, this tiny town of few. I brushed aside the faded ivory curtain. There was the old maple tree, naked winter arms still in worship to a wide sky. There was the mountain, a breast of the earth, still sheltering the old house. To the left, there was the road and the home that now sits on the first piece of property Jim, and I bought when we moved here. To the right, there was the road that wended past a weathered shed and then uphill and into a curve.

I felt certain, as my eyes followed the road, that there were unknown curves ahead. I hoped they were gentle. But the fullness of life is perfectly imperfect. I am not afraid. I know the love that I am made of will see me through everything.

As I turned to leave the upstairs bedroom, I spotted a small plaque on the wall. It was a quote from the writings of Emmet Fox,[35] an Irish spiritual teacher in the early 1900s who held a bright light of love and hope to others during the Great Depression. I have long admired his writings. It seemed fitting that he spoke to me from the walls of that house, a crucible for this book:

> *If only you could love enough, you would be the*
> *Happiest and most powerful being in the world.*

LINDA SANDEL PETTIT

Thank you for reading *Leaning into Curves!*
I hope you enjoyed the book and will leave a review on your reading platform of choice. Doing so helps other readers find great books and spreads the message of the Wild, Intuitive Way of Love.

Join Linda's community on Facebook: @thewildintuitivewayoflove
Follow Linda on Instagram at: @lindasandelpettit
Find her on LinkedIn
https://www.linkedin.com/in/linda-sandel-pettit/

For more about Linda, her events, and services, and to read her blog, please visit www.lindasandelpettit.com
You can sign up for her mailing list or leave a message for her on the contact page.
https://lindasandelpettit.com/contact/

ABOUT THE
AUTHOR

D R. LINDA SANDEL Pettit's life's work is listening—to the
wisdom within, to the wisdom that is expressed in heartfelt
conversation, to the wisdom of Life, and to the wisdom that Love
is. It is listening that empowers her words in writing, spiritual
mentoring, and compelling public speaking. She is a global influ-
encer at the common boundaries of psychology and spirituality.

As a mentor, Linda listens and intuits how to point others
toward powerfully creating life from Love. She is skilled at shap-
ing a safe crucible for transformative change. She revels in working with awakening souls who are ready to lean into curves after
disruptive experiences of loss. Linda guides them to trust the intuitive way of love through rebirth to optimal self-expression and
creativity. As a mentor, she has been called "fiercely sensitive and
sensitively fierce."

Linda's work rests on a psychospiritual understanding known
worldwide as the 3 Principles shared by Sydney Banks, and on
Beingness, a way of living shared by Steve Hardison in *The Ultimate Coach*.

Linda's creative writing is published in the anthology *Stories of the muses: Become a better writer.* *Leaning into curves* is her first book. Her second book is in production.

Linda holds a doctorate in counseling psychology from West Virginia University [1991], a master's in counselor education from Siena Heights University [1983], and a bachelor's degree in journalism from Michigan State University.

She is married to Bill Pettit, MD, a psychiatrist, and recognized teacher of the 3 Principles. They make their home in Phoenix, Arizona and are over-the-moon about their family: five children and their partners, eleven grandchildren and three great-grandchildren. Linda loves bike-riding, swimming, walking, reading, writing and coffee!

Follow Linda on Facebook, Instagram, Medium and LinkedIn. Find her website at: www.lindasandelpettit.com.

Read more from Linda Sandel Pettit:
To download a bonus chapter "A Bookbag Named God" from
Linda's next book, in process, scan the QR code below:

Linda's writing is also featured in:
Iliffe-Wood, M. Hollows, JB. (2022). *Stories from the Muses:*
Become a better writer (Method Writing with Jules Swales.)
I W Press

ACKNOWLEDGMENTS

M Y HEART IS full of gratitude for all the mentors, teachers, allies, friends, family, and disruptors who have shaped me and are interwoven, named or not, into *Leaning into Curves.* You know who you are, and I love you.

I acknowledge all of you who read the chapters in which you are mentioned, made suggestions and corrections, and graciously gave permission for me to name you

I acknowledge my beloved daughter, Laura, and my exquisite grandsons, Luke, and Alex. You were my reason for starting this book. Laura, because you and your father are at the heart of my being; Luke, and Alex, because I wanted to leave you the story of your amazing Grandpa Jim, who you never met in this life but who I know watches over you with so much joy! Thank you, too, Laura, for our photo shoots—a gift of your love.

I acknowledge my writing teacher, Bella Mahaya-Carter. You read the first of my chapters and your encouragement kindled the flame for writing this memoir.

I acknowledge my Method Writing teacher and dear friend, Jules Swales. You helped me find my deeper voice, the truth of who I am, as a woman and writer. You gave me the tools of storytelling. You edited the stories multiple times and pushed me to go deeper. I acknowledge, too, all the fellow writers in your classes who have taught me with their presence, feedback, and their sharing of brilliant creative genius!

I acknowledge my dearest friend, Maryann Dreske. You have been my writing hallelujah chorus for over fifty years. You are truly Pan del Cielo, bread from heaven, in my life. Your practical wisdom saved this book from getting lost in the weeds.

I acknowledge my dearest friend and colleague, Sarah Hook-Nilsson. Your quiet observations and unfailing willingness to read and comment on multiple drafts helped me to be more thoughtful, clearer in my writing, and to trust my gifts.

I acknowledge Shannon O'Neill of O'Neill Editorial, [www.oneilleditorial.com] my editor. I chose you for your practical, thoughtful presence, and that was so perfect. Your manuscript assessment became a guiding beacon for crafting the story arc, themes, and characters of *Leaning into Curves.*

I acknowledge Christopher Vogler, who authored the phenomenal book, *The Writer's Journey: Mythic Structure for Writers,* for your artful and insightful articulation of the hero's journey in story.

I acknowledge Elizabeth Jarrett Andrew, who authored the book *Living Revision: A Writer's Craft as Spiritual Practice.* Thanks to you, I learned to see revision as creative an endeavor as the laying down of the first draft, maybe more so. Revision became an enticing joy—a good thing, since this book was revised eight times over four years!

I acknowledge Ria Iliffe-Wood, founder, and head of IW Press Ltd, who I met in my Method Writing classes. Your own writing is breath-taking and your support and guidance through the publishing process buoyed me through tasks that sometimes felt dreary or were foreign to me!

I acknowledge Sam Horn, CEO of Intrigue Agency, author, speaker, coach, and communications expert, who sensed the value and importance of this book's message as a "life raft" in modern times and helped me to stand strong for its worth in the world of marketing.

I acknowledge my sister, Carol Deedler, a fellow creative, who cared deeply about me and the value of this project.

I acknowledge my first writing teacher, Sister Corinne Weiss. I called her "Chief," and she called me "Sassy." It was she who first named a gift that was hidden to me.

I acknowledge Lone Pine Publishing, Judy Banks, and Shane

Kennedy for permission to quote the teachings of Sydney Banks, HarperCollins for permission to quote the poem, "Love" by Emmet Fox, and Benjamin Hoff for permission to quote from *The Tao of Pooh*.

I acknowledge artist and friend, Coizie Bettinger, who created the original, and beautiful, artwork for the cover of *Leaning into Curves*—a perfect capture of my vision for it.

To those of you on social media who kept cheering me on... your love meant more than you can ever know.

And last but first, I acknowledge my beloved husband, Bill. You waited patiently through many days when the door to my office was closed as I pounded the keys to spin my stories. You were a cheerleader, and a consummate editor when you finally read the manuscript. The fullness of this story could not have been told through the eyes of deep, deep love, had I not met you. I love you with all my Being.

BOOK CIRCLE QUESTIONS

T HIS IS A great book to bring alive in your own life via a book club or circle. Whether you are certain of it or not, you have your own story of the intuitive way of love. What would happen if you learned to trust Love even more?

Many book clubs or circles begin with a friend or two, or three, deciding to get together for coffee, or a meal and to discuss a book. Perhaps you could enroll a friend or two in the idea—and watch everyone enrich, expand, and get inspired!

Here are some questions to guide your discussion of *Leaning into Curves*. *Tackle them all or pick a few here and there that interest your group*. I wish I could be a fly on the wall listening in! I know my love for you would grow even bigger!

I invited you to grab a cuppa of your favorite beverage...and enjoy your sharing.

Chapters 1–7

How do you define intuition? Share an example of an intuitive experience.

What experiences have you had of feeling connected to others across lifetimes?

What do you think of Linda's definition that intuition happens when the eyes of Love, the spiritual eyes, fly wide open?

In our early years, we develop a "starter kit"—a constellation of beliefs about *ourselves, others, and the world.* This kit is shaped by our ethnicity, culture, religion, and life experiences. What are some of the beliefs in your starter kit?

As a young child, Linda asked God to "know what the fullness of life means." As a child, what did you or would you have liked to ask God for?

Linda speaks of the "Divine Mother." What meaning, if any, does that have for you? What are your thoughts about the gender of God?

What, for you, is the relationship between spirituality and religion?

What is beautiful about your religious heritage? What feels difficult or distressing?

How has the way you think about God changed over your lifetime?

What was your first *spiritual* experience? [Might or might not be religious.]

What are your thoughts about a punishing and/or a forgiving God?

What is the meaning, for you, of "leaning into curves" as a metaphor for successful navigation of life?

What clues in childhood did you have about what your soul longed for—to be, to do, to experience?

Chapters 8–17

In her twenties, early in her relationship to Jim, Linda wrote in her journal, "...in love, all that I do is of you, God. I am the I am. We are inseparable. The beauty and growth evolving in the form our attraction must be you in action."

Her sense that we are "love, or God, in motion" is already forming up. What is it like for you to think about yourself as a manifestation of God?

Linda's mother has been a devout Catholic all her life. Yet, Linda's relationship with Jim stimulated an insight that caused her to reconsider the dogma and dictates of religion. This is often referred to as "gnosis"—following one's own knowing. How have you negotiated "gnosis" and relationships with social, religious, or cultural "rules"?

What's your sense of what people mean by the "now" or "living in the now"?

What's your take on the notion that when we live in the now, in the present, in a quiet mind, we can access all knowledge from the past and sense the future?

Who in your life has seen something in you that you couldn't see for yourself?

What did they mirror to you?

What are your "flight paths of your own choosing"?

What landscapes, places and spaces call to you? How have you known, honored and embraced those callings from intuitive love?

What values and ways of being characterize "your people"—your kindred spirits, your tribe?

Chapters 18–26

What clues have helped you know when you were "off track" in your life?

What angels/mentors have helped you on your hero/heroine's journey?

What is easy for you about listening? What is challenging?

Share your story about how you met your partner. Or share about the partner you dream to share your life with.

Share something about yourself that will surprise and delight people—something about you they might never guess. Share an adventure.

How are you a creator of miracles?

Does the Divine plan flow through you? Do you co-create a dream with the Divine creator behind life? What do you think?

When you think about your own life, what are your turning points? How did you realize you were at a fork in the road?

What do you think about W. H., Murray's comment about commitment?

What experiences do you have of making a commitment and realizing a dream?

What examples from your life can you share about how a bridge often often materializes AFTER you jumped, after you committed.

Chapters 27–35

How do you know when you are pushing yourself, pushing life too hard?

When have you felt overwhelmed and broken? Can you see any ways that you created that state of being versus being the victim of external, unchangeable circumstances?

If you've done therapy, what was your experience like? Was it helpful, or not?

What experiences have you had of a life-changing intuitive knowing?

Describe a time when you have followed your heart and risked stepping outside your comfort zone. What did you learn?

What "critical incidents" or "life accidents" have had long-term consequences for you? What have you learned from them?

When you think about life without the "creature comforts" we take for granted—electricity, running water, heat – what comes up for you? How would you cope in an extended period if those were unavailable?

Chapters 35–38

If you were to slow down to the speed of love, what in your life would be different?

What estrangements in relationship have you experienced? If those are not healed, what would it take to mend and transform them?

Can you see times in your life when difficult experiences or dark times have yielded gifts that you could put into service for yourself and others?

What does the term, "the beauty way," living in harmony with all things, mean to you?

Linda heard, "Relax. You are guided, always, by unseen hands. LOOK and SEE." What meaning might that hold for you?

What stops you from asking for help?

Describe a time when human angels showed up to help you along.

When have you been given a "second chance" in life?

Chapters 39–50

How aware are you of guiding synchronicities in your life?

What does having a "light heart" mean to you?

What do you think about the idea that the body sends us "love letters"—symptoms, pain, discomfort, etc.—when we are not in alignment with our spirit, souls, and hearts?

How can it be that people move from lack of forgiveness to forgiveness in an instant? What does it take to have a "change of heart"?

Linda writes, "In the sudden absence of that [life] essence, I glimpsed the nature of God, an energy without form. Intelligent. Wise. Alive. Breathing." What does that mean to you?

What experiences, if any, have you had of visitations from loved ones after death?

Linda writes, "consciousness is eternal." What are your thoughts about that?

What are your experiences of loss and grief?

What are your experiences of being blind-sided by life? What do you think about Linda's thought that loss cannot repress or destroy the beauty of life?

What are your fears about death and dying? What would you like to have on your mind when you die?

What holy places involving death, places of sacred learning, can you mark in your inner landscape?

Which of the life lessons in the eulogy for James Noel Pfeffer speak to you?

What are your thoughts about *gratitude* and *awareness of beauty* as antidotes to grief?

What are your thoughts about premonitions? Is life laid out before we live it?

Do we arrive here with an agreement to participate in certain experiences in life so that we, and the souls we move through life with, can evolve?

How have your experiences of grief and loss reshaped you? What do you think about the notion that the inner feminine in all beings knows how to ride the spiral through the "life-death-life" cycle?

How does it feel to consider that you will find the exact thought you need to face death with courage and surrender?

Chapters 51–56

What experiences, authors and teachers have most contributed to your spiritual understanding?

What examples in your life support the adage that "when the student is ready, the teacher appears"?

What does the phrase "life is a mystical dream" mean to you?

Describe an experience you've had when your heart has said, "you know" and your head has said, "no you don't." Where do these thoughts come from?

Which do you listen to more often?

What are your judgments about practitioners of healing intuitive arts? If you listen from judgment, what will you see?

Describe a chance encounter with another person that, in the end, changed your life in a positive way.

Chapter 57 – Epilogue

In chapter 57, Dr. Pettit first describes the 3 Principles of Mind, Thought and Consciousness. Notice if you have any initial reactions and discuss these.

What are your thoughts about the notion that *Thought*, the principle we use to *think*, is a spiritual power?

What makes sense to you about the statement that, "we are creating our experience moment-to-moment from the inside-out?"

What are your thoughts about this statement, "the life of a thought is only as long as we think it"? Does "trauma" exist if we are not thinking about it? If we listen to life and to ourselves from the "place" or "thought" that we are traumatized, are we that? If we listen from a "place" or "thought" that we are never broke and have nothing lacking, are we that?

Linda speaks of the appearance of the turtle as an auspicious omen in her life.

What are your omens?

How do you deal with sharp differences in your intimate partnerships?

If you're so inclined, watch together one of two videos where you can listen to Sydney Banks, either *The Great Illusion* or *The Experience at https://sydbanks.com/longbeach/* Have a chat about them.

The 3 Principles describe how we all have different realities because we *think* differently. This is seen as just a FACT of human life. How can we bridge this inescapable reality?

In what ways do you live in a prison of your own making by harboring upset feelings created by your own thinking?

What do you think about the notion that the intuitive way of love is serving up solutions all the time, but we don't notice them because we're too busy thinking?!

What do you think about the notion that intuition is logical and rational and that everyone can access it in equal measure, just by noticing it?

Describe one of your own life-changing insights—one that has helped you flourish in life.

Linda describes God as a "formless energy, a spiritual intelligence, a Truth, Love, which takes form in many ways—in the thoughts we use to create separate realities, in our bodies, in nature, in the all-ness and is-ness of life." How does that fit ornot fit with your understanding?

What Black Madonnas—angels who have sorrowed and suffered with you, and offered healing—have graced your life?

How do you experience "love in motion"?

In what ways are you and your life "perfectly imperfect"?

DELICIOUS READING LIST

Andrews, E. J. (2005). *Writing the Sacred Journey: The Art and Practice of Spiritual Memoir.* Skinner House Books.

Andrews, E. J. (2018). *Living Revision: A Writer's Craft as Spiritual Practice.* Skinner House Books.

Banks, S. (1983). *Second Chance.* Fourth Edition, Lone Pine Publishing.

Banks, S. (1989). *In Quest of the Pearl.* Lone Pine Publishing.

Banks, S. (1998). *The Missing Link: Reflections on Philosophy and Spirit.* Lone Pine Publishing.

Banks, S. (2001). *The Enlightened Gardener.* Lone Pine Publishing.

Banks, S. (2004). *Dear Lisa,* Lone Pine Publishing.

Banks, S. (2005). *The Enlightened Gardener Revisited.* Lone Pine Publishing.

Bettinger, D. & Swerdloff, N. (2016). *Coming Home: Uncovering the Foundations of Psychological Well-Being.*

Chandler, S. (2019). *Creator.* Maurice-Bassett.

Chandler, S. (2017) *Reinventing Yourself.* Career Press.

Coelho, P. (2014). *The Alchemist: 25TH Anniversary Edition.* HarperOne.

Cormier, S. (2018). *Sweet Sorrow: Finding Enduring Wholeness after Loss and Grief.* Rowman and Littlefield.

Estes, C.P. (1992) *Women Who Run With the Wolves: Myths and Stories of the Wild Woman Archetype.* Ballantine Books.

Hammerschlag, C. (1989). *The Dancing Healers: A Doctor's Journey of Healing with Native Americans.* SanFran.

Hammerschlag, C. (1994). *The Theft of the Spirit: A Journey to Spiritual Healing.* Simon and Schuster.

Hardison, A. & Thompson, A. (2021) *The Ultimate Coach.* Zeebroff Books.

McMeekin, G. (2000). *The 12 Secrets of Highly Creative Women: A Portable Mentor.* Conari Press.

Pransky, G. (2107). *The Relationship Handbook: A Simple Guide to Satisfying Relationships. – 25ᵀᴴ Anniversary Ed.* Pransky and Associates.

Quiring, L. (2015). *Island of Knowledge.* CCB Publishing.

Quiring, L. (2016). *Beyond Beliefs: The Lost Teachings of Sydney Banks.* CCB Publishing.

Scovel Shinn, F. (2016). *The Complete Works of Florence Shinn.* Martino Fine Books.

Scovil Shinn, F. (2013). *The Magic Path of Intuition.* Hay House Inc.

Vogler, C. (2007, 2020). *The Writer's Journey: Mythic Structure for Writers—25ᵀᴴ Anniversary Edition.* Michael Wiese Productions.

Watterson, M. (2021) *Mary Magdalene Revealed: The First Apostle, Her Feminist Gospel & the Christianity We Haven't Tried Yet.* Hay House Inc.

Wesselman, H. (1999). *Medicinemaker: Mystic Encounters on the Shaman's Path.* Bantam.

Wesselman, H. (2010). *Spiritwalker: Messages from the Future.* Ballantine.

Wesselman, H. (2011). *The Bowl of Light: Ancestral Wisdom from a Hawaiian Shaman.* Sounds True.

Three Initiates (2018). *The Kybalion: Hermetic Philosophy.* Tarcher Perigee.

END NOTES

Chapter 3—The Big Ask

1. The Catholic Primer. (2005). *The Baltimore Catechism.*
    www.catholicprimer.org

Chapter 5—The Dark of My Eye

2. IMDb. https://www.imdb.com/title/tt0565126/

Chapter 6—Confession

3. (2002) The Yankee Doodle Boy. Library of Congress, Washington, DC.
    [Manuscript/Mixed Material]
    Retrieved from the Library of Congress, https://www.loc.gov/item/
    ihas.200000020/.

Chapter 7—First Kiss

4. Simon, S., Howe, L. Kirschenbaum, H. (1972) *Values clarification.* Hart
    Publishing Co.
5. Bolles, R. & Bolles, M. (1977). *What Color is Your Parachute?* Ten Speed
    Press.

Chapter 12—Psychodrama

6. Whitehead, A., (1929). *Aims of Education.* Free Press, Reissue Edition
    [January 1, 1967]

Chapter 13—In Service

7. Ferguson, M. (1980). *The Aquarian Conspiracy: Personal and Social
    Transformation in Our Time.* Tarcher: First Edition.

Chapter 16—Foreshadowed

8. Rohr, R. & Ebert, A. (2001). *The Enneagram: A Christian Perspective.*
    Crossroad.

Chapter 18—The Fishbowl

9. Egan, G. (1975). The Skilled Helper. *A Problem-Management and
    Opportunity-Development Approach to Helping.* Brooks Cole Publishing.

Chapter 25—Jumping Off

10. Murray, W. H. (1951). *The Scottish Himalayan Expedition.* J. M. Dent.

Chapter 28—Chronic Distress

11. American Psychiatric Association. (1987). Diagnostic and Statistical Manual of Mental Disorders (3RD ed., revised.)
Chapter 32—Fire and Water
12. Sandel, L. M. (1991). *Self-understanding and empathy development in seasoned psychotherapists: A qualitative study.* Graduate Theses, Dissertations and Problem Reports. 9707. https://researchrepository.wvu.edu/etd/9707

Chapter 33—Humpty Dumpty

13. Hammerschlag, C. (1989). *The Dancing Healers: A Doctor's Journey of Healing with Native Americans.* SanFran.

Chapter 37—The Beauty Way

14. Hammerschlag, C. (1994). *The Theft of the Spirit: A Journey to Spiritual Healing.* Touchstone.
15. Turtle Island Project. http://ww.turtleislandproject.com/carl.html

Chapter 42—Story of Death

16. Beecher, L. F. https://en.wikipedia.org/wiki/Gone_From_My_Sight

Chapter 50 — Heartwood

17. Heartwood in the Hills, founded by Jude Binder and Frank Venezia. https://www.heartwoodinthehills.org/
18. Estés, C.P. (1996). *Women Who Run with the Wolves: Myths and Stories of the Wild Woman Archetype.* Ballantine Books.

Chapter 52—Uncle Mikala

19. Wesselman, H. (1999). *Medicinemaker: Mystic Encounters on the Shaman's Path.* Bantam Books

Chapter 55—Valentine Shakeup #1

20. McMeekin, G. (2000). *The 12 Secrets of Highly Creative Women: A Portable Mentor.* Conari Press.
21. Pettit, S.S. (1987). *Coming Home: A Collection of Poetry.*

Chapter 56—Valentine Shakeup #2

22. Pettit, S. S. (1987). *Coming Home: A Collection of Poetry.*

Chapter 57—Coffee with Salad Dressing

23. Banks, S. (2000). Long Beach Lecture Series - Streaming Video; *The Experience*. Retrieved from https://sydbanks.com/longbeach/
24. Banks, S. (2001). *The Missing Link: Reflections on Philosophy and Spirit*. Lone Pine Publishing.

Chapter 58—Popliteal Fossa

25. IMDb. *Fried Green Tomatoes*. https://www.imdb.com/title/tt0565126/

Chapter 61—Meeting the Teacher of THOUGHT

26. MentorCoach LLC; www.mentorcoach.com
27. International Coaching Federation. Retrieved from: https://coachingfederation.org/about
28. Banks, S. (1987). *Second Chance: An Amazing Story About Endings and Beginnings—and the Miraculous Power of the Mind*. Lone Pine Publishing.

Chapter 62—Separate Realities

29. Hoff, B. (1982). *The Tao of Pooh*. Dutton Books.

Chapter 64—Boats on a River

30. Banks, S. (2005). *The Enlightened Gardener*. Lone Pine Publishing.

Chapter 65—Wisdom Sources

31. Banks, S. (1989). *In Quest of the Pearl*. Lone Pine Publishing, p. 43

Chapter 66—Flourishing

32. Banks, S. (2001). *The Missing Link: Reflections on Philosophy and Spirit*. Lone Pine Publishing.
33. Banks, S. (2001). *The Missing Link: Reflections on Philosophy and Spirit*. Lone Pine Publishing, p. 120.

Chapter 68—Catherine of Siena

34. Oxford University Press (2017). *Oxford Essential Quotations [5th ed.]*, edited by Susan Ratcliffe.

Epilogue

35. Fox, E. (2009, 1940). *Power Through Constructive Thinking*. HarperOne

INDEX

Milton Keynes UK
Ingram Content Group UK Ltd.
UKHW051152240324
439902UK00005B/184

9 781916 701103